PRAISE FOR TAMAR E. CHANSKY

"An excellent book, one of the best of its kind . . . This book has the potential for helping thousands and thousands of children, their parents, and their families."

—JUDITH S. BECK, PhD, President,
Beck Institute for Cognitive Therapy and Research,
and Clinical Associate Professor of Psychology
in Psychiatry, University of Pennsylvania

"The master of providing clear, accessible, practical advice and guidance for wise and loving care of the anxious child."

—JEFFREY M. SCHWARTZ, MD, author of *Dear Patrick*

"Tamar Chansky, PhD, has done it again—written another incredibly helpful, practical book. *Freeing Your Child from Negative Thinking* offers specific strategies for parents (or any adult) to use with children and describes variations on these strategies for younger children and older adolescents. Every parent who has a pessimistic, negativistic child should read this book! As parents use the thinking and behavioral strategies that Dr. Chansky recommends, they will undoubtedly find that they themselves are becoming more optimistic and positive, not only toward their child but also more generally in their own lives. I highly recommend this wonderful book."

—JUDITH S. BECK, PhD, President, Beck Institute for
Cognitive Therapy and Research, and Clinical Professor of
Psychology in Psychiatry, University of Pennsylvania

"Many youngsters are burdened by self-doubt, negative feelings, and depression. Their lack of confidence and sadness typically trigger feelings of confusion and distress in their parents as the latter struggle to find the best approach to help their children develop a more optimistic, resilient outlook. Tamar Chansky's book *Freeing Your Child from Negative Thinking* offers a wonderful resource for parents. In a very skillful manner, Dr. Chansky explains the roots of negative thinking, but most importantly, she offers specific, realistic strategies with actual dialogue that parents can use to minimize their child's negativity. Her empathy and understanding for children and parents is evident on every page of this very readable, practical book. It is a book that parents of children of all ages will read and reread as they seek to help their children perceive themselves in a more hopeful light."

—ROBERT BROOKS, PhD., Faculty,
Harvard Medical School and co-author of *Raising Resilient Children and Raising a Self-Disciplined Child*

"Tamar Chansky gives parents a dynamic approach to helping their children escape thinking badly about themselves and their world with thoughts ranging from mild negativism to clinical depression. Her insightful and creative techniques, based on scientifically grounded cognitive behavior therapy, are, on any given day, helpful not only for parents and their children but for all of us. Next time I want to blame myself for something that went wrong, or feel terrible about something I did, I will open this book and I know I will soon feel better."

—MYRNA SHURE, PhD,
author of *Raising a Thinking Child*
and *Thinking Parent, Thinking Child*

"Tamar Chansky has distilled cutting-edge research on optimism, pessimism, depression, and resilience into an incredibly thoughtful guide for parents. Her book is full of suggestions about what to look for and what to do (and what not to do) that parents should find engaging and accessible. Reading this book should ease the worries of both parents and their children."

—BARRY SCHWARTZ, author of
The Paradox of Choice and Professor of
Psychology, Swarthmore College

"In a clearly readable fashion, Dr. Tamar Chansky combines clever phrasing (for adults) along with "kid speak" to communicate with youth. From having worked with anxious youth who struggle with all of the possibilities (too many), Dr. Chansky shifts to the negative youth who see no future—the youth who mistake one thing for everything. She walks the reader through discussions that focus on how negative experiences happen to everyone, and that they are 'manageable' and 'temporary.' This book is not a review of the scientific literature, but it is a readable set of guidelines and understandings that are informed by it."

—PHILIP C. KENDALL, PhD, ABPP,
Professor of Psychology and Director,
Child and Adolescent Anxiety
Disorders Clinic, Temple University

"For every parent who wants their child not to feel bad, here is an excellent book to feel great about. In *Freeing Your Child from Negative Thinking*, Dr. Chansky abundantly gives parents powerful, easy to apply tools to ensure the emotional health and success of any child. I hope no parent trying to help their child to get ahead misses out on reading this wonderful book packed with valuable advice."

—JEFFREY BERNSTEIN, PhD,
author of *10 Days to a Less Defiant Child*

"[A] gifted writer and clinician . . . Chansky takes the reader by the hand and guides them through the complex maze of thoughts and emotions in a way that is wise, compassionate, and knowledge-based. This is the gift of *Freeing Yourself from Anxiety*."

—DANIEL GOTTLIEB, PhD, author of *Letters to Sam*

"If a brain were to come with operating instructions, it would consist of these pages."

—THERESE J. BORCHARD, author of *Beyond Blue*

FREEING
YOUR CHILD
FROM
NEGATIVE
THINKING

FREEING
YOUR CHILD
FROM
NEGATIVE
THINKING

Powerful, Practical Strategies
to Build a Lifetime of Resilience,
Flexibility, and Happiness
from Toddlers to Teens

SECOND EDITION

TAMAR E. CHANSKY, PhD

ILLUSTRATIONS BY PHILLIP STERN

LIFE
LONG

Copyright © 2019 by Tamar E. Chansky, PhD
Illustrations copyright ©2019 Phillip Stern
Cover design by Amanda Kain
Cover photograph by Maddie Eisenhart
Cover copyright © 2020 Hachette Book Group, Inc.

The lines from "love is a place" copyright 1935, ©1963, 1991 by the Trustees for the E. E. Cummings Trust. Copyright © 1978 by George James Firmage, from *Complete Poems*: 1904–1932 by E. E. Cummings, edited by George J. Firmage. Used by permission of Liveright Publishing Corporation.

Da Capo Lifelong Books
Hachette Book Group
1290 Avenue of the Americas, New York, NY 10104
HachetteBooks.com
Twitter.com/HachetteBooks
Instagram.com/HachetteBooks

Printed in the United States of America

Second Edition: January 2020

Published by Da Capo Lifelong Books, an imprint of Perseus Books, LLC, a subsidiary of Hachette Book Group, Inc. The Da Capo Lifelong Books name and logo is a trademark of the Hachette Book Group.

The Hachette Speakers Bureau provides a wide range of authors for speaking events. To find out more, go to www.hachettespeakersbureau.com or call (866) 376-6591.

The publisher is not responsible for websites (or their content) that are not owned by the publisher.

Print book interior design by Jeff Williams.

Library of Congress Cataloging-in-Publication Data
Names: Chansky, Tamar E. (Tamar Ellsas), 1962– author.
Title: Freeing your child from negative thinking : powerful, practical strategies to build a lifetime of resilience, flexibility, and happiness / Tamar Chansky, PhD ; .
Description: Second Edition. | New York: Da Capo Lifelong Books, 2020. | Revised edition of the author's Freeing your child from negative thinking, 2008. | Includes bibliographical references and index.
Identifiers: LCCN 2019032769 | ISBN 9780738285955 (paperback) | ISBN 9780738285962 (ebook)
Subjects: LCSH: Self-esteem in children. | Resilience (Personality trait) in children. | Child rearing. | Parenting.
Classification: LCC BF723.S3 C48 2020 | DDC 649/.7—dc23
LC record available at https://lccn.loc.gov/2019032769

ISBNs: 978-0-7382-8595-5 (trade paperback); 978-0-7382-8596-2 (ebook)

LSC-C

10 9 8 7 6 5 4 3 2 1

For Phil, Mer, and Raia—
the heart of my happiness

And for my mother, Elissa,
my first and best teacher of all things resilient

Contents

THE WORK OF HAPPINESS
BEGINS ON THE INSIDE

All parents want their children to be happy and want to give their children the best. How we define *giving* and the *best* and even *happiness* itself informs our parenting approaches and ultimately makes a big difference in our children's well-being and fulfillment in life. When we give our children the opportunity to see how they can get things for themselves—working hard, persevering, taking risks, overcoming disappointment and adversity, then we bring out the best in them. The ultimate contentment comes from having the ability to act, to see that one can manage oneself, hold one's own. But what if your child's thinking doesn't allow for contentment? What if the very ideas—default and automatic—racing through your child's mind don't grant a fighting chance to see what is possible, what is accurate, what is good—and, in fact, it is fighting with those very thoughts that leave kids feeling defeated every day? Welcome to the world of kids with negative thinking.

OPENING UP THE VAULT

For nearly three decades, I have been listening closely to the sounds of anxious children—their worries a constant barrage of questions, fraught with what-ifs, like a frantic opening and closing of doors on their future: "What if this happens?" "What if that happens?" "What if that goes wrong? What if I mess up?" "What if I fail?" Always a question, always about the worst-case scenario. But as the years went on, I started to hear a different story—from children plagued by negative thoughts. In contrast to the frantic flurry of possible disasters to avert, children with negative thinking had no questions and all the answers, and none of them sounded good: "There's no point." "I give up." "It's always like this." "Nothing ever works for me." "Everything's ruined." Or simply, "No."

Instead of the clamor of what-ifs, I heard the silence of finality sealing shut a thick vault, all the treasures locked inside, as these kids not only expected the worst but *accepted* the worst. Parents would stand around that vault, trying to gain access. "But you're good at so many things; this is no big deal," they'd plead. But guarded by the insidious partners of hopelessness and impossibility, these kids remained, shut down, unreachable, convinced there was no use in trying to make it different. Accepting the worst leads to no satisfaction; on the contrary, it leads to sadness, even "pre-sadness," as one teen called it. When kids repeatedly predict that things are going to go badly, they begin to get sad *in advance*, anticipating the defeat before they even start, borrowing ahead on the disappointment just like anxious kids borrow ahead on worry. The possibility that things could turn out well is irrelevant; they've already decided, it's pointless.

When I say to these parents, "Your child has depressive thinking," they quickly counter, and rightly so, "But he's not depressed." I explain how their child is demonstrating what Dr. Aaron Beck, the father of cognitive therapy, called in the 1970s the depressive triad: negative views of the self, the world, and the future. Dr. Beck codified this triad as a three-part punch: *I struck out at baseball; I hate myself* (one blow); *baseball is stupid* (the next); *I stink at everything* (and down they fall).[1] An hour later, this child may have moved on and is asking with a cheerful smile, "What's for dinner?" as if nothing has happened. Meanwhile, the parents, completely wrung out from a lifesaving mission to wrestle their child out of the hole he had seemingly dug himself into, are mystified. They scratch their head and sigh, but they don't feel completely relieved because they have a hunch that they won't be in the clear for long: The depressive triad will be waiting around the corner for the next disappointment, and *kaboom*—another attack of the negative brain will knock their child down again. So, although these children are not *depressed* per se, it is clear that with all these repetitions of the pattern of everyday ordinary events leading to damning conclusions about the youngsters' abilities and prospects—damned by their own lightning fast (mis)interpretations, they are *depressives-in-training* and they are not happy about it. Part of their misery is that the solution seems out of reach—they are convinced they can't be happy or successful because they believe that big changes have to happen on the outside: better grades, nicer clothes, more money, more friends, better hair, better toys . . . and today . . . more likes on Instagram!

The truth about happiness is this: It always begins with the work you do on the inside. It always has. What will determine our happiness, to a great extent, is how we seek out meaningful experiences, help our kids discover what is meaningful for them and, perhaps most important, keep that discovery process going. Kids need the flexible habit of mind to accurately narrate the challenges and disappointments they face and to learn to expect them. To learn to not stop at the global first take, "I'm a failure!" and come back to that inner conversation with a much more accurate and focused assessment of the damages. If we want kids to develop this flexibility, they have to know to look for it. They need to hear consistently that there are different ways to narrate a situation. Then they won't stop at the first version, as we know that with negative thinking on board, the first is always the worst!

As kids learn to pivot their inner assessment from seeing things as difficult rather than devastating, as uncomfortable rather than unacceptable, they can get back on track more quickly. Equipped with flexible expectations and accurate explanations for when things don't go as expected, kids can acquire the emotional agility to successfully navigate their path in life.

We have to help them by reinforcing flexible expectations and accurate explanations. Stay clear from teaching that leading charmed straight-A, all varsity, picture-perfect social media lives makes kids happy. That picture doesn't exist in real life! Happiness comes from having a sustainable understanding of how life works: Moments of struggle are not wrong, they are not mistakes that shouldn't be happening, and having the "I can't, I won't, it's not fair, everyone else is better, nothing's good" thoughts are not wrong, either; they are part of life. I tell the kids I see that these thoughts and experiences are not personal—they're not a Johnny or Julie issue, they're a human being issue. Everyone hears those thoughts and has those feelings; it's just that for kids plagued with negative thinking, these thoughts and feelings don't just have the first word, as may happen for any of us, but they have the last as well. By deciding the meaning of events for kids, negative thinking is running the show inside your child's mind.

Parents of kids with negative thinking know that roiling feeling—alternating between concern and disbelief—watching kids crumble, shut down, or melt down in the face of even small disappointments or hints of criticism. We ask ourselves how something so seemingly small could become so big and, more important, how we can stop this from ruining our children's lives. If we could look behind the scenes in the brain, we would see that the mind is laying down tracks, neural shortcuts jumping from point A to point Z. When something goes wrong for these children, it feels permanently and unchangeably wrong, it impacts everything, and they usually see it as all their fault: Nothing bad can be *temporary* or *occasional* or *specific* and *manageable*. In the 1980s, Dr. Martin Seligman of the University of Pennsylvania identified this pattern of understanding experience as a pessimistic explanatory style: negative events are explained as *permanent* (not temporary), *pervasive* (relating not just to that specific domain, but spilling over into everything), and *personal* (their failure), what we will refer to as the 3 P's. He found that children don't outgrow this style but actually grow into it, using it to explain an ever-widening circle of events and aspects of their life. Eventually with all these rehearsals and practices of the 3 P's, this thinking habit becomes automatic, seemingly impenetrable, and so convincing to children that it is the gateway to true depression.

Over time, this high-speed brain connection becomes so efficient—like any habit—that even if a child doesn't want to think that way and doesn't believe these ideas in his heart, he is still convinced of them, just because they are the answer that got there first over and over again. The alternative ways of looking at circumstances, which these children could use to go on a much more inviting, realistic, and promising track, remain hidden; the children are either too discouraged to look for these transfer stations or don't even know they are an option. Feeling intensely bad from what their thoughts are telling them and not seeing a way of being able to impact that bad feeling only compounds children's feelings of helplessness and hopelessness. Seligman and his colleagues found two things: (a) You can protect vulnerable children from developing depression by *teaching* them the skills to look for that other track; and (b) the protection this training provides holds even years after the training is finished; children who learned these skills had half the rate of depression of the children who hadn't learned the skills.[2]

While it's more challenging for those kids to change their relationship with those thoughts because the thoughts are coming at them fast and furious all day long, they can develop an inner translator so that those automatic negative thoughts are not the interpreters of their world and their place in it. Instead, they can learn to pause, recognize the patterns, and recognize the sound of those absolutes, the "I'll never, you always, I can't, I quit!" mode the brain has slipped into and get the system back on an accurate track—having the flexibility to do so is how our kids can have contentment in life.

Most important, in happy lives, things do go wrong—sometimes big, sometimes small—and we know that. The key to a sustainably successful life is how you frame the problem from the get-go. Is the hurdle in front of you a problem, or a challenge? An opportunity to grow? When things go "wrong," kids can get caught up in the idea that it *shouldn't* have happened, that things *shouldn't* go wrong. It feels like an injustice to them, if not an emergency. You can help teach them that it isn't either. It's okay to be sad. It's okay to lose. It's okay to be disappointed. Help them to change the conversation in their head and with you to know that it isn't a *wrong* moment, it's a hard moment. Rather than blaming themselves—*I'm so stupid!*—keep it impersonal: *that's so frustrating!* Keep the significance of that event small and don't rewrite their future and past based on the tough moment they're in. It's really the conversation about these feelings that matters most in promoting your child's resilience and satisfaction. If this sounds hard to believe and somewhere deep down you think your child is using this to try to get attention, your child isn't grateful enough, or something like that, those things may be true, too, but that's not the reason your child is acting that way. You have the opportunity to teach your child how things work, to expose and change the conversation in your child's mind, which in turn changes the conversation your child is having with you. You can teach this resilience, but only if you practice it, too: Changing the apparent or immediate meaning of struggle, failure, disappointment and seeing it as one step in a many, many-step process that we—parents and children together—only move forward throughout life.

We need to teach our kids to remember that when they are having the stuck feeling, this is a "thing" to learn to fix, like learning to fix a stuck zipper or untie a knot. When this "thing" happens, they need to learn to summon their inner executive who says, "I feel stuck." "Is it helping me to think their way?" "Is this true?" "Is it helping me?" "What do I want to think instead?" And in so doing, instill in your child or teen the sense that happiness and well-being don't happen on their own, and must be actively pursued.

NOSE FOR THE NEGATIVE

Many kids come by happiness naturally, although even for the sunniest kids, it's still not a given all the time. For others, happiness is entirely contingent on things working out exactly as expected, without a single hitch. As soon as one thing goes off the track, it's the end of the world as we know it.

What should we be doing for the kids with a nose for the negative, or for any kid for that matter? We could keep trying to make life work for our children, make them feel better, bend over backward, walk on eggshells, and do a daily minesweeping to keep all systems go. As all parents of a child with a negative bent know, there's always that one more thing that we didn't think of. The *nose for the negative* is like a bad allergy to adversity or discontent so a child notices potential obstacles in the most minute detail, sees them as foregone conclusions, and is thrown into a tailspin ahead of time, before anything has actually gone wrong. Trying to "just be positive and hopeful" (or asking kids to be that for themselves) doesn't work and often backfires. It's like applying paint to a poorly prepared surface: No matter how excellent the paint, it simply won't stick. As we'll see, the opposite of negative thinking isn't *positive* thinking: It's possible thinking, helping your child see the myriad opportunities that await just on the other side of the rapid-fire pessimistic conclusions that her negative thinking supplies. And when your friends and relatives chide you to just be "more firm" and use "tough love" with your child's "crankiness" or "spoiled" behavior, they are completely missing the point: These kids would *love* things to be different; they don't want to think, feel, or act this way; it makes them miserable. They just don't know what else to do.

Enter: parents. I have seen just how competent and influential parents can be in changing the course of their child's life once they have a road map through the twists and turns of their child's negative mind. My hope is that these pages will equip you with the words, pictures, and ideas for this journey, and that they will inspire your creativity and tap into your strengths, not just fixing your child's life, but teaching the mindset and worldview that change is possible and how to get there.

NEUROPLASTICITY: CREATING NEW TRICKS AND NEW TRACKS

How can we change a pattern that has become so automatic? The brain gets good at whatever it does the most. This is what Jeffrey Schwartz and Sharon Begley describe in their book *The Mind and the Brain*[3] as "the survival of the busiest." Whichever neural circuits are tapped into most often have more brain resources devoted to them. So, if our kids are running daily laps around the pessimism track, they will become sprinters—effortlessly reaching conclusions that are at once airtight and totally undermining. But by the same token, if we begin to create some new hubs in their explanatory landscape—hubs that say, "Some things are temporary," or "It's one thing; it's not everything," or "Don't stop at your first thought; think in twos!"—they will get very good at heading toward those new circuits in their thinking. Over time, they will become able to manage the ups and downs without falling flat, and eventually those new, healthy, realistic thoughts will meet them halfway and may even beat out the negative ones. So: new answers, new tracks, happier kids.

The problem is that parents may feel daunted by learning how to help their child create these new tracks. Their responses to this point— frustratingly ineffectual—have been either to rush in with reassurance or, after reassurance leads nowhere, to get fed up and say, "Enough!," or "Get a grip!" which leaves them feeling like horrible, insensitive parents. Parents' uneasiness and uncertainty about how to approach their child is not lost on the child and only rocks an already struggling, unbalanced vessel. On the one hand, parents see their child suffering and want to make it better; on the other hand, talking about what is bothering their child feels like a process that could spiral into a complaining fest on a good day or, worse, a bottomless pit in which the child—holding onto his negativity like a heavy anchor—is not only *not* ready to let go but is going to take his parents down with him.

PARENTS CAN TEACH THE LESSONS

Parents are always the first responders to their children's distress. In my own practice, I have repeatedly seen how parents, armed with the right tools, train their scared and anxious children to think differently and learn to recognize and outsmart the worry traps in their mind. Similarly, parents of children and teens who are either negative by nature or otherwise vulnerable to depressive thinking can learn how to recognize and respond powerfully to their children's slipping into that locked vault and can teach them how to learn the combination, open the vault, and stay in touch with their treasures—even in the face of the occasional, but inevitable, disappointments or failures. Rather than keeping their fingers crossed that their kids won't get tripped up by the vicissitudes of life, parents and children alike can tackle the tangles head-on, as they set their navigation system to the way out.

To buffer our children from getting stuck in negative thinking, the key is to *get specific*, and narrow down the overwhelming, global problem to one specific trigger, event, or situation, setting in motion a process to find an accurate interpretation of its significance and meaning. Children don't know that they are feeling so overwhelmed because they are seeing their situation magnified one hundred times. Even something as familiar as a strand of hair can look unrecognizable (and even creepy or daunting) under a microscope. By learning to adjust the microscope's controls—realizing that there *are* controls that they can put their hands on metaphorically—children can eliminate the distortion and shrink the problem back to its actual size and see a different picture, an accurate and therefore more manageable one. So, we teach kids to cultivate the two-track mind: for young children, that means to put down the negative glasses and pick up the "competent glasses"; for teens, this translates to not going with that first pessimistic reaction and taking a second look by asking themselves the "million-dollar question" of what they truly believe the significance of that adverse event to be. Then, after they have looked at different perspectives on the situation, we can help them "mobilize" and choose to be an agent of change on their own behalf. Names like Disaster Man or The Exaggerator help children reduce the tyranny and authority of their negative thoughts to their proper place—and to see them as just one among many possible interpretations of the situation. While it's campy, teens can benefit from these concepts as well, even if with a smidgen of age-appropriate sarcasm and disdain.

FINDING THEIR WAY THROUGH
THE THICKETS OF UNHAPPINESS WITH YOUR HELP

Our Changing World

We live in uncertain times. In the ten years since this book was first published, the general climate of fear, anxiety, and our sense of an insecure future has not shown any signs of letting up and in many ways has intensified. Much has changed for all of us, but perhaps most dramatically in the lives of children. As I write these words, a news alert pops up on my phone announcing that 2018 was the worst year for gun violence; ninety-four tragic school shooting incidents, a nearly 60 percent increase from the previous record in 2006 of fifty-nine. Lockdown and active shooter drills have become a regular part of our children's daily reality.

There has never been a more urgent time in our history for these lessons. The statistics below indicate the staggering scope of devastation caused by childhood depression:

- Depression costs the United States $210 billion a year in medical expenses and lost productivity. This has increased nearly five-fold in the last ten years.

- At any one time, 10 to 15 percent of children and adolescents have some *symptoms* of depression; 11 percent may meet for a diagnosis of a major depressive episode.

- At any given time, as many as one in every thirty-three children may have clinical depression. The rate of depression among adolescents may be as high as one in eight.

- Preschoolers are the fastest-growing population for depression; over 1 million are clinically depressed.
- Every 100 minutes, a teen takes his own life.
- Twice as many girls develop depression as do boys.
- Suicide is the second-leading cause of death among young people aged ten to twenty-four.
- Suicide rates are twice as high for black children under age twelve as for white children.
- LGBTQ youth are three times more likely to contemplate suicide than are heterosexual youth.

Beyond the dire statistics and tragedies, it's perhaps the profound changes in the technology of daily life that pose the most predictable challenges for parents of kids struggling with negative thinking. We just need to survey the blinking lights and power cords around us to see the technological advances we've enjoyed in the last few decades, but this has not translated by any means into better mental health for our children; in fact, some suggest that it is those advances—and specifically the rise in smartphone use—that are at the heart of the surge in symptoms of depression (up 33% in the five years between 2010 and 2015) and teen suicide attempts (up 23%), and teens who committed suicide (up 31%).[4]

It's especially difficult for parents to think about negative thinking in kids at a time of turmoil when parents themselves are struggling to know what to do with their own doubts, fears, and default overwhelmed state. Many of us may try to cope with our uneasiness by clinging to the belief that if we do everything we can, we can *make* our children happy. But if it were even possible for your kids to be happy all the time, *that in and of itself would be a problem*! You'd be working too hard, and your kids won't learn how to manage temporary unhappiness if they never get in the trenches and practice.

Ten years ago, only the most precocious or fortunate kids held devices in their hands. Now, kids and teens never have a free hand as they are swiping, clicking, posting. Their very understanding or definition of what constitutes life has changed—young kids are constantly angling for more time on their screens, and social media often ends up defining their worth and determining their mood. For teens, their popularity, inclusion, and measure of happiness is calculated by the ticker tape of likes on their Instagram. Parents can feel daunted by this third party in their parenting. Or they can take it on. By helping kids and teens understand how habits form in the brain, we can also teach them how to dismantle that faulty wiring and reconnect the wires differently, more accurately, and ultimately with a much more fulfilling and broader view of life. In short, we can teach children how to create new habits: getting perspective, accepting that things are hard (especially at first, but even after that, too), problem solving, experimenting, and asking for help at the right times make us more effective and even independent.

These lessons are not new but never more needed. What has stayed the same is that parents want to make the world right for their kids. We want our kids to thrive, to grow, to learn how to take care of themselves, to succeed, to have a meaningful life—to be happy. External pressures have always been there in some form, but importantly, as we've said, happiness is an "inside job." We can supply our kids with a loving environment, great education, and social support, but the way they frame their successes and especially their disappointments will determine their mood and their actions.

DON'T IGNORE IT, DON'T AIRLIFT THEM OUT, BECOME AN EXPERT

The very good news is that parents of children who are negative by nature *can* nurture their kids to learn a better way of thinking. By implementing the strategies in this book, parents will learn, not only how to turn their unwitting depressives-in-training into experts in depression prevention, but also how to enable their children to hold their own—in their mind and in the world. Their children will develop the flexible mind-set that obstacles do not signal "time to quit" but are surmountable and can be approached from many different angles. This is the formula for resilience, resourcefulness, and happiness in life.

We can't simply ignore negative thoughts because the more we try to ignore something, the more it will come stampeding back. But we also don't need to stop our thoughts, and we can't. There isn't a switch that we can flip. It's a process. If, rather than ignore, you are prepared to recognize negative thoughts—line yourself up with their true significance (or lack thereof!)—and see them as a universal, knee-jerk reaction to doubt, then they cease to be a personal crystal ball for our future. As I tell kids, if I think there is a bear next to me, I won't be able to (and shouldn't be able to!) ignore it. If, however, I realize that it's a picture of a bear (coming from my imagination and thoughts, not a threat), then it's easier (with diligent practice) to dismiss it and say to myself—*that's just a thought, an idea, not a fact or a threat. I can let it be, thoughts come and go, there's nothing I need to do about it.*

CATCHING IT WHEN IT'S SMALL:
SEEDLINGS OF DEPRESSION

When we moved into our first home, we had to literally see past the enormous, overgrown yew tree that had taken over much of the front yard and entirely blocked the view from the sunporch. It was a monstrosity. It was ugly. It had to come down. When I was showing my late father-in-law, an esteemed man of science, the problem, I said, "And to think it probably just started out as a little seedling." He chuckled and said patiently, "Yes, dear, everything does." I imagine that the intention of those who planted what had now become a behemoth bush was to keep it small—a manageable pruned hedge—but clearly things had gotten out of control. We wouldn't want to scare our kids off by being the "negativity police," reacting to every sigh, rolling of the eyes, or unpleasant comment, but we do need to be vigilant in catching these seedlings when they are small, before they take over. And to make sure that if our children's negativity blocks their view, they are able to prune back their thoughts and let the light of reality in.

The purpose of this book is to make you an expert on how negative thinking gets built, so that you can teach your child how to handle disappointment and adversity in the same matter-of-fact way that you would teach lessons like looking both ways before crossing the street. These skills include what to do with the intense feelings negative thinking creates, how to dismantle the logic of faulty wiring, and how to re-wire and rebuild a more solid and accurate system of interpreting events. In addition, you will learn how to create a framework to detect and appreciate positive, fulfilling experiences in your child's daily life. When you have a clear, behind-the-scenes understanding of why your child is behaving in a certain way, you also become a more *credible* tour guide to your child. If you want him to explore new territory in his thinking and behavior, you need to be very familiar with it yourself.

As you read this book, you will have your ear tuned to such negative buzz words as *always, never, no one,* and *everyone.* You will come to know with an engineer's precision how your child's faulty conclusions were constructed, and you will have the tools to help your child dismantle them and rebuild more accurate (realistic) perspectives. You will also learn to highlight the positive moments to help your kids methodically reconstruct how they contributed to things going well, so that they can do it again. You will learn a new language and create a communication system with your child to unpack disappointments, unhappiness, or blues and keep interpretations of such adversities accurate and their impact small.

TABLE FOR TWO, PLEASE! TAKING CHARGE OF NEGATIVE THINKING IS A TWO-PERSON JOB

These lessons can be taught. But only if you practice them, too. As you work through this book, you may find yourself using these strategies on yourself, and that's good! This is what I call the "table for two" of interactional optimism, and it is central to this book. Recognizing the mutuality of our interactions, we can make choices that contribute to the upward spiral of optimistic thinking—for all. If you are not taking charge of your own negative thinking about your child and reining in those "Why is he *always* like this? Why is he *never* happy?" thoughts, it will be hard for your child to rein in his. You can't really *make* someone change, but you can change yourself. So, on the flip side, don't be surprised as you work on editing your own thoughts, if you start seeing unexpected possibilities in your own life popping up in the corner of your mind's eye, or you start hearing your own negative thinking as less than the final word, and more as a cue to do your own fact-checking. You will start to feel lighter, your communication with others will improve, and you will be more authentic when you work on these issues with your child—you are, after all, fellow travelers on the road of life.

If you are deliberate in identifying and modeling these new ideas and strategies, you can lay them out—like stepping-stones. Then, your child will be more likely to choose to take a walk down this path rather than the path of great resistance. Whether you understand these lessons already or they are new to you, the temptation to get upset with your child's negativity is real and wired in. He's struggling and it feels like an emergency in your mind. It's not the stress of now so much, it's the helplessness and fear you feel overlaying or extrapolating this moment into his whole future; everything moves at lightning speed. You are going to learn to slow down, step back from the moment, and see it as *just this moment*, not the rest of your child's life—or yours. In those vital steps, the emergency resolves itself. As you work on your own thinking and behavior, your kids may notice. For example, you may be yelling at your child, "You never clean up your room!" and then catch yourself and say, "Wait, that was too *global*; what I meant to say is that you *rarely* clean up your room, or, more specifically: I'd like you to clean up your room, *now*." Your kids will feel happy, vindicated, and intrigued—as if watching Halley's Comet—witnessing that rare and spectacular event of a parent correcting herself, and they'll also start wondering what this whole "global, specific, temporary thing" is all about.

No matter what your starting point—if your child gets stuck occasionally or regularly, or thinks in metaphors or prefers concrete logic—you will find the tools to work on that inside job of happiness, so grab your highlighter pen and get started.

PART ONE

Changing Your Child's Mind

1

UNDERSTANDING NEGATIVE THINKING

Wired to Quit (Too Soon)

FROM THE CHILDREN:

There is a mean voice that yells at me in my head, saying I'm stupid and I can't do things. I want to make that voice go away, but I don't know how.

FROM THE TEENS:

There has to be something really, really big for me to be happy, but I can get unhappy over nothing at all.

FROM THE PARENTS:

Everything can be fine with Mark and then suddenly everything is terrible—there's no in between.

Eva is so hard on herself. We don't care about grades, well not that much, but we could tell her she could get all C's and she would still push herself. She doesn't think she is smart.

FROM THE SCIENTISTS:

The revolution in our understanding of the brain's capacity to change well into adulthood does not end with the fact that the brain can and does change. Equally revolutionary is the discovery of how the brain changes. The actions we take can literally expand or contract different regions of the brain, pour more juice into quiet circuits and damp down activity in the buzzing ones.

—*Sharon Begley*[1]

When we first hold our children in our arms as infants, we imagine the life we want for them when they grow up. Will they be a scientist, we ask of the children with intense focus and curiosity; will they be an artist, we wonder of the children who draw beautifully. Will they find meaningful relationships, love, happiness? We all want the best for our children. What we likely don't think about is how, for those dreams to come true, learning to effectively and adaptively handle disappointments, obstacles, and frustrations needs to be a daily task on the to-do list of all kids. It's how they learn and grow. Although some children ride out these bumps with decent shock absorbers, for children with a nose for the negative, a low threshold for disappointment, and a keen radar for the bumps, the ride can easily be ruined. They take those bumps hard, fall into those holes deeply, dwell on them, and pull other people down with them. But adding insult to injury, they don't just fall; they make a whole new theory about themselves and *why* they fell. There are no coincidences, nothing is insignificant: *I'm stupid, I deserve it; see, I told you nothing good ever happens to me.* There are no isolated events; one false move changes everything. It's as if the person who they were—their talents, their smarts, their perspective—two seconds prior to this adverse event fell through a trapdoor beneath them and, in a flash, they lose everything. Their thinking is in powerful absolutes that command authority and suggest that, like it or not, this is just the way things are! And because those thoughts don't come with an introduction—"The following message is sponsored by your unreliable negative brain"— they believe what they hear, word for word. It is a truth that—while it makes everyone miserable, kids and parents alike—becomes instantly set in stone. Unbeknownst to them and their bewildered parents (and however much they really do want to be happy and help themselves), all their efforts seem to make the problems worse rather than better, deepening the hole of unhappiness.

PART ONE: FROM THE INSIDE OUT

Negative Thinking:
When Something So Wrong Feels So True

Negative thinking is notoriously inaccurate, exaggerated, and harsh. Take a moment and think what you said to yourself the last time you made a big mistake. If your very first thoughts were "It's okay; I can fix this," go straight to the head of the class. If instead, your initial reaction sounded more like "How stupid of me; what a jerk; this is a disaster; everything is a disaster," know that you are in good company. These fits of impatience and harsh judgments let most of us blow off steam and continue on our day. We don't drop everything when we hear them and start taking notes: "I'm a *j-e-r-k*; say that again, please?" We don't give them that authority. The negative is fleeting, the logical is lasting.

The Happiness Equation

It is crucial to understand that our lives are much more complex than any research study can ever reflect, so no one factor, or even ten factors, can define or predict what our life path will be. To reinforce this fact, in his book *Authentic Happiness*, Martin Seligman provides a user-friendly format to capture the idea that we can do much to become the driver on our path in life, even if we have some strikes against us:

$$H = S + C + V$$

Our enduring happiness (H) is a function of the combined values of our set point (S; genetics or inborn tendencies), our circumstances (C; whether we are rich or poor, ill or healthy, oppressed or privileged, etc.), and the thoughts and actions that are under our voluntary control (V).[2] Sonja Lyubomirsky of the University of California and colleagues Ken Sheldon and David Schkade have conducted extensive research on these factors and quantified the relationship between them as follows: Our happiness is 40 percent under our voluntary control, 10 percent due to our circumstances, and 50 percent due to our set point.[3] The optimists reading this will be reassured that we can, with great hope and confidence, protect our children from depression, and enhance their happiness in life. Those who are skeptical that 40 percent can make a difference should imagine what 40 percent control over the weather, the stock market, or our government would be like; 40 percent might start to sound like a very solid figure.

For children and teens with a negative thinking bias, the ratios are reversed. Through no fault of their own, their negative reaction doesn't become just a temporary stop, a first negative knee-jerk followed by a more reasoned, freed-up reaction; instead, it becomes the default, the first, last, and final word. If someone were actually coming at them—a bully, for example—they might do a "Nope, not today!" But they just don't know that they have that choice with their own thoughts. When kids hear their string of negative thoughts, self-accusations, and judgments over and over, like a sinister advertising jingle, they begin to believe them. The way out of that spiral is to help kids get distance from the thoughts, expect them, and change their relationship with them. When kids learn to recognize and "tag" thoughts as the negative brain jumping in, they are able to dismiss the thoughts and know that intrusive negative thoughts are nothing for them to trust. Instead of insisting that things have to go *right* or else they are *wrong*, kids can incorporate flexibility in their narrative and reinterpret the situation: I would *prefer* that things happened differently than they did, but I will figure out how to deal with it.

Some kids get stuck in this thinking only occasionally. Other children seem to be permanent residents in the land of what's wrong, finding relief only in those fleeting moments when everything is just right (although typically, parents can't relax in those moments because they are waiting for the other shoe to drop, or they know that a total meltdown is just a broken shoelace away). Whatever your child's situation—whether she is stuck in a negative place or just passing through—you can help safeguard her from these debilitating patterns of thought. Kids can break free from negative thinking when they identify it not as the "truth" but as an automatic first reaction, which they can counter by cultivating a more neutral, accurate, or even hopeful second reaction. Parents, equipped with the right information can be powerful agents of this change in their child's thinking.

Portraits in Negativity: Who Is the Negative Child?

Just Passing Through: The Occasionally Devastated, Typically Happy Child. In even the happiest of kids, you can see the lights of their spirit and conviction dim, or more aptly, shut off altogether, in the throes of a negative spin. These kids, whether five or fifteen, may have an easy-going temperament, they might even sparkle and dazzle, they may be very resourceful, excited, and engaged in many aspects of their life, but a curve ball of any size throws them for a loop. Instead of landing quickly on their feet, they get disoriented. Perhaps because these kids cope well most of the time, the degree of distress they experience can be especially embarrassing, disconcerting, or uncomfortable. And because a negative mood may feel very foreign to them, they may be more reluctant to learn about how to handle it and just want somebody to make it stop. Parents of the occasionally negative child need to learn that rather than removing the offending circumstance or feeling, they need to help their child see that he can make it through by learning the skills of resilience.

Glass Half Empty: The Negative Magnet. Some kids with a negative bias feel the impact of their mood more consistently, and those around them feel it, too. Adversity doesn't have to befall these children to make them unhappy; they produce their own constant flow of negative comments about whatever passes by their screen: "That's for breakfast? Gross!" "I have to drive with Cassie today? I hate Cassie." "I have to go to Target after school? Why do I always get dragged around on errands?" "Why do I have to eat dinner with the family, it's so *boring*." Life feels like an imposition to them. Their high irritation quotient over the day-to-day details only makes their fuse shorter when more serious challenges arise. The constant barrage of "no" or "bad" ripples the negativity out into the family who feel like they're walking on eggshells. Working on seeing the daily annoyances more neutrally will give them more of a buffer when something big comes along.

The Anxious-Negative Child. Kids who are plagued by what-ifs throughout their day, who anticipate harm, danger, or failure around every corner, often succumb to negative thinking when, exhausted, they give up on preparing for each imagined disaster and begin to feel hope-less about their ability to manage their life. Their default response to any new situations is "no" because they don't want to risk being unprepared, or caught off guard. Over time, life gets smaller for these kids as they feel frustrated with their inability to take a risk, and instead shut down op-portunities that they see their peers enjoying. These kids need to address the negative thinking first, and then they can successfully tackle the underlying source: their anxious thoughts.

Perfectionist Pressure Cooker. A tyrant in your ear might be kinder than a perfectionist—at least, a tyrant has to sleep from time to time. When everything must be "just so," it is impossible to have a good day. First graders, convinced that every letter must be just right, refuse to put any marks on the page or erase and rewrite until the paper is torn. Teenagers, bleary-eyed from lack of sleep, unable to turn in anything less than the (unattainable) perfect project, melt down in the face of the impossibility of completing homework each night. Constantly rebounding from all the perceived failures (of both oneself and others) makes it hard to notice the successes because they are so few by comparison. Perfectionists typically become very irritable from trying to absorb all the disappointments and pressures their mind creates for them each day. Lowering the stakes, not the standards is key. Redefining what excellence means, focusing on growth and improvement not perfection, these are the new ideas that kids need to incorporate into their thinking.

Exploders. Anger is one way that kids express their negativity. When your child's brain is essentially saying, "I'll give you fifty reasons why this won't work" (when two pros and two cons would have sufficed), the negativity may come out with a vengeance. Because negativity has been picking on them, as in playing a game of hot potato, they throw the blame on you.

Imploders. Some kids are very invested in keeping their mind-set and problems private from others at school, but they are ready to lose it when the last bell rings and they get in the car. They may demand, "Roll up the windows! Now!" before they burst with everything they are upset about. Their teachers and sometimes even their peers may have no idea that their thoughts are beating up on them. Their negative thinking takes its toll invisibly, creating an internal prison of limits, restrictions, and enough discouragement and disappointment to keep them on the sidelines of their lives.

Most poignantly, whatever scenario parents may find in their home, they often describe their children with a negative mind-set as "unreachable." Negative thinking creates an absolute airtight seal in the mind, preventing any other possibilities from getting in. Seeing kids trapped by what are self-imposed and illogical limitations, criticisms, and predictions, parents are drawn on instinct to rational engagement—try to pull off those limitations by countering them with facts—"it's not true that you're not smart; of course you're very smart," their pleas sheeting off the spirit of their shut-down child. When their child is surrounded by an impenetrable certainty that all is *not* well, parents feel they have no access and therefore can offer no relief. Like people who have been brainwashed, kids in the throes of negative thinking are convinced that what they are hearing in their head or saying to themselves is true, and their parents' attempts to comfort them or disagree may only bring on more negative propaganda.

As we'll see, engaging with the content is not the best strategy. At least, not to start. The first step is to connect with your child's suffering through empathy. Lean in. Let her know you see her—you see her struggling, then she won't have to try so hard to convince you of her difficulties. You aren't agreeing that her perceptions are true, you are recognizing that these are her perceptions—these are truly the feedback she is getting from within. You may not even understand the perceptions, but you *want* to understand. Connecting with your child first, letting her know you are on her side, helps you then externalize the problem in a way that gives your child some breathing room and the possibility for perspective. Then, focusing on "who's talking" or "who's narrating the story of what happened" can follow. For young children, you can do this by externalizing the problem and referring to the source of the negative thoughts as Mr. Meany or The Criticizer or get distance by putting the conclusions through the "reality checker": "I lost this race, therefore I am a bad swimmer, therefore I should quit the team" versus "I am a strong swimmer who lost this race; I did my best time ever; my opponent just did better; quitting the team doesn't make sense because the team needs me." For teens, this may mean helping them take a step back from that first assessment and decide whether they want to have their thoughts keep leading them in that direction, saying things like, "Those are some pretty tough thoughts there." "Those conclusions may make sense, but let's see, can we test it out a little. . . . " Parents will do well to remember that table for two, leave your pessimism (why are you always so negative!)

at the door, breathe, and help your child get distance from her thoughts the way you're trying to, too. Remember, too, that simply arguing with your child's negative conclusions won't work. Kids will likely feel worse, not better, because you are correcting them and not hearing how bad they are feeling. If parents are open to taking the scenic route—taking the long way through their child's thought process and inviting them to come help with the fact-checking, then they will likely follow.

PART TWO: CAUSES AND CORRELATES OF NEGATIVE THINKING AND DEPRESSION

We need to be clear from the outset that we have robust methods to reverse the epidemic of depression in our culture and prevent the needless suffering of children and adults. So, while the statistics on depression in the Introduction are reason for grave concern, the research on treating and even preventing depression presents a very different picture—one of great hope and specific actions that can be taken to maintain every child's firm grip on her or his right to a fully functioning life.

The Overprotective Brain: Evolution at Work?

Is it possible that negative thoughts and even depression have a protective function, an evolutionary purpose? At first glance, it is hard to envision how shutting down a system, giving up, isolating oneself, and all the other negative behaviors that accompany depression could be adaptive in any possible way. The opposite would seem to be true. But evolutionary psychologists suggest that depression at one time may have, in the words of Dr. Edward Hagen of Humboldt University, functioned as a "labor strike,"[4] as if the person is saying "I give up," so that others will take over when the coping system is overwhelmed and needs time out.

Consider the case of anxiety (a close cousin of depression), which can be too much of a good thing, *overprotecting* us from danger so that we begin to fear things that we need not. Every anxiety has a "kernel of truth": A fear of dogs or snakes may be unrealistic in its degree, but not absurd, and our goal is to shrink the feeling of risk back to its appropriate size. Similarly, negative thoughts signal to us that something went wrong, but in supersizing the impact and finality, we think that the engine has fallen out and is beyond repair rather than that something unexpected or even unfortunate happened and perhaps we just need to downshift and reevaluate our direction.

Negative tendencies in the brain, with all the best intentions to protect us from failure, get in our way either by sending the give-up message too soon in an overreaction to a small disappointment, or by prolonging an otherwise appropriate negative reaction far beyond what is reasonable or useful. Helping children understand that these disproportionate reactions are a potential programming error rather than an accurate reflection of the situation will begin to get them off the hot seat and in a better position to do a system reset to a more workable interpretation of for the situation they are in.

Could It Be Cultural?

"It was the best of times, it was the worst of times." Charles Dickens's words may be the most apt description of the United States and other developed nations that are both the richest economically and the poorest in terms of depression and other mental health conditions. As we juxtapose the highest median income in history with the highest rates of depression, researchers are investigating whether there is a correlation. Could the pressure and expectations that seeking greater and greater material security places on us line the pathway to increased stress, anxiety, and depression? Our competitive culture, powered by capitalism and advertising, leaves us feeling empty and anxious, and we fill that void with things, and more things. If the slogan on a playground-equipment delivery truck is any indication, children have been dragged into the rat race, too: "My child has a bigger imagination than yours."

We have seen a generation blamed for helicoptering, the hyperbolic parent doing everything for their child on a silver tray, and for kids not knowing how to manage themselves. And yes, those parents exist. They do. But let's be honest: We all have found ourselves in those moments of getting ahead of ourselves and our kids. The child who is studying the ants on the sidewalk—she's going to be a scientist! Before you know it, she's signed up for classes at the Science Museum, outfitted with a microscope and the works. There is nothing wrong with this, and there is much that is right. We delight in our children's growth. We have these visions for our children and that's wonderful. Here's the thing. Kids have different needs and parenting is not one size fits all. We just have to check ourselves that we aren't inadvertently saying hurry up and get there! because of our own fears about the future. Yet, even that is understandable. It's what we do with those fears that counts.

When we parents anxiously feel the pressures of economic and other uncertainties, are our children shouldering the fallout? In psychologist Madeline Levine's *Teach Your Children Well: Why Values and Coping Skills Matter More Than Grades, Trophies, and "Fat Envelopes,"*[5] the follow-up to her groundbreaking *The Price of Privilege: How Parental Pressure and Material Advantage Are Creating a Generation of Disconnected and Unhappy Kids,*[6] Dr. Levine suggests that parents can become part of the solution, rather than the problem, by reevaluating their priorities and learning to manage their own anxieties and pressure-filled lives. Until parents realize that pushing children to the endgame of good grades, college, and jobs as the marker of success isn't what kids need, the number of kids with significant emotional challenges will continue to grow. The formula for lasting success and happiness doesn't come from the superficial high of a good grade on a test, it comes from developing the emotional skills over time to take reasonable risks, to rebound from the struggles, to connect with others, to grow. The focus in schools on test grades and perfect attendance doesn't help. When it comes to academic stress, parents, children, and educators are all in the pressure cooker together. Children feel the crunch earlier and earlier with hours of homework, stress out to the point of throwing up before tests, check their GPAs the way some adults check the stock market, and only take classes in which they are sure to do well to preserve that GPA. All this happens even before the key to the college admissions machine is inserted in the ignition. As much as families and secondary schools may manage the stress of getting children into college, colleges also feel pressured to find classes that are appropriate for the "zoomers," the students who have already taken advanced college-level classes in high school. Who is being served by all this pressure on our children? When and where do we start to alleviate it? As one secondary school administrator pointed out, in the rigor-equals-success equation "no one wants to be the first to break the cycle."[7]

While it may take decades for the system to right itself, the health and well-being of our children is at stake; they can't wait—and they don't have to. We can decide what is best for our families, what factors contribute to lasting fulfillment, and we can begin to weave them into our lives today. Glancing ahead to the strategies for sustainable optimism in Chapter 12, you will find ideas for championing growth, but not at the expense of your child's well-being. This approach is not about lowering our standards or expectations for our children, but about taking a very serious and careful look at what is at stake when we leave children unprepared for the demands and ravages of a flawed educational system.

The Impact of Stressful Events and Everyday Stress

As much as we try to shield our children from stressful events, they are unfortunately an inevitable part of life. In addition to the ordinary pressures of having to do well in school or being overscheduled, children are exposed to such traumatic events as crime, accidents, or the death of a family member, or they live with chronic stressors whether of an individual nature, such as illness, abuse or violence, or the protracted impact born of systemic issues, such as poverty, racism or other debilitating prejudice. Truly, today, the landscape of daily life for all children is rapidly changing. The world they face is not the world that we knew growing up. Along with taking attendance and turning in homework, active shooter and lockdown drills have become part of the reality of daily life for our kids. In addition, many children realistically fear discrimination and bullying for the color of their skin, whom they love, what they wear, or how they pray.

The realities of these times further emphasize the need for resilience skills. In many instances, it isn't that our children are inventing the possibility of negative events; these do happen. But even and especially when there is a reality component to the risks, there is still much that children and teens can do and must do to stay safe and grounded—both physically and emotionally—in the face of ambient hostility. Beyond a certain point, focusing on risk puts us in a precarious place emotionally. It is more adaptive to focus on safety than on risk. Kids can understandably feel upset about the negative aspects of the environment they live in; this upset may make them feel powerless. The challenge for children and teens (and the parents who support them) is to be smart about safety, but not dwell on it. Instead of focusing on what they can't control, they can focus their attention and energies on engaging in meaningful activities and connecting with others who share similar values. This ensures that the preponderance of their attention is on things that matter to them rather than getting pulled into negative conversations in their own mind.

A staggering 62 percent of US children will encounter a significant traumatic event in their lifetime.[8] Traumatic events can have many different consequences in social-emotional functioning, though less than a quarter of kids will go on to develop a diagnosis, such as posttraumatic stress disorder.[9] As tragic as it is that we can't prevent traumatic events from occurring, given the differences in numbers of exposure versus disorder, fortunately there are other factors that we can cultivate in our kids to buffer the effects of trauma.

As we learned earlier from Dr. Lyubomirsky's equation (see box, page 19), external circumstances account for only 10 percent of our overall happiness level. The very hopeful message, the basis of the science of cognitive behavioral therapy, is that although we can't control the events that happen to us, we *can* control the story we tell ourselves about those events, and therefore we hold the key to the impact they have on us. It is understandable that the first story we tell ourselves may cast us as the victim. But with time and reflection, we can more accurately and even hopefully revise that story to emphasize how we've overcome as opposed to how we've been wronged.

Interestingly, just as the Chinese pictograph for *crisis* is made up of two terms—*danger* and *opportunity*—studies have found that many children, contrary to what we might expect, actually find opportunities for growth and strength amid adversity and hardship. Whether enduring open-heart surgery or chemotherapy, living with a chronically ill parent, or experiencing a natural disaster, children's coping repertoire may be expanded and their resiliency increased by the ordeal of personal challenge.

Adapting to new circumstances, flexibly generating new solutions, staying hopeful by staying in the present, and focusing on what still works rather than on what is now broken are the skills that, even on the best of days, are in short supply for the negatively wired child. In the face of a trauma, any child would be expected to ask, "Why is this happening to me?" Children who pull toward the negative make that very normal question a hub around which this event and others spin, thinking, "Bad things always happen to me," or blaming themselves for their situation.

Rather than adapting to changes and finding alternative activities, children may get stuck on the loss of what they were once able to do, or what they think *should* be happening, getting deeper into a hole of impossibilities. Inaccurate explanations weigh such children down and become a pathway to depression. But that pathway can be diverted to a healthier track by accurate thinking, flexible problem solving, and managing negative emotion.

Peer teasing, bullying, sexual harassment, and overt aggression are a group of stressors whose impact are time and again underestimated and dismissed as benign "kids will be kids" behavior. In fact, these experiences are often traumatic, tragically so in too many instances, and are a very strong predictor of cognitive vulnerability to depression.[10] Although the strategies throughout this book will be helpful for building peer-stressed children's assertiveness, studies on bullying suggest that skillful, strategic *adult* participation is essential in any peer-bullying intervention, so for further reading on this important issue, please see the resource guide at the end of this book.

Even children who are spared the harsher experiences of life are exposed to daily dosages of stress from the pinging of texts, app alerts, overbooked calendars, five a.m. swim practices, or backbreaking schoolbags. Children not only shoulder their own stress but get the fallout from parents' overbooked lives. Furthermore, they have few of the choices and little to none of the authority of adults: They can't skip a meeting to eat a meal or catch up on sleep. With more to do and less time to do it in, sleep suffers, nutrition suffers, and the result for many children is emotional overload. A stressed system is more prone to quick assessments ("Everything stinks in my life!") than to accurate ones ("I'm hungry and I don't understand my math homework!").

The cost of this overload has been well documented. As we saw in the Introduction, the level of depressive symptoms and emotional disorders has increased precipitously in recent years. Dr. Jean Twenge, who had reported in a 2000 study[11] that the typical schoolchild during the 1980s reported more stress than psychiatric patients did during the 1950s, found in 2017 that depressive symptoms increased a steep 50 percent in teenage girls, and 21 percent in boys in the years between 2012 and 2015.[12] Dr. Twenge points to the concomitant rise in social media use as a culprit, and we will address this directly in a later chapter.

The take-home message is that we can't protect our children from every risk, but we can take the stress temperature of our household and commit ourselves to establishing a sustainable family lifestyle, even when that means making unpopular choices. By setting up an infrastructure—basic expectations for such things as sleep, healthy food, hard work, and play; discussing healthy, reasonable guidelines for social media and technology use—we can create a physical and emotional buffer zone for stressful events, so that our children can manage the additional demand. The exercises throughout the book, in particular in Chapter 12, "Everyday Optimism" (page 287), will help you create a sustainable, depression-proof life for your child and your family.

The Influence of Family Factors

Parental Depression. One of the early tasks of life is developing a trusting attachment to a parent figure. Within this relationship, a basic sense of safety grows: "I am cherished; my needs are met; I will be taken care of." The elements of that safety are experienced and registered nonverbally through a process of tracking and mirroring (when a child smiles, you smile; when she looks upset, you look upset, too).[13] These empathic data points accumulate and help form an internalized, secure home base from which children begin to venture out—whether it's to a caregiver's arms, the playground, or eventually, their first job. To an infant, parents are the world; research has found infancy to be a "sensitive period" for being impacted by parental depression and the development of what are known as internalizing symptoms later in childhood—anxiety, depression—as this period sets up the framework for the infant's internal emotional regulation system.[14] Parents who are depressed, just like parents who have any incapacitating medical problem, become paralyzed and overwhelmed by their own struggles, are depleted emotionally and physically, and tragically, often neglect the needs of their children. In fact, children of depressed parents are two to four times as likely to develop depression than are their peers with parents without depression.[15] Fortunately, when parents are treated, improvements are readily seen in their children as well.

Family Conflict and Criticism. In *Hand-Me-Down Blues*, clinical psychologist Michael Yapko[16] points out that the family can play a vital role in both the "nature and nurture of depression." At different stages of development, different influences may be felt. In infancy, as we have seen, a basic sense of trust and confidence is affected; in younger children, emotional regulation is impacted. In preschool-aged children, low levels of positive emotion (positive mood states, social connection, and engagement), but not high levels of negative emotion, have been associated with depression in mothers.[17] As children get older, they are more keen at picking up on family cues and can exercise greater self-control. As a result, they learn to tiptoe between two worlds with very different rules: enjoying themselves away from home and then needing to "leave their smile at the door" because it is understood that "happiness is not spoken here." Yapko points out that not only are many of the standard exchanges of childhood—good news, a good grade, a joke, a funny anecdote—lost in families that are under depression's rule, but kids also either begin to devalue these experiences themselves or blame themselves for getting excited about events because, converted to the economy of the household where suffering is the gold standard, these measure up as a deficit.

A negative family environment doesn't cause depression, but it may interfere with a child's development of the coping strategies he needs to buffer himself from adverse events. Researchers have identified the following disruptive factors in a negative home environment: a high level of conflict, harsh criticism, weak attachment bonds, and low responsiveness and attunement to children's emotions.[18] It is important to know that when these issues are approached in treatment, family relations improve, children's internal coping also improves, and adolescent depression may be reduced.[19]

Parenting Style. Is there a parenting style associated with depression or negativity? Parents who are themselves unhappy, negative, or depressed can create a toxic environment where children absorb and reflect a similar style of perceiving and interacting with the world. For example, a father who is unhappy about his job and who thinks, "It doesn't matter what you do, the world is unfair, and there's no point in working hard," spreads that unhappiness to his child by discouraging or invalidating the child's enthusiasm about a project or by not paying attention to it. A parent who is a perfectionist responds harshly to her child's hard-earned B+ because it isn't an A. In either example, the children may absorb the wrong messages from their parents: "What you do isn't important," or "You failed because it wasn't an A." Some children naturally buffer those messages, but other children begin to talk to themselves the same way. Over time, these patterns of responding become automatic thinking habits—as effortless as they are destructive. As parents, the more we work on our own negativity and model adaptive responses the more our children will feel free to do the same.

Even parents who are not intentionally critical or negative may foster depression or negativity less obviously. In over fifty years of research, parenting-style researcher Diana Baumrind has identified two key dimensions of parenting behavior. The first, *parental responsiveness* (empathy, availability, listening, warmth, supportiveness), is associated with the goal of fostering individuality and self-regulation by staying attuned to children's needs. The second, *parental demandingness* (discipline, behavioral control, expectations), refers to the "claims parents make on children to become integrated into the family whole, by their maturity demands, supervision, disciplinary efforts and willingness to confront the child who disobeys."[20] Baumrind adds a third factor that can be present in any of the styles: *psychological control*, the "how" of parenting interventions, or the degree to which we are intrusive with our interventions. Waiting for an apology would be "low" control, while using guilt induction or shaming to get a child to behave would be considered "high" on the dimension of psychological control. One can imagine that if our goal is a self-regulated, responsible child, intrusive actions of psychological control will undermine that goal. And in fact this is the case. The following chart describes the four styles.

CHART 1-1

	Indulgent	Authoritarian	Uninvolved	Authoritative
Responsiveness	High	Low	Low	High
Demandingness	Low	High	Low	High
Control	Low	High	Low	Low

Indulgent/Permissive Parents

Focusing on responsiveness to children's needs, these parents are lenient, may overly identify with their children's demands, and as a result do not ask for responsible behavior. Result: These children are more likely to have high self-esteem but poor judgment and are more likely to be involved in problem behaviors and to not persevere in school.

Authoritarian Parents

These parents are high on demands but low on responsiveness. Therefore, rules, which require no explanation, are always more important than what may be going on with the child. Result: Children in these families tend to be obedient and to perform well enough in school, but have a higher risk of depression, poorer social skills, and lower self-esteem because their emotional needs are not met.

Uninvolved Parents

These parents are high in neither demand nor responsiveness, and in general, their children are left to fend for themselves. Result: In contradiction of Jean-Jacques Rousseau's idea of children's finding their own way, they need help, and children in this category perform poorly in all domains: socially, academically, and emotionally.

Authoritative Parents

This style is consistently identified as most highly associated with socially competent, well-adjusted children who have lower levels of problem behavior or depression and anxiety across all stages of development. Authoritative parents are high on demands and accountability but low on control, and they are not restrictive or intrusive. They take on the complex challenge of being supportive of and attentive to their children while still expecting compliance with rules that are based on logic rather than "because I said so." Discipline is about learning, rather than punishment. As a result of this modeling, children of authoritative parents are able to find a balance between external demands in their own life for achievement and conformity, while still keeping their individuality and autonomy. Authoritative parenting is the model on which the interventions in this book are based.

Genetics

> The most important message our research can make is that experience is as strong or stronger than anything that is inherited.
>
> —STEPHEN SUOMI, PhD, National Institute of
> Child Health and Human Development[21]

It has long been thought that depression runs in families. Years of research, across multiple studies, have concluded that if one person in a family is depressed, it is likely that another family member will have depression. In one study, depressed teens were five times as likely as nondepressed teens to have another depressed family member.[22] If one identical twin is depressed, the chance is as much as 50 percent that the other twin will be diagnosed as well. With technological advances, researchers have found that rather than a single gene being responsible for depression, the genetic influence is expressed through the interplay of many different genes.

If your family has a history of depression, know that the skills you will learn here will play a crucial role in buffering your child from developing depression.

Biochemical Influence

The notion of depression as a chemical imbalance has become so accepted that even some of my youngest patients, who can barely spell or reach the sink without a stool, are completely comfortable using the phrase "chemical imbalance" to explain why they are depressed. In fact, these young scientists are not entirely wrong, but neither are they entirely right. For instance, the function of some antidepressant medications— for example, the popular selective serotonin reuptake inhibitors, or SSRIs—is to correct an imbalance in the brain by making more serotonin (a chemical messenger) available in the system. But if there are, in fact, lower levels of serotonin in the brain of someone who is depressed (this assumption has not been scientifically proven), these lower levels may be a *consequence* of depression, rather than a cause. The relationship between behavior and neurotransmitters is reciprocal, a two-way street: Serotonin impacts behavior and mood, but behavior impacts serotonin levels as well. When our mood is low, we may have less serotonin available, but when we make changes in our mood or behavior, they register as changes in brain activity as well. In other words, our biochemistry both reflects how we have learned to respond to situations and may dictate our tendencies to respond in certain ways.

This process of changing brain mapping through changes in behavior is what neurobiologists refer to as *neuroplasticity*. And it is why we can have confidence that if we engage in cognitive behavioral techniques (our "V," or voluntary efforts), "depression can be cured," in the words of Martin Seligman.[23]

In their book *The Mind and the Brain*, UCLA psychiatrist Jeffrey Schwartz and medical reporter Sharon Begley[24] have documented the powerful impact of neuroplasticity: the dynamic changes in the allocation of brain space and resources in response to whatever activity we do a lot of. The index finger of a blind person who refines his skill with Braille or the thumb of a video game fanatic, by virtue of their practice, have larger regions of the brain dedicated to those body parts than will those who don't engage in those activities. In the clinical realm, Schwartz found when working with patients with obsessive-compulsive disorder (OCD) that changes in the prefrontal cortex, the thalamus, and the caudate nucleus were visible on a PET scan after treatment; these patients' brain looked (and therefore functioned) like those of people without OCD. What is important is that these changes were just as significant in patients who took *no* medication as in those who did. Changing behavior and mind through behavioral exercises actually changed the brain and, most important, continues to change the quality of life for millions of people who suffer with OCD. Similar results have been found with depression: As mood improves, there is increased activity in the left prefrontal cortex, the part of the brain responsible for positive feelings and problem solving. So, when our children begin exercising their flexibility and resilient responses, their brain is attentive and will create a new map or game plan, allotting more "staff and supplies" for the regions that will best support those activities.

Cognitive Style

Our explanatory style—the way we narrate the circumstances and events of our life—impacts us every day. Is a forgotten book a hiccup or a disaster? It depends on your explanatory style. Research has consistently documented the robust connection between negative thoughts and pessimistic style and the development and maintenance of depression. Although we can imagine that it would be helpful to have an optimistic or resilient style to get through a significant trauma or stressful event such as a move, a parent's illness, a car accident, or the death of a loved one, those events are fortunately rare in a child's life. But explanatory style can either buffer or bother a child during the hundreds of small moments and social exchanges in any given day. A child who is negative or in a bad mood or even depressed may baffle you, and you may not understand where the mood comes from, but tracking down the threads of her attributional style makes it clear that she is racking up negative points all day in processing the vicissitudes of life. An event as innocuous as choosing a broken plastic fork in the cafeteria may be the only evidence the child needs to confirm that "nothing good ever happens to me; I always get the worst of everything." With your help, that same child can learn to set aside that first reaction, choose a new fork, and even get a chuckle because the quality control is not what it used to be. Applying these skills to shield themselves from their own misinterpretations will keep children with a default negative mind-set moving forward on the road of life, rather than getting waylaid in the ditches.

CONCLUSION

There are many pathways into negativity, including cognitive style, stressful events, and genetic vulnerability. But we ultimately have the tools to construct a life outside the box of this way of responding. Now we begin.

2

CHANGING YOUR CHILD'S MIND

Talking Back to the Negative Brain

I feel like there is an evil guard dog barking in my head every time I say something to make myself feel better. I feel like I can't do a single thing to talk that dog down.

—eighteen-year-old girl

We get into an argument every day. He says, everything went bad today, and I insist that can't be true. I'm not trying to fight with him, but somehow he's got to fight with himself.

—father of fourteen-year-old boy

CULTIVATING THE TWO-TRACK MIND:
IT'S NOT THE THOUGHT, IT'S WHAT YOU DO WITH IT

We don't see things as they are, we see them as we are.

—Anaïs Nin

There's nothing either good or bad, but thinking makes it so.

—William Shakespeare

When it comes to flexibility, many children seem to have an on/off switch. During a video game, when children encounter an evil guy or hit a dead end, they've got flexibility in spades. Their resilience is fluid. They know there are options: That's the whole point of the game. Faster than you can say, "Turn it off, it's time for bed," they've escaped the villain, found the treasure, saved the world, rerouted, and forged ahead in a new direction multiple times. But when these same children hit a glitch in their own lives, they don't pick up their controllers or look right and left for their options. They crumble, they get stuck, and it's "game over." Children use cognitive flexibility playing computer games because they see the options right there—colorful, dynamic and inviting—and they want to win. When they encounter an obstacle, they don't get scared or discouraged; they get determined and competent. And the more they play, the more competent they get. So, herein lies our challenge: If we want our children to persevere in the face of adversity, we need to help them seek out the options, to make those options more inviting, and help our children see that in withstanding the challenges of navigating through the dark lands of their own thinking, they can win. Just as fish don't know they are in water, they just swim, children who tend toward the negative often don't know they're thinking negatively—they're just thinking. The first step in changing negative thinking is *knowing* when it's happening. Once children recognize the sound of their "negative brain," they learn that following those messages leads them to a dark place they don't want to be. Instead, they can choose to call on their "smart brain" for another interpretation of the story that will lead to a more promising pathway. This is what cultivating the two-track mind is all about: Just because you start with a negative thought doesn't mean you need to stay stuck with it. You get to choose what to think. Negative thoughts should be treated as *hypotheses*—questions or theories to be proved or disproved—rather than *decrees*. Especially as children learn that negative thoughts are reliably unreliable (however speedy) reactions, they will be less tempted to pull up a chair and listen. So, it's not the thought, it's where you go next. Much as we can't control who calls us on the phone, we can't control the calling of negative thoughts, but we *can* decide how carefully we listen, how long we stay on the phone, and who we keep on our speed dial.

In this chapter, you will find many strategies and exercises to help your child find his way out of the maze of blind alleys and think holes of the negative brain by learning how to spot the traps, generate arrays of alternatives, and navigate to his goal. Because we will use these "thinking differently" elements in the master plan in Chapter 5, jot down your favorites or the ones you can imagine easily using with your child to serve as a quick reference and reminder.

Noticing the Negative Voice: The Uninvited Guest

We would all be a bit suspicious, if not deeply disturbed, if our internal voice started saying things to us like "Everything is great! You are simply fabulous and will be forever more! Everything you do is terrific! Absolute guarantee!" We would want to see some ID before letting those crazy ideas in the door. And yet, when our internal voice says to us, "You're a failure; everything's out of control; you can't fix it; you should give up," we push aside all evidence to the contrary and give that voice the VIP treatment. What is most debilitating about negative thinking is that those voices slip in the back way, unannounced, and start taking over the sound system and manipulating our feelings. As psychologist William Knaus says, "How can you tell if a thought is depressive? You can tell by its results. You feel worse."[1] Falling prey to emotional reasoning, we mistake *feeling bad* as validation for the accuracy of the thoughts, when actually it's just a natural and temporary reaction to hearing something unpleasant; it doesn't permanently change the reality of what is true. We need a bouncer at the door of our mind who informs us through the intercom, "This is your negativity talking. This is not a voice to be trusted," to protect us from the effects of just letting that voice in. Fortunately we don't have to hire a big guy to protect us. We can protect ourselves. We have choices. We don't have to give preferential treatment to our automatic negative thoughts.

As we move into this chapter on talking back to negative thinking, we see again that the goal isn't to make the thoughts stop (we can't just reach in and do that!), or to deny the presence of the thoughts, or even to fight with the thoughts. We must change our *relationship* to them: Although the negative brain is programmed to see the problems, flaws, and disappointments, we can nevertheless pick ourselves up and look at things through a different lens. We can't help that the first negative thought jumped in, but we can train ourselves to not pile on ten more. The thoughts are just one of many interpretations of a story, and making a habit out of considering just one or two of the alternatives (minus the distortions) releases you from the moment of being stuck.

What You Need to Get Started

Mind-Set: Get Your Child Interested in the Process. Kids are excellent at spotting *our* foibles—like when we occasionally hightail it through a "pink" light—so, they just need to know what to look for in their own thinking. In this chapter, parents will learn not only how to be a distortion detector for their kids, but also how children can become expert at thinking critically and detecting distortions themselves.

Because no one likes to be told he or she is wrong, especially someone who is already feeling terrible about him- or herself, it's best to make these lessons impersonal. And they are! These negative thoughts are not something unique about your child, these are universal human reflexes. Rather than framing these exercises as correcting the "wrong thing" that your child is thinking, enlist his curiosity about finding the "tricks" the mind can play and his creativity in finding alternatives. Kids with a pull toward the negative are already self-critical, so you must be clear that your child is learning about the machinery of his wonderful brain— which doesn't always cooperate with him. He can't help what he sees first; that's his wiring, but in understanding how the brain works, he can change where he takes that story *next*, freeing himself from negativity.

Materials: Gathering Your Child's or Teen's Thoughts. You and your child are going to need to compile a list of her negative thoughts for many of the exercises here. For young children, you will help with the "gathering," with teens, you can model the strategies and give them the choice to show you or not. Often it's helpful with teens to give a generic or impersonal example, "people in that situation might think at first 'x,'" "it wouldn't be surprising if people in that situation were thinking 'y' to themselves." Some kids are talkers and could report enough negative thoughts for the whole neighborhood. Other kids may be less aware of their thoughts, or less comfortable sharing. For those children, it will help to do a "thought sample." You can explain that a thought sample lets you know what you are saying to yourself, so each evening for a few days, or at random times, ask your child to write down in a notebook two or three thoughts. You can help her focus: "What were you thinking when you were feeling your worst and your best today?" or "If we put a microphone to your head, what was your mind saying during those times?" Once she is in the habit of tuning in to her thoughts, you can do this exercise only as needed.

OUTSMARTING THE TRICKS THE BRAIN CAN PLAY IN NINE LESSONS

Lesson One: Teaching Your Child to Think out of Both Sides of the Brain

The brain has two sides, which respond to very different input. When we are afraid or confronted with a negative situation, circuits in our right prefrontal cortex are firing away, whereas in more positive situations, the action is in the left brain.[2] Interestingly, this lateralization of the brain is not just a human phenomenon: When a dog sees a "friend," it wags its tail to the right (because the left, or happy, side of the brain is in charge); however, when danger approaches, the tail goes to the left (because the brain's right side is on the job).[3] You might share this information with your child to bring it home (unless, of course, he is afraid of dogs). In humans as well, the left prefrontal cortex is active when there is something safe to approach, whereas when the right side is buzzing, as with anxiety or negative thoughts, we avoid or don't approach. The goal is to create passageways, a bridge over troubled water, to help your child travel from one side of the brain to the other. At first, kids will need reminders to instruct themselves to "pivot," or "switch sides," or "cross over," but the more they practice switching perspectives, the more automatic that action will become, and over time, the brain will learn to switch on its own.

Flexible-Thinking Exercise. There are many ways to help kids learn to differentiate negative thinking from more accurate thinking. For younger children, you can use different stuffed animals to mark the difference:

The cranky puppy and the happy bear can both be looking at the same situation—spilling the milk—and have two very different versions of the story. Or you might draw or find two pairs of glasses, the fuzzy glasses that see everything as bad, and the sharp glasses that see how things can work out. For older children and teens, you can take a sheet of paper, draw a line down the middle, and ask them what they want to call the two sides of the brain. Give examples, such as titling one side "Negative Thoughts" or "Meany Brain Thoughts" and the other side "My Good Thoughts," or "Smart Thoughts." For teens, it may help to think of a very pessimistic character in a movie, or a person they know (it will help them feel more comfortable knowing they're not the only one, and at this moment, they're not on the hot seat!) and for the other side, a very logical person they know. You can then have your teen narrate a situation from these two different perspectives. You can also have your child draw a picture with thought bubbles like the one in the illustration, to distinguish the two types of thinking and to show that it's not about having to "get rid" of negative thoughts, it's about remembering to pivot to find more accurate thoughts. When he sees them side by side, your child can compare one version of the story with the other and choose the one that's truer. He can "thank" his overprotective side for caring so much—teens can do this with a little sarcasm—and then get his smart side to "teach" his overprotective side when it makes sense to jump to conclusions, and when it doesn't.

NEGATIVE GLASSES

This always happens. Everybody thinks I'm a loser. I never do anything right.

Stress temperature 100

COMPETENT GLASSES

Accidents happen. This is a small thing. It means more to me than it does to them.

Stress temperature 25

Stress level 0-100

Lesson Two: Optimism and Pessimism: Observations and Explanations

Part One: Observations: Choosing to See What Is Actually There

> A pessimist sees the difficulty in every opportunity;
> an optimist sees the opportunity in every difficulty.
>
> —Winston Churchill

Long ago, we had an emergency-room visit when our younger daughter, Raia, about four at the time, bumped her head at the dinner table; fortunately, when all was said and done, one single stitch was required. With hours spent waiting in a busy urban children's emergency room, it was after midnight when we finally left the hospital. As we were buckling Raia into her car seat, she exhaled and said, "Well, that was fun." Fun? Not exactly my version of the story, which was more like "Will this leave a scar? How's our daughter at home? I should have been paying more attention. I'm so tired, how am I going to function at work tomorrow?" Raia was firmly grounded in the moment, taking it for what it was, whereas I was scrambling in all the different dimensions of parental time and space. The Dalai Lama teaches that we can't stop events from happening, but there is no one fixed way to view them. The suffering that we subject ourselves to about them is entirely optional. That night, I had clearly left my Buddhism 101 notes at home, but young Raia had them well in hand.

Two Views of a Doughnut

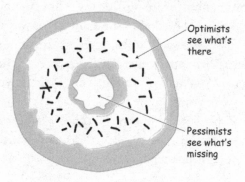

Optimists see what's there

Pessimists see what's missing

One need look no further than the floor at a one-year-old's birthday party to know that we can see great flexibility in any situation. Much to the amusement of the doting adults, the star of the show is usually delighting in the tangle of colorful ribbons, papers, and boxes more than the gifts themselves. Unfettered by preconceived ideas of how things *should* be, the birthday boy calls 'em like he sees 'em and goes for the most fun. Although we may all wish to live with the Zen-like present-centeredness of new life, we are, after all, perpetually living and at the same time making up theories or stories about that life—essentially living in a running commentary. We are free to recast the same facts in many different narratives, yet those with a negative warp immediately home in on what's wrong, overlooking what's right. That running commentary is, bar none, the single most important contribution to how we feel. To paraphrase the Greek philosopher Epictetus, "We are disturbed not by events themselves but by our perceptions of them." Life becomes increasingly unpleasant for children with a negative mind-set, not because they are cursed with greater adversity, but because they are saddled internally with a negative running commentary.

By the time children start kindergarten, they have started not just to *feel* the moment but to try to make sense of it. The resulting theories are the woof and warp of their outlook on life. Two children at a Scoopy-Doo ice-cream parlor have their poorly secured scoop of rocky road slip off the cone. Both are understandably upset. One child cries, "It wasn't on right, so it fell. Can I have another one?" This is the optimistic child's point of view: a factual account of the current problem and problems have solutions. The pessimistic child adds something extra: "Why does this always happen to me? This store is so stupid! Everything's ruined. This is the worst day of my life." The story in the pessimistic child's mind inserts extraneous material from outside the script, attributing intention, permanency, and a global quality to something that was a small accident, plain and simple. By the same token, parents can model theories. The optimistic parent: "It happens. Let's go in and see if they'll fix it." The pessimistic parent: "You're never careful," or "Why do you always get so upset? That's it, we're going home!"

Your child will become an optimistic thinker by learning to keep her thinking accurate, catching on to distortions, and having the flexibility to see what's there, not just what's missing.

Flexible-Thinking Exercises. Playing games that involve going back and forth between positive and negative is one way to cultivate flexible thinking for dealing with adversity. It can also be a lot of fun as the shaggy dog stories are spun. For example, in the game "Unfortunately, Fortunately," you and your child each write down five sticky situations on cards and put them in a hat. Each person in turn draws a card, says the unfortunate circumstance (e.g., "Unfortunately, the movie I wanted to see was sold out"), and then the other person generates a fortunate counterpart ("But fortunately, I went to see another movie"), and they go back and forth for several rounds: "But unfortunately, there were only seats up front." "But fortunately, I got a seat, and there was no gum under my seat." "But unfortunately, there was sticky stuff on the arm of the chair." "But fortunately, it wasn't summer and I was wearing long sleeves." "But unfortunately, my brother sneezed on me." "But fortunately, I had a napkin." Your young child will enjoy playing this game and may not even realize that he is exercising his flexibility muscles. This concept can be conveyed to teens, by saying, "I guess this could be a good moment for the fortunately/unfortunately game" without asking them to play (remember, long-distance learning where one isn't on the hot seat works best for everyone, but especially teens). You could give an example from your own life—when unfortunately, you forgot to bring to work the casserole you made for the potluck, but when you served it at dinner instead and it didn't taste so good, it was fortunate after all!

Another way of cultivating flexibility is to create a "magnet of good." Because sometimes finding the good in a situation is like finding the needle in a haystack, a strong magnet comes in very handy—sometimes for the whole family. You and your child can draw a superstrong magnet (demonstrate the concept of the strong pull of a magnet on your fridge door first, if necessary) that will help you find the good. You can practice this game by generating with your child several mishap situations—or even just reviewing the last couple of "bad" days he had, and seeing whether the magnet can turn up any surprises. After your child describes an unpleasant day or situation, say, "Let's pull out the magnet and see what hidden good parts stuck to it." The biggest surprise may be that the memory of the bad day has faded significantly in your child's mind. The next time your child (or your spouse) has told you her or his version of author Judith Viorst's *Alexander and the Terrible, Horrible, No Good, Very*

Bad Day, you can pull out the good magnet (either real or imaginary) and see whether your child wants to give it a try.[4] Ask him to power up the magnet to locate and pull out all the exceptions to the rule of "bad day," for example, what actually worked out okay.

The same principle may be used for an older child, if you change the metaphor to a reality detector or a good detector similar to the wands and scanners at airport security. When listening to your child talk about all that is wrong, you could suggest that the detector in his brain seems to be set to beep only at problems, meanwhile not letting him see anything else in his life: "Let's see if we can reprogram it in your favor." Notice that you are not placing blame on your child for his involuntary narrow-mindedness. When you say, "It's kind of not fair to you that your mind is doing this to you," your child is more likely to follow your suggestions.

Your teenager will likely think the magnet and wand ideas are lame, but authenticity from adults scores big points, so with just a slight modification you can own that "lameness" and make the lesson impersonal (or, about you, just not about them): "I know this is lame, but I can't help but think if there were only a wand or magnet that could show us what is good instead of pointing out all the bad, ya know what I mean?"

> The next time your child is struggling with a tough moment, suggest, "There are a lot of 'unfortunatelys' stacking up. Can we see if there are any 'fortunatelys' in this situation?"

Part Two: The Hammer and Nails of Our Explanations: Constructing Theories That Box Us In or Set Us Free

Wrestling an airtight explanation away from your child during a negative spin may feel tougher than loosening a toddler's grip on your cell phone when it's ringing and it's your boss. In both cases, you know your child needs to let go, but you also know she's not going to without major unpleasantness. Just as retrieving your phone means giving your toddler something else to grasp, rather than unwrapping the phone from her hand finger by finger, switching your child off the negative track means asking the right questions so that she can seek out a more inviting direction, rather than telling your distressed child point by point why her perceptions are wrong.

In Chapter 1, we saw how Dr. Seligman and his colleagues identified the 3 P's of pessimistic thinking: explaining the adversities of life as *permanent* (unchangeable, unfixable), *pervasive* (not just the missed homework but everything in life), and *personal* (my fault). In the mathematics of pessimism, P + P + P = overwhelmed, hopeless meltdown. The following exercises will help kids do a new math, correct each faulty conclusion about the events in their life, and create an equation that is specific, accurate, and, most important, solvable. Seligman's approach is to evaluate thoughts along those three dimensions and endeavor to keep the explanations accurate, as optimistic thinking is not about sugarcoating the truth or simply wishing for the good. A good place to start is listening for words expressing extremes and absolutes, such as *nothing, everything, always*, and *never*; these are typically red flags for cognitive errors. When you start replacing those with words like *some things* or *sometimes*, you are on the road to more accurate thinking. Once you become familiar with this concept, you and young child can have some fun with it, creating a character, changing your voice: "Joe on the dispatch. I think we have some false accusations, some jumping to conclusions, and some all-or-none thinking here. We need some logic and truth—*and fast!*" For older kids and teens, reflecting those supersized words with empathy as a fellow traveler in life can go a long way: "It's the never, nothing, everything attack; that gets me, too, sometimes. I know it's not true, but it sure does feel that way in the moment . . . It never feels as bad later, I try to fast-forward to that realization as quickly as I can." Teens may be surprised that you're not challenging them on the negativity, and that you're normalizing their experience. And they'll learn from your example how to pivot and not buy in to the negative version of their life. We will now look at each of the 3 P's and identify ways of talking and working with them.

Playing with Permanent: Next Stop Sometimes Land. Kids with negative thinking habits often don't like the gray areas of life. Everything is either all or none. *Maybe, sometimes, right now,* and *temporary* are not in their vocabulary, as in "Sometimes I do well at bat," or "Sometimes my friends are nice to me," or "Sometimes I read well." So, help your child look for the *sometimes* in life—in your own life, in your child's life. You can help young children draw or construct their own "sometimes" shaker; when your child is telling you that things are "always" bad or "never" good, suggest a good shake of the "some" shaker on the situation and see what it looks like then. With teens, as always, own the campiness of the idea, and demonstrate how *you* use it, rather than insisting that they try: "I am having the feeling that I am *always* cleaning up after you kids. Where is that "some" shaker? I could really use that!"

It is human nature to protect ourselves from adversity. Paradoxically, we sometimes protect ourselves by expecting adversities because there can be no unpleasant surprises if we expect the worst. The fine print of that pessimist's guarantee includes being unhappy and missing opportunities by playing it safe. When your teenager fumes that soccer is stupid and she's not going to try out for the team because last year she didn't get picked; ergo, she'll *never* get picked, she is trying to protect herself from being taken by surprise (or rejected), but she is also depriving herself of the opportunity to ride that learning curve and see that things could work out, and get easier, over time. This type of thinking may feel better in the short run, but left unchallenged it engenders hopelessness, undermines confidence, and narrows your child's world. If, instead she sees a situation as temporary, there is the possibility of the next time going differently, and lots of room for improvement or positive change, which she can anticipate and work toward.

Some people...
Some of the time...
Some things went well...

Shake "SOME" today on your ALL-OR-NONE thoughts!

Flexible-Thinking Exercise. Play the Pencil or Pen Game to represent qualities or events that are changeable or permanent. Write out ten adverse situations and ten situations with positive outcomes, and as you comment about them, decide whether the comment should be written in pencil, if it could change, or in pen, if it will be the same way forever. Hint: Most things will be written in pencil. For example, if you miss the bus, your comment "I always miss the bus" or "The bus is always early" would be written in pencil, since it's not true all the time. If you do well on a test, the comment "I'm a good student, I work hard" (if that is true, obviously) would be written in pen, because even though there may be blips here and there, these are enduring qualities. Because pessimistic kids tend to misattribute successes to *temporary* factors ("The test was easy"; "The teacher was nice to me"), rather than to permanent ones, it is important to exercise your child's skills in making accurate attributions for successes as well as disappointments. In presenting these ideas to teens, it's best to talk about yourself or a celebrity or famous athlete, "I know it's hard not to generalize and feel like tough moments are a sign of how things will be forever, but you know Beyoncé lost on *Star Search* when she was a kid, and well, when my boss is not thrilled with an idea I present, my immediate reaction is: 'I stink (or in their terms: suck)' and then I think, wait, did I think that five minutes ago? No. So, I've learned to correct myself, I don't suck, this moment kind of sucks, but it will pass."

You can suggest that you and your child create a new word bank with such words as those that follow, and post them on the fridge or on the bathroom mirror as reminders.

New Word Bank Ideas: sometimes, right now, at this moment, this time, not yet, occasionally, for now

Playing with Pervasive: It's One Thing, Not Everything! When one thing goes wrong, it seems like everything is wrong. Kids with pervasive explanations see the consequences of an adverse situation as spilling over into everything they do. There are no boundaries, no isolated events;

everything is connected. So, messing up one assignment becomes, through a lightening-speed reaction: a chain of imagined terrible consequences, messing up the year, their future, and the rest of their life. Or when Mom gets mad because you forgot your homework, it's the broad sweep: Mom hates me, instead of the specific (and small) part: Mom wants me to remember my homework!

Although it feels as if there are dominoes connecting all the events of your life, and when one falls, they all come tumbling down, it's not true: There's a gap. Encourage your child to be accurate when stating the consequences of her actions: "How many dominoes are really knocked down? Where is the gap? Where does it stop?" So, when one thing goes wrong you can encourage your child to get specific and say, "I messed up a part of this assignment. I'm not messing up the class, my career, my future, my life. I'm not going to be living at my parents' house forever. I may just get a disappointing grade on that one assignment."

When something goes wrong, we tend to catastrophize (that is, imagine ongoing, disastrous consequences for a manageable event), generalize, or otherwise let that one bad apple spoil the whole bunch. This concept can be illustrated in a game called Trunk, Branch, and Leaves. Draw or have your child draw a picture of a tree, then label the parts. Imagine that he is upset that a project at school didn't work out as well as he'd like and he is saying, "I stink at school. I don't care anymore." Show him the drawing and ask, "How much of the tree is damaged? Is

Domino Theory

Explains how something feels, not how it works

that project like one leaf or the whole trunk? Is the tree going to fall? Does the project ruin you as a student? Or is the project more like a leaf—one of many opportunities, some of which will work out and some of which won't, but the tree is still strong?" When your child engages in overgeneralized thinking, you can playfully relabel the situation by saying, "Uh-oh, do we really need to cut down the whole tree? Is it a branch that's the problem or just one unfortunate leaf?" You can help drive home the point by saying, "I bet the negative brain would say it's right to conclude that a baseball player should leave the team because of one bad game, or that a teacher is a bad teacher just because one of her classes was boring—but I bet you know better!"

Borrowing an art history lesson on pointillism can help older children and teens understand how insignificant the C+ is, the embarrassing moment in gym when you dropped the ball and it seemed like everything froze and all eyes were on you, as your team lost the game in the grand scheme of their life. These events are but a small dot in the big picture of your life—not remarkable, not even noticeable. Look up together the nineteenth-century French painter Georges Seurat's most famous work: *A Sunday Afternoon on the Island of La Grande Jatte*—the one with all the Parisians with umbrellas, looking out from the banks of the River Seine. It's made up of millions of tiny dots (points, thus the name *pointillism*), which you can see up close. If even a hundred of those dots were painted the "wrong" color, or were missing dispersed across the painting, we wouldn't notice, it's the big picture that matters. So it is with those gym class snafus and vexing pop quiz grades, they do not change the intricate and beautiful masterpiece in progress that is your child's life!

New Word Bank Ideas: sometimes, some things, one thing, this part, this assignment, partial disaster, part success, what worked, what didn't work

Playing the Blame Game: It's Not Always About Me. Not only do negative-minded kids think the sky is falling, but they might tell you that they deserve for more of it to fall on them because the sky is mad at them for something. Personalizing adversity means that when things don't go right, or go as expected, one person is the cause. Say a teacher isn't smiling one day: "She's mad at me. She hates me." The real reason is that her husband has just had surgery. A friend simply forgets to call one night: "She doesn't care about me. She doesn't want to be friends anymore." When everything that happens in your child's day reads like ten things the world hates about him, he gets understandably upset. Change the world, or change the thinking? In the following exercise, help your child or teen differentiate between problems that are about him or that are not about him and are instead due to other people or circumstances.

Help your child to be a detective and examine the situation. Although his *first* thought is based on feeling, "It's all my fault," he can be encouraged to look for his *second* thought based on the facts. For young kids and teens alike, it can help to represent this by having them create a pie chart and ask what part of the situation or outcome was due to something they did (forgot to bring home book the night before the test) versus what part was due to something or someone else (had a field trip that day so didn't have time to stop at locker before the bus).

- Why did this situation not work out the way I'd hoped?
- What might I have done to make it not happen?
- What do I think is my part?
- What parts may be about someone or something else?
- Would it have worked out for everyone this way?

> New Word Bank Ideas: partially about me, partially someone else's responsibility; part I could control, part I couldn't control; something temporary about me (not permanent); something specific about me (not general)

Putting the 3 P's All Together. The illustration on the next page brings the 3 P's together and, by a process of narrowing down, helps your child go from feeling a huge, overwhelming problem to seeing the one specific straw that broke the camel's back. Negative thinking supersizes the problem; smart thinking is about getting specific and narrowing down the problem. Once the specific issue has been identified, your child can

Unpack—Shrink—GET SPECIFIC

(Which package would you accept?)

"My math test was a disaster so I won't get into college!" → "I stink at math!" → "I just didn't understand some word problems." → "I need to practice word problems."

set about deciding what to do about it. You may wish to have your child create her own "Problem Shrinker" or trace the one here and learn to put the problem in the smallest box.

Lesson Three: The Power of Nonnegative Thinking

It is a common misconception that positive thinking is the secret fix to negative thinking. Although this misconception makes intuitive sense, decades of cognitive research have yielded the unexpected result that what differentiates those who are depressed from those who are not is *not* the presence of positive thoughts (both groups may have these) but the presence of nonnegative or neutral thoughts, which have a buffering effect on depression. Imagine if you were running a race and had fifty people booing and only ten rooting for you. The solution wouldn't be to increase the number of fans; if you just quiet the booers, all will be well. Neutral thoughts are factual: "I'm working hard. I'm doing my best." Or they are coping or strategic thoughts: "Watch for that corner"; "Keep your breathing steady." Even though there are days when parents feel desperate and would practically beg their child to say a-n-y-t-h-i-n-g positive rather than a complaint, it doesn't work to demand the positive, just go for neutral. We need to remember that, like us, when faced with a disappointment or frustration, a negative-thinking child's automatic *first* thought is likely to be inaccurate and negative. The following lessons will help to free up your child or teen from that first thought and either go for a strong, logical second thought or simply disengage, neutralize the first thought, and move on. Either way, kids will escape getting pulled into a depressive spiral and will instead get moving in a direction full of possibility.

Flexible-Thinking Exercises

Rephrasing

"That broccoli is so disgusting!" "Charlie is such a slob!" Who would think that those unwelcome comments could provide grist for the mill of changing negative thinking? Rather than volleying back parental corrections—"That is so impolite" (about the broccoli), "What an awful thing to say" (about poor Charlie)—look at these declarations as excellent opportunities for your child to practice flexing his "neutral" muscles. Invite your child to *rephrase* his comment in an unbiased form, by simply saying, to your young child, "Hmmm, let's try that again; how could you say that with different words?" (Usually even young kids know with that little nudge of a reminder of manners that they can rephrase their statement more kindly.) For older kids and teens, you can say, "I'm detecting some strong reactions here, but could I ask that you try that one again, this time a tad more neutrally?" Sometimes with teens, less is more; just saying, "Excuse me?" in a neutral tone is enough for them to realize they need to try again. What may seem like an exercise in good etiquette is actually cultivating the discipline of observing life without judgments, criticisms, and comparisons. For example, the examples of negative comments could be rephrased humorously as follows: "This darkish green treelike vegetable is the champion of bitterness, and it is remarkably tough"; "Charlie is a great collector of things and keeping things neat and organized is his next great challenge." Asking children to become impartial observers of things outside themselves will be especially crucial when the judgments and criticisms are aimed at them. So, practicing "rephrasing" early and often will serve them well in the heat of a negative moment.

Younger children may need some further instructions, such as "Can you say it the way Mommy or Daddy would?" You can bring out the same tact and diplomacy in an older child by asking her to summon her inner sportscaster or newscaster: A good announcer is going to stay close to the action, describe it accurately, and keep his or her judgments to a minimum. Once your child understands this skill, have her practice it on herself. When she says, "I'm stupid, I'm a failure, I'm a loser," ask her to rephrase more accurately: "I'm tired. I'm struggling with math. I'm getting frustrated. I probably shouldn't be working on this now."

The Big Thank You, Yes!

The second strategy for working on neutral thinking may sound counter-intuitive but it's by doing nothing short of simply accepting it—not agreeing with it—but accepting its presence rather than fighting it. Buddhist psychologist Tara Brach writes in her book *Radical Acceptance*[5] that saying yes to our anger, pain, or sadness is not endorsing and en-couraging it. We're not saying it's great to hate broccoli or Charlie or homework. What we are saying is yes, this is how I am feeling (right now—don't forget, feelings come and go, it's temporary!), end of story. Rather than turning that negative view into something we should feel bad about, doubling the negatives and using our energy to try to cheer ourselves up, or vigilantly pushing the uncomfortable feelings away, we are just saying, "Yes, this is how I feel right now and it's okay to feel that way." This approach is consistent with the teachings of the Dalai Lama about the difference between pain and suffering: When we reduce our inner commentary about our pain, we can use our energy to manage the pain rather than to fight our feelings about it. Think of how much attention and energy we waste by saying, "I hate being sick. I can't be-lieve I'm sick. This is so horrible. Why is this happening?" Just saying, "Yes, it's a total drag to be sick. Yes, I'm sad that I'm missing the party" is the essence of hugging our own experience. The effort that it takes to push away the negative feeling doesn't give anything back. But saying yes immediately gives you a feeling of relief: You don't have to fight anymore. Try it yourself first, even right now: just say, yes, or even just nod your head. See how your body naturally exhales? Imagine if you had those brief interludes throughout the day; how different you might feel. Then try it the next time you break a glass, burn the dinner, forget to pick up the dry cleaning. Imagine dropping your anger and letting go of your tension and saying yes, this is what's happening right now. This idea may seem in Dr. Brach's terms, radical, but in action, the results are compelling.

Lesson Four: How Negative Talk Leads to Negative Walk

It is bad enough that negative thinking puts a damper on one's mood, but it doesn't stop there. It barricades the doors and windows and imbues the room with the impossibility that anything could be different from how it is now. Rather than being motivated to prove the internal negatives wrong and stand up to the barrage of internal insults and accusations, negative-minded kids give up, close up shop, and smolder. Like watching an explosion build in slow motion, you see your kindergartner move from trying to draw a cow to "I can't draw a cow" to "I can't draw anything" to "I hate drawing and I quit!"—and before you know it the tears come, and you have to duck to avoid the markers being thrown across the room. If only someone had said, "Cows can be tricky [specific] and that's okay; especially at first [temporary]; I can help you practice, or we can try something else [action]." Children prone to negative thinking believe that when mistakes happen they have to give up. Negative thoughts echo down the hallway of the child's mind all because he forgot his history book and he has an open-book test. Cornered by thoughts and feelings of failure, he is immobilized, and the perception of not having successes becomes a self-fulfilling prophecy. An alternative is right around the corner: "I spaced [temporary]; bad move on a day like today [specific]; I've got to borrow a book! [action]." As a child's thinking becomes more accurate, options open up for actions to be taken and the chance of success increases.

Flexible-Thinking Exercise. All aboard the two tracks of the brain train. To introduce this concept (see the following illustration), have your child choose an adverse situation to work on. To start, make it an issue that is comfortable for him, rather than one that presses the hot-seat button.

The Brain Train

To lend distance, you may even want to start with an adverse situation of your own ("I forgot Grandma's birthday" or "I shrank Mom's favorite sweater"), especially if seeing parents as "fallible," too, is a validating, if not exciting event for your child.

Next, go a little closer to home: If your child struggles with negative thinking about grades but has clear thinking about friendships, use the brain train on friendships first. Beginning with something your child feels accomplished about has added benefit. First, fill in the situation box, and start with the negative track first because that is what your child is used to and likely the most available response. Ask him what his negative brain would tell him about that situation, how it would make him feel, and then, given those thoughts and feelings, what she would do. Actually, actions on the negative track are typically inactions: "I would miss the show"; "I would stay in my room"; "I wouldn't call anybody." Once he has completed the negative track, have him take the same situation and run it down the positive/neutral track, asking him, "What would be different and more helpful, or accurate or more positive? What would your coaching brain tell you? How would you feel, and then what would you do?"

The most important aspect of the brain train is to teach children that the two tracks present a choice, and it is theirs to make. Highlight that the same situation—for example, not getting the lead in the class play—has two very different outcomes depending on what track your child chooses to pursue and cultivate: One is missing out, and one is getting a great but different experience. They hold the power in their hands to decide which way to go. Ask your child which track he'd rather ride on. He can't help that he didn't get the part, but he can decide what that event means to him and where to go next. It's not the negative thought (or even the negative event); it's what you do with it.

You can copy the drawing in the illustration, or your child can draw his own. You can also refer to this metaphor without the drawing: "Wow! Which track are you on? Do you know where it's headed? It really sounds as if the negative track picked you up and is taking you for a ride. I wonder what this would look like on the other track. Can we see?"

To demonstrate these two tracks with older children and teens, start where they are. They are convinced that they totally embarrassed themselves in Greek mythology class when they mispronounced *chimera* with a "ch" instead of "k." Let them ride that first track. You can say, "Okay, I know you're upset and you know that I don't think you're a fool, total or otherwise, but let's go with that thought—imagine if someone else mispronounced something—what would their negative track sound like? 'I'm a total loser because I didn't know how to pronounce that word; I feel so embarrassed; my action is that I am going to disappear in that class and pray the teacher never calls on me again.' 'Now, what would the accurate track sound like? They didn't know that word, this happens all the time, no one will remember, million-dollar bet—that didn't make history, and if they are thinking that way, they'll probably feel calmer, and their action, they don't have to hide and can walk into class head held high.'" Point out that it is the thought or interpretation that makes all the difference in how we feel and what we do, so take time to run a few interpretations down the track; don't stick with the one that gets their first. Negative thinking is fast, but not accurate.

Lesson Five: Undoing Emotional Reasoning: Separating Facts from Feelings

"I am the worst parent in the world!" How many times have we felt that way? Whether it's the *mean* worst parent, who says no to the teenage sleepover when "everyone else will be there," or it's the *neglectful* worst parent, who sends a child out without an umbrella oblivious of the forecast for rain, or it's the *too busy* worst parent, who misses half the class play because a meeting ran late, after the first few hundred times of feeling this way, parents begin to recognize it as a temporary feeling state—although an uncomfortable one, a moment of *agony* at times—which is usually forgotten as quickly as the last meal. If we had to prove our "inferiority" in a court of law, we would be hard-pressed. We have come to recognize the distinction between facts and feelings. For children, however, like us on a bad day, feelings blur facts like rain on a sidewalk chalk picture. Everything gets murky. Kids are what they feel, and they feel it in every negative fiber of their body. So, a six-year-old convinced that he is "so stupid" because he made a mistake and called a friend a bad name is awash with regret for his action, but the mistake has nothing to do with being smart or not and, perhaps most important, there is much he can do to fix the situation. A teenager is convinced that she is "pathetic" because for a few minutes at a party, she didn't have anyone to talk to and was walking around like a "total loser." Although she felt uncomfortable in that moment, that does not set her identity or destiny in stone; it's a feeling, albeit a strong one, not a fact.

While parents often rush in and say, "Don't say that," or "Don't feel that way," or, "That's not true," remember that when we are poised to be crowned on our worst parent runway, we wouldn't listen to any of that advice ourselves. The essential lesson here is that *just feeling that way (a lot) doesn't make the feeling true*. Feelings are temporary. You can feel like a fool, a jerk, a dummy, but that feeling wave washes over you and washes out, and like the rock on the shore, you're still there—you haven't changed. Kids need to understand that *anyone* hearing that internal tirade, "This isn't going to work; this always happens; I'm a loser," would feel bad about him- or herself, but feeling that way doesn't make those statements true. It's just that such thoughts—as when they're watching a scary movie—have temporarily manipulated their feelings. From this perspective, instead of talking your child out of that feeling, you can first empathize and thoroughly and freely bear witness to the *feelings* he is having (remember, this doesn't mean that you agree that those ideas are true). Given how rotten he is feeling, the endorsement will actually feel good: "I know you feel really bad, awful in fact. That's how caring people feel when they do something they're not proud of, but we all do things like that—even me. I feel terrible when I make a mistake like that, but it doesn't turn me into a bad person. It's just like a zap—a bad-feeling zap—that will go away, but it will pass a lot faster if you don't keep rezapping yourself by reliving it. Another thing that will help it pass is if you think about the facts: What was your mistake, and how do you want to fix it? That kind of thinking happens in the smart part of your brain, so when you switch on the smart part, the feelings part fades out." We will be looking in Chapter 3 at more ideas for how to handle big feelings for kids who get the "zap" experience frequently.

Flexible-Thinking Exercise. You can help your child separate her feelings from the facts by asking her, "How much of you *feels* upset that you are a bad person [or other accusation]?" Your child is likely to say 100 percent. Next, ask, "How much of you really *thinks* and believes that you are literally the worst person in the world, that everyone would vote against you based on this event?" Have her make a pie chart like the one in the illustration and color in the proportions. Giving your child room, both to express the intense feelings and also to see them as distinct from her beliefs and predictions, will allow her to make the switch to logical thinking. No matter how strong the feelings are, they don't change the facts. Then, you will not need to reassure her that she is not a villain; the facts will speak for themselves.

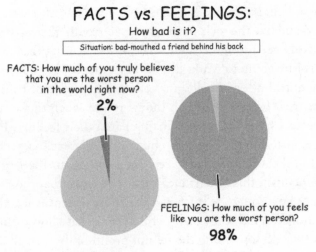

FACTS vs. FEELINGS:
How bad is it?

Situation: bad-mouthed a friend behind his back

FACTS: How much of you truly believes
that you are the worst person
in the world right now?
2%

FEELINGS: How much of you feels
like you are the worst person?
98%

When the facts are in charge, you're in charge.

Lesson Six: Trends and Outliers

When one thing goes wrong, do you make a new rule about how things work? Or do you keep your basic understanding and add the caveat that "sometimes" there are exceptions? Children prone to negative thinking tend to generalize from the exception, rather than from the rule. It takes just one mistake, one data point, to create a negative theory, whereas it takes many, many good happenings to see a positive trend. As one child explained, "I can't see a positive trend. If something good happens, I assume it's just a coincidence. But if anything—just one negative thing happens—I'm sure it completely ruins my reputation." Whether it is the straight-A student who sees herself as a failure when she gets that first B or the athlete who is ready to quit after one bad race, these kids need to know the difference between rules and exceptions. In the following illustration, we see a child concluding that "her friend doesn't like her" because one day her friend didn't say hi to her (she didn't notice her, but that piece of data was overlooked). Looking at the graph, ask your child what is the trend, or which has the most points: that the friend likes her or doesn't like her.

Flexible-Thinking Exercise. To help your child understand that having an "exception" to the rule doesn't mean changing the rule, generate a list of adverse situations with him. You can think of a few embarrassing or frustrating moments such as those in the following list. Then ask, "Does this usually happen?" If not, think of a few similar situations where things turned out well. After you have collected the "data," help your child draw a graph of what constitutes a trend (what is most typical) and what constitutes an outlier (what happens sometimes or even has happened only one time):

- My voice cracked during my audition; does this mean you are now a bad singer?
- I forgot my homework two times; does this mean you are now a bad student?
- I got an "unprepared" for gym today because I didn't have blue shorts; does this mean you are now an irresponsible person?

- Jasmine didn't save a seat for me at lunch today; does this mean now that Jasmine isn't your friend?

- Once kids get the idea that flukes, exceptions, or outliers are to be expected and do not change or cancel out all the data points that came before, when an isolated event does happen and your child begins to rewrite the story of their talent, cognitive abilities, or friendships, you can cue them (after acknowledging their upset) with a simple, "Wait, trend or outlier?" and cut down greatly on their experience and the duration of their distress.

Trends and Outliers

Examine the evidence to support your conclusion

Does my friend like me? Yes—Thursday was an off-day

Lesson Seven: Relabel the Problem as the Negative Brain

Negative thinking is so automatic and, as we've just seen, can engender such strong emotions that it is difficult for kids to get enough distance to see an event for what it really is. Parents can help their child step back and rescue her gifts of smart, rational thinking by not confusing the child with the negativity itself. This strategy of externalizing the problem, first introduced by the founder of narrative therapy, Australian therapist Michael White, defines the *problem* as the problem, rather than the child as the problem.[6] So, rather than saying, "You're being so negative," which essentially gives a child no choice but to prove it, parents can relabel the moment as the "negative brain" taking over. Not only does this help kids restore some distance and perspective, but it also gets them off the hot seat and recasts the parent as an ally against this troublesome third party of Mr. No—the real bad guy ruining her day. Relabeling utilizes a "consider-the-source" strategy and can cut the seriousness of the thoughts by using a humorous name or a funny accent—a cowboy, Mickey Mouse, or a Scottish brogue—that changes the experience of those thoughts dramatically. Relabeling begins to demote the validity of the negative thinking, encouraging the child to not trust it as the "truth," but as the annoying, upsetting, overprotective, or just sort of ill-informed voice that it is. See for yourself: Say to yourself in a serious voice, "I have so much to do, it's going to be a disaster"; then say it again with a funny accent. Parents can relabel by saying things like "I see that magnifying glass; whoa, is it exaggerating the bad," or "Watch out, I think the Exaggerator is trying to be in charge again," or with an older child, "I think the filter isn't working; only the brain spam is coming through." With teenagers, this process is less about "renaming" the negative (unless you allow them free rein to find colorful monikers for this cognitive interloper), it's more about seeing teens as being harassed by the negative voice in their head, rather than thinking that they are doing this on purpose or for attention. Creating separation between the thoughts and your teen may simply sound like this: "Those negative thoughts are pretty unrelenting right now, aren't they?" Or "Your brain is trying to make an air-tight case," or "Those negative thoughts are so fast and just won't give you a break right now." Or "Those negative thoughts critiquing your every move, that's what they sound like for everyone, but they aren't true and they aren't about you." As we'll see in the master plan in Chapter 5, relabeling is an essential step toward ensuring that your child knows that you are working with her, not against her.

Flexible-Thinking Exercise. Have your child choose a name for his negative brain: Mr. Sad, Meany Mouse, Magnifier Man, Fun Blocker, The Critic, whatever your child likes. Introduce the idea by reminding your child of a time when he was stuck in a negative-thinking hole: "Remember when you said you were 'stupid' because you drew on the table by accident? You don't feel that way now, right? But what would you call that voice in your head that made you feel that way then?" Next, have your child draw a picture of the character and even choose a voice for it. He can then generate some boss-back talk for his exaggerator brain and write it down on cards or a big note on the fridge, like "You're not the boss of me; you make me feel bad; I'm not listening to you; you see everything as awful; you need new glasses!"

Lesson Eight: Positive Events Deserve Accuracy, Too!

Kids with a negative thinking style not only find a way to make worse anything that's bad, but also make bad anything that's good. It's not them, it's the mind-set. What that sounds like is to downplay any accomplishment and distort and twist all the credit out of it, so that "I got an A on my science project" becomes "It wasn't that great because the teacher is an easy grader" (not giving credit to herself), "It doesn't mean anything—the next grade could be bad" (seeing the success as fleeting or temporary), and "I got a B on my French test, so I'm still not a good student" (specific). The optimistic formula for positive events is *permanent* causes ("I do well on tests"), *personal* ("I am a good student; I know how to study"), and *pervasive* ("I'm not just good in verb conjugation; I'm strong in French").

Flexible-Thinking Exercise. To lightheartedly point out the necessity of viewing the positive positively, have your child name a few successes she admires in others—her favorite film, her favorite athlete, the best day of the year—and describe them pessimistically, using the 3 P's as her guide. For example, in pessimistic terms, the success of the film adaptation of L. Frank Baum's beloved book *The Wizard of Oz* would be described as a lucky try, a favor from the film studio, not such a big deal because not all of Baum's books were turned into movies.

Challenge your child to say the most positive, expansive, permanent, and personal things about her accomplishments, while still being accurate and truthful. Take the "Problem Shrinker" drawing from Lesson Two on page 53 and reverse it: Start with the small way that your child is describing her triumph or success and help her enlarge on it. Repeat frequently!

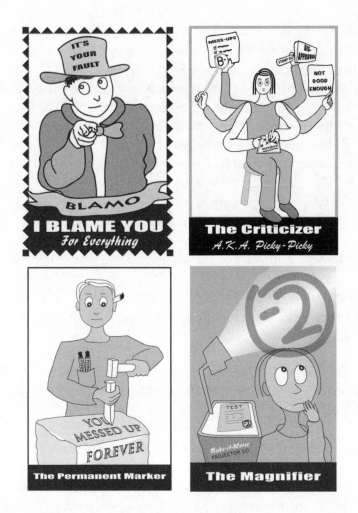

Lesson Nine: Catching the Error of Their Ways: More Thinking Errors

You can teach your older children the following cognitive errors—and encourage them to use these as a guide to correct the work of their negative brain.

All-or-None Thinking. Children with all-or-none thinking are missing the shades of gray between what is black and what is white. Things are either all good or all bad, perfect or failing. The key is finding the middle ground. When your young child says, "I'm a bad swimmer," you can draw a big circle and ask her to color in the part that she is "good" at in swimming, then the part that she is "not as good" at, and, finally, the "in the middle" part—what she is perhaps learning but hasn't mastered yet—choosing a different colored crayon for each. Talk to your child about the behaviors that make up each part of her circle and, in the process, help her move to a more balanced view of herself. Ask your older child to identify the partial successes in a disappointing event. As in the example below, help him name what worked, what didn't, and what he would do differently next time.

Here is an example based on losing a baseball game.

First thought: I am terrible at everything. I'm quitting baseball.

Parent's response: You're feeling really bad right now. Do you hear the *everything*? Let's take a minute to think whether some things in the game went well.

Specific thought: I did hit that double, but then I missed the ball when that guy stole third. I guess my hitting is okay, but I've got to work on fielding.

Catastrophizing. When we jump to conclusions and play out disastrous scenarios based on one small event, we are borrowing trouble from the future that will likely never materialize. The antidote to catastrophizing is to slow down, narrow the spill of destruction, look at the original problem, and brainstorm what can be done to address it. Here is a situation in which a teenage girl doesn't have a new outfit for the dance.

First thought: Everyone's going to think I'm lame for wearing my usual clothes. I bet no one will ask me to dance. Everyone else will have new clothes. I'll just stand there looking pathetic. I'll be a social outcast, and no one will want to eat lunch with me or sit with me on the bus.

Parent's response: I know you're feeling really disappointed about not buying a new outfit. Do you think that all those things would really happen, or do you think you might feel uncomfortable, but some other girls won't be wearing new outfits, either? Let's snap back the problem to the present and refocus on what we know is the problem: You need to figure out an outfit for the dance.

Second thought: I'm not happy about not having something new to wear, but probably people won't care—they're too busy paying attention to themselves! Maybe I can put together something that I like out of the clothes I have.

Mind Reading. "I know you hate me. You yelled at me!"

"She didn't ask me to put my work on the board. I know that she thinks I'm dumb!"

Has your child the gift of a sixth sense? Or is she caught in the cognitive error of mind reading: being convinced—without any proof—that she knows 100 percent why people are acting a certain way and specifically what they are feeling about her. Arguing doesn't work, her mind is jumping to conclusions and convinced she's right. Instead, ask your child to role-play being the one whose mind is being read, and interview that person:

"Do you really hate Margie?"

"No."

"Okay, what are you thinking about her?"

"I'm just frustrated that she didn't clean up her toys."

"Okay, that's good to know."

Flexible-Thinking Exercise: Switch Shoes!

With young children, switch shoes to make the exercise fun. Your child can imagine or draw the shoes of the person he is worrying about, "step into them," and make up the voice and words of that person. Often, just switching into play mode is enough to loosen the negative grip. If it doesn't, helping your child to decenter from his view into someone else's can increase the accuracy of his perception of the other person's reactions.

For older children, think of this as the Freaky Friday intervention, named for the classic Disney movie in which a warring mother and daughter are forced to understand each other to undo a spell that has switched their bodies. Have your older child "blink" and switch with the person he is making theories about; have him say what that person is feeling so that he can hear for himself that it sounds extreme or even absurd.

Magnification and Minimization. Like walking through a hall of mirrors at an amusement park, the negative mind can generate distortions of insignificant negative events, making them seem grotesque and insurmountable; it can also shrink the importance of a child's accomplishments and make them seem so trivial. As one child said, "Proud? I don't know what I'm supposed to be proud of; when I look, I can't see anything." Parents can respond, "I know you feel as if it's nothing, but I don't think it's you. I think it's the mirror playing tricks on you. What would your friend see if he looked in the mirror? Can you think of someone who would be very happy to be seeing what's there?"

In the following situation, a classmate gets a writing award at school:

First thought: I'm not really good at anything at school. Anyone can do what I do.

Parent's response: You're feeling really disappointed about that award. It feels like that one fact cancels out all of the things that you've accomplished. Disappointment can do that, but remember the disappointment is temporary, but all of your accomplishments up to this point are permanent, even if it feels as if they get washed away just because of this, they don't. Maybe this is an opportunity to think back and savor the writing projects you really enjoyed or were proud of.

Second thought: I guess I am an okay writer, I did get that essay published in the school newspaper. I guess it is just disappointment— but it feels big.

Parent's response: Yes, it does feel big right now, but that feeling will fade over time, especially if you can work hard to keep this disappointment small, like the isolated event it is.

Flexible-Thinking Exercise

Ask your young child to draw or construct three different mirrors: a minimizer, an exaggerator, and a real mirror. Creativity is welcome in this project whether the mirrors are drawn wacky, scary, or silly. You can also invite children to give their own names to the mirrors: the mirror of doom, the meany mirror, or the power mirror. Children first choose three things that they feel bad about. Have them write down what those things *feel* like in the exaggerator mirror, then have them write down what they *feel* like looking in the mirror of truth. Do the same for three things they would like to feel proud of but don't: Write down what they *feel* like in the minimizer mirror, then switch over to the real mirror.

Help a young child whose inner exaggerator is making her feel bad about a mistake to distinguish between the whole of who she is and the tiny part that had the problem. She can represent the relative size by coloring in a picture of herself and circling the small part that made the mistake. Don't be surprised if she needs to do two drawings. If she colors in the first one "all bad," you can explain that this is how she *feels*. Then, encourage her to do a second drawing of how *you* see the mistake. For fun, the mistake can be represented by, perhaps, a freckle on her arm. You can explain that unlike freckles, the mistakes actually fade away. If your child doesn't like to draw, you can use differently colored dried beans, beads, or similar materials to make a graphic representation of the teeny-tiny-ness of her mistakes.

CHAPTER CHECKLIST

Once you can identify the common potholes of negative thinking, you can help your child to climb out quickly, rather than dig in further. Always end on a good note: After all the two-track mind work is done, ask your child to say the new, rational thought—the one she would choose—loud and clear, and with conviction (even if it takes a few tries to sound convincing)!

Red flags for negative thinking and negative mood:

- Exaggerating and extending the importance of an adverse event
- Blaming self for something that was caused by external circumstances; blaming big for small things
- Generalizing that whatever happened always happens
- Becoming easily angry with self
- Not trying activities unless sure can excel
- Thinking bad things always happen, good things never happen
- Trouble tolerating mistakes, disappointment, or losing
- Shutting down in the face of any obstacle

Formula for accurate thinking and better mood:

- Identifying the actual cause
- Keeping the event in perspective—an isolated event, without exaggerating
- Not generalizing from one example because once isn't always
- Looking for what worked, not just what didn't work
- Thinking about what this will mean to you in a week, a month, five years

3

WEATHERING THE STORM OF BIG, NEGATIVE FEELINGS

Inviting Them In, Working Them Out

In the last decade or so, science has discovered a tremendous amount about the role emotions play in our lives. Researchers have found that even more than IQ, your emotional awareness and abilities to handle feelings will determine your success and happiness in all walks of life, including family relationships.

—John Gottman[1]

I turn my back for a second and Hannah is melting down. I never saw it coming. What happened? I am afraid of how vulnerable she is, but I also don't want to be on the receiving end of her emotions. How can I help her if I really want to hide?

—mother of a twelve-year-old

INTRODUCTION: EMOTIONS: IN THE WAY, OR ARE THE WAY?

Years ago, when I was first writing this very chapter on big feelings, my then six-year-old conveniently went into a total meltdown. She had been playing with her treasured brand-new sparkly Rapunzel computer game for an hour when I reminded her she needed to stop. That's all it took. You'd think I'd told her she would never be able to eat ice cream again! Real tears streamed down her face, she yelled at me that it wasn't fair, she stomped and shook her fists, she was so frustrated. It was one great big bowl of bad. The tight feeling in my throat was not heartburn from lunch; it was stress. On the verge of my own internal meltdown, I felt myself stretched between scrambling to figure out how to make her happy again (not just because I desperately needed to get back to work) and wanting her to follow the rules (one hour on the computer is the house rule). As I sat on the stairs with her, and she ceremoniously gave an indignant "no" to all my suggestions of what else she could do to pull out of this, it suddenly dawned on me: I wasn't taking my own advice! I had just written about how we need to help children see that their feelings are temporary and manageable, and there I went trying to fix it, and in the process was just fueling her growing fury.

Suddenly, I realized that I needed to do nothing except let her sit with and ride out her feelings without distracting her or trying to find the nearest exit, while she was in the process of learning the life skills of accepting that things would not always be exactly as she wanted them to be. We both needed to, in the words of meditation master Jon Kabat-Zinn, *de-identify* from our feelings and see them as a fleeting storm passing through our steady sky. The more I calmed myself, reminding myself that it wasn't the emergency that it felt like inside, the more I could be that sky—steady and stable—as Hurricane Raia blew through. And rather than trying to steer her away from what she *was* feeling, my steadiness also allowed Raia to reestablish her own base—her own sky, through which her tantrum gale-force winds were blowing.

I said, "Raia, you are really upset, aren't you?" "Yes," she said. The first yes! "You love that game, don't you?" "It's hard to stop, right?" Yes and yes. "Are you ready to feel better?" "No," she said, "not yet." Ah, "not yet"; that sounded promising to me. "Okay," I said, "will you tell me when you are?" "Yes." Another yes! I sat for a few more moments on the stairs as she sniffled a bit, and then I invited her to bring a book and sit next to me on the couch while I resumed my writing. Within a few minutes, she found some musical instruments in the living room and was back in her flow. We had averted the crash of two storm systems and all was calm again, all by finding the way to get to the nodding head of "yeses" in a sea of "nos."

In retrospect, I am deeply grateful for that episode. Although different in magnitude, it had all of the same elements as the scenes that my families bring to me each week, and it helped me recall both how easy it is to cling to our Mr. or Ms. Fix-It role when it comes to our children's feelings, and how hard it can be to remember (even when we are writing a book about it) our job as spotters, coaches, and loving holding environments for our children's feelings, so that with our support they can learn to work their way through the dark twists and turns of their emotions for themselves. This is a lesson that we may need to relearn frequently, but in the long run, our children will benefit greatly from our study.

In Chapter 2, we looked at cognitive strategies to address negative thinking patterns. In this chapter, we focus on the heart, or what might be best described as the "in your face" side of negativity: the feelings. Children with a negative thinking style get in deep with big negative emotions—typically lacking the skills to work their way out—and pull parents in, too. In a swimming pool, kids are allowed in only as far from the shallow end as they can handle. But these kids, by their wiring, not their will, get in over their head with emotions before you can even say—*wait, what just happened?* They melt down, they flounder; as parents, we see them floundering and instinctively jump in to rescue them—trying to make it all better. But that rescuing reinforces our children's beliefs that those feelings are wrong. That they shouldn't be there. That they are overwhelming, unmanageable, and even unsafe, rather than a natural part of life from which they will learn and grow. What if instead they floundered, tried a few new moves, and then prevailed? Our goal is to build true resilience—teaching our children not to fear the water and to stay afloat with their own feelings, especially when things get choppy. So—suit up, because we're going swimming.

PART ONE: PREPARING THE TEACHERS

Our Feelings About Feelings: Why Parents Must Be Prepared

As parents, we pass down certain emotion-processing habits, intentionally or otherwise. It is best to know what our kids are learning from us. Here's a quick test. Choose from the following list the answers that best describe what lessons your kids have learned from you: Negative emotions, such as anger, sadness, or frustration, are:

- Something we learn from
- Embarrassing! Don't show them!
- Too painful to bear, and should be avoided
- A terrible experience that we all hate
- A self-indulgence
- Nothing we can do anything about
- A signal to ourselves about what is going on in our world
- Normal, temporarily uncomfortable, but a necessary part of life

We would be hard-pressed to find anyone whose feelings about feelings (their own or others') have not run the gamut of any of those replies—from welcoming with open arms to the emotional equivalent of running for cover. Because of how big and deep the feelings get for children in a negative spin—whether this is their home base or they are just visiting—they truly need tour guides proficient in the ins and especially the outs of uncomfortable feelings. If we are unsure about how to manage our own feelings, would rather not talk about them, and brush them under the rug, we are going to be at a disadvantage when it comes to equipping our highly emotional kids with the expectations and strategies to ride the wave of intense feelings. Worse, because life is a two-way street, if we don't know how to navigate our own emotional vehicle, we and our children will be two unmanned cars out on the road careening toward a collision.

None of us would want our kids to learn math from the teacher who has a math phobia; we would wrangle through a stampede to get the teacher who loves math, can point out the neat tricks, even show kids the beauty of how things work. To be that good a teacher about feelings for our children, we may need to take a review class. Fortunately, the lessons are simple, and putting them into practice in the heat of a major moment will be much easier if we are familiar with the strategies and put them into action in the smaller moments of our day.

Why We Fear Feelings: We Want to Make Them Stop

When my niece Allison, now an adult, was three years old, her baby brother, Isaac, was born. Making casual conversation while driving home from the hospital with little Allison in her booster seat, her father asked her how it felt to have a little brother. She paused for a moment and then with all sincerity answered, "It feels like vomit." Was it the sleep deprivation, the idea of sharing her toys and parents with a brother? It didn't matter. It felt awful.

What we fear about feelings—especially big feelings—is that they are complex and messy and, perhaps like vomiting, are unpleasant and unexpected and *feel* uncontrollable, like something very *wrong* is happening. Children can exhibit the same panic in response to big feelings as when they are about to get sick; you know the look of "What's happening to me? Make it stop!" In these situations, parents can run around trying to get their children to feel better with the same urgency they would as if they were putting out a fire. But what message does that behavior send, since fires are dangerous and feelings are not? Or parents can empathize and comfort their children, talk through what happened, and by their calmness lend confidence that this is normal, manageable, comprehensible, and solvable. While the first choice may sound appealing, thinking there is something wrong or urgent about our children's feelings will convey that message to them, and they will be calling us for roadside assistance every time they hit an emotional bump.

The Goal: Don't Remove the Feeling, Remove the Fear of the Feeling

Rather than approaching our children's negative feelings as something *wrong* that they need to get out of quickly, we need to show them how to safely go in, so they can receive the important information—however encrypted and uncomfortable—that they were getting from themselves. Feelings are not an enemy attack; they are more like an interoffice memo, and we don't want to intercept or scramble the message so that our kids lose an opportunity to learn how to take care of their own needs. For example, when a child says, "Everybody hates me," hidden in the heart of that statement may be something like "I need to speak up more because I'm feeling ignored." Or "I hate myself, everything's terrible" may come down to "I have to forgive myself for mispronouncing a word during my oral report." So, our goal is to *strengthen* our kids' internal communication system, not obscure it.

Picture the "Problem Shrinker" illustration in Chapter 2. The only way kids can transform their problems from the humongous package that won't fit through the front door into a manageable one they can hold in their hands is by hearing themselves think and feel. Job One is taking the mystery and fear out of our kids' feelings, teaching about feelings as matter-of-factly as we teach our youngest about how a visible boo-boo works: It will heal. "In how many days will it heal?" an inquisitive preschooler asks. After the first twenty or so boo-boos, they know the drill. You get a bandage (even if the scratch is more on the ego than on the epidermis), and pretty soon it won't hurt and will feel better. We often teach children this by demonstrating with our own boo-boos. Children are satisfied with those explanations, in part, because parents deliver them with conviction, unambiguously, and with great authority. They come to know what to expect. Although they aren't going to be happy about the wound, it isn't alien to them, and they can anticipate the outcome.

By the same token, as we will see in a moment, our understanding will help our children learn that they can ride out the waves of their emotions: "This is manageable. It is temporary. It is normal. I can handle it. It will pass." Once the feelings have passed then we can get to the business of figuring out a solution for what got them so upset, sad, or angry in the first place. Keeping in mind that the end is in sight helps make it come even faster.

Kids Are like Cars: Accepting Temperamental Style and Negative Emotions: Why Some Kids Are More Prone to Big Feelings

One more point before we dive in. The feelings of some children are unmistakable: The child wears them on his sleeve, he is not subtle about them, and they make a deep, lasting impression on his mood (and sometimes on the mood of others). The feelings of other children register more like a Mr. Magic erase board: Pull up the sheet and whatever was there is now—poof!—gone. We've all witnessed the extreme differences in various children's emotional expression in the grocery aisle, at birthday parties, and maybe even within our own families. This emotional style is not based on *choices*: One child doesn't choose to be "difficult" any more than another chooses to be "easy." It is based instead on their temperament: a wired-in-at-birth blueprint of their tendencies, like the default settings in your car. We come to expect the car to be slow to warm up, or jumpy, or reactive, or to take the bumps and curves well, or not. We wouldn't take the car to the mechanic to fix these characteristics; we don't get mad at the car, we accept these characteristics because we know they can't be changed and—here's the punch line—we adjust *our* behavior to them: we brake earlier, we slow down on the curves, and so on. If we approach our children with the same understanding that we have for our cars, and, ironically this may prove rather difficult, we'll all be in better shape. Having compassion doesn't mean letting your child's temperament wreak havoc on your life. What it does mean is that, rather than faulting kids for being who they are and responding the intense or unwelcomed way they do, you're going to help your child learn to manage those reactions as constructively as possible.

PART TWO: THE LESSONS

As mentioned, an additional stressor for children with "big feelings" is that they feel frightened or upset by those feelings, so in this section we look at the key operating principles of our emotional system. These lessons will help parents—children's frontline emotional tour guides—to tell them where they are, why they are there, and, most important, how to get to the other side of what they are feeling.

The Simple Truth About Feelings: What Goes Up Must Come Down: Strong Feelings Pass

Whether we're scared, mad, sad, surprised, or even happy, our nervous system responds strongly to our signals, *at first*, but then over seconds, minutes, or sometimes hours, the feelings fade and get weaker. Humans are wired to have strong reactions because their body is always ready to protect them, but as they see that they are safe, the strong feeling signals fade. Look at the accompanying illustration (you can have your child draw a picture of waves, a roller coaster, a mountain, or the like): The big feelings go up and up really fast, but then they always come down. You can help reinforce this message with young children by asking them to think of a specific time when they were really mad: "Do you remember

Feelings Over Time

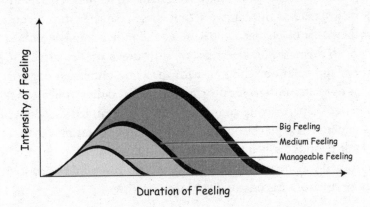

Intensity of Feeling

Big Feeling
Medium Feeling
Manageable Feeling

Duration of Feeling

when someone else finished the leftover pizza and you were really mad?" They may have forgotten, so don't be surprised by a brief burst of renewed emotion. "Well, let's make up a story about you and the pizza. How does the story *start*?" "I was hungry, and I went to the fridge to get the pizza. It was gone! I was really mad!" "Right, now let's turn our imaginary pages and go to the *middle* of the book. What happened?" "You made me macaroni and cheese instead." "Right. That was good, wasn't it? Now, let's go to the *end* of the story. Were you still really mad about the pizza?" "Well, I told Jack to not eat my pizza again, but I wasn't mad." "Exactly. Feelings start out strong, but then they fade. Next time you are mad, you might think to yourself, 'In a few pages (or a few minutes!), I'm going to feel a lot better, especially if I figure out how to fix the problem.'"

The Other Simple Truth About Feelings: Emotion Gets There First

"Think, think, think," says Winnie-the-Pooh. "I can't *think* when I'm *feeling*," says nine-year-old Nate. Who is in charge? How is it that kids like Nate, sweet, thoughtful, caring children, can totally lose it and then be completely remorseful minutes later, without learning to control their feelings before they happen? Winnie-the-Pooh, taking a *top-down* approach, summons his higher brain functioning to solve problems. Nate, like the rest of us, is destined to react sometimes to things in a big way "before he knows why." It turns out that the brain developed so that feeling is wired to come *before* knowing. As neuroscientist Joseph LeDoux, author of *The Emotional Brain*,[2] explains, the feeling brain was there long before the thinking brain got here. This is the reason we may find ourselves suddenly very angry or upset and may also see these out-of-proportion reactions in our children. The first responder—the amygdala, which controls our fight-or-flight response—makes quick but not accurate assessments of the danger in a situation (with an emotional reaction of fear that relates to the risk, with anger that relates to whether needs are being met or understood). So, we may "fly into a rage," only to find a few minutes later, when the message has worked its way up the fifty flights of stairs to the executive suite, or the higher brain functioning, that the picture no longer looks like life or death but is manageable. Older children and teenagers may appreciate this explanation because they will know that such strong reactions are not crazy; they will also appreciate your understanding that they are not in total control of their reactions. The one in charge, the amygdala, is operating on the wisdom of the ages, but not necessarily on the exigencies or needs of the moment, and as much as we may try to *think straight*, the amygdala, not concerned with the fine-grained distinctions of learning and memory but programmed to survive, has chosen a reaction for us—in a matter of a thousandth of a second.

So, working with our wiring, when we respond to our kids' *first* feelings as the whole story we distract them from getting down to analyzing the real problem that they can do something about. Give them time to cool down from those strong first feelings, and then let the higher brain sort through and determine what started it all.

How to Make Feelings Pass Efficiently: Monitoring and Modulating

While it may seem from the previous description that our emotions are in charge, it is more accurate to say that our emotions are in charge *first*, and that we can do many things *second* to work ourselves through the surge and back down where we want to be, perhaps with a greater understanding of our reactions, but certainly in a zone that feels more comfortable for us.

Monitoring: Anchors and Thermometers: How Big Is the Feeling? How Big Do You Want This to Be? Part of your communication with your child is to try to move your child from *being* the feeling to talking himself (and you!) through it. Intense feelings fully engage us and we are not open to information. To help a child to step down from that state gradually, parents can first acknowledge the feeling: "You are very upset right now," or "You are having a lot of feelings right now," then ask him, "How big does it feel *right now*?" Give the anger, sadness, or frustration a number from one to a hundred or a size: small, medium, large, essentially, to take his "emotional temperature." What is most helpful about this intervention is that it includes the expectation that things can change. Without such anchors a child may not be able to distinguish the subtle shift when his feeling begins to fade. So, if you ask, "What is your temperature now?" and again ten minutes later, the good news, which *he* discovers *himself*, is that his temperature went down. A second aspect is to have anchors or reference points: "What size does this *feel* like: small, medium, large, or supersize? How big do you *want* it to be?" By making these distinctions you are introducing the idea that how he's feeling is *changeable*: he doesn't *have* to feel the way he does. In a calm moment, have your child make a chart of things to say and do for the small, medium, and large settings of unpleasant emotion. For young children, you can make the chart with various faces from neutral to very unhappy; for older children, you can simply use a scale from small to supersize, or from one to ten.

THE STRESS THERMOMETER

"This is unbearable" — 10

"This is hard, but I can handle it" — 5

"No problem" — 0

Modulating: What Makes Big Feelings Bigger? What Makes Feelings Better? When your child is already worked up, having to listen to you or argue with you is like telling the amygdala, "We're under attack; send more troops!" So, letting your child cool down when she is upset, rather than having to explain herself to you right away, is a good strategy. Sometimes just talking about the causal event (even when you aren't arguing with her) seems to push a child's anger temperature up higher because she is re-living the situation and feeling attacked all over again. At these times, you can say, "I know you're so upset, and it seems as if you're getting more upset talking about it. Do you think so? Do you want to take a break from talking about it for a minute and do something else?" The something else should not be a thinking activity because that puts more demand on an already taxed-out, maxed-out brain. Taking a few deep, centering breaths and blowing them out slowly helps to ease the strain. Physical activities are better. Play a quick game of catch with a nearby pair of socks; shake out your arms and legs to break up the tension. Because reestablishing a safe, calm environment is essential before any other action can be taken, we will later look at exercises for accomplishing this.

Behind the Feeling: A Problem That Hasn't Been Solved, Yet. As was said earlier, feelings are a message, so once children have calmed down, we are ready to decode the message and work on the real issue, what started the emotional fire in the first place.

We all understand the basics of problem solving: Define a problem, generate solutions, and choose the best option given the circumstance. We use that model over and over throughout the day as we encounter obstacles. But when it comes to managing our kid's distress, often we don't problem solve at all. Instead, we campaign. Our teen is melting down, saying, "Everybody at school hates me, I have no friends!" and we desperately want him to feel loved and connected (and also may think his social life is not as bad as he's saying). As much as we'd like him to let go of his negative beliefs, mostly we'd appreciate it if he would just sign our own solution on the dotted line, and the sooner the better. Going in with our mind made up that his perceptions are wrong is trying to fix one negative with another. The more comfortable we can be with our children's discomfort, the less we'll need to rush them out of it. If our children sense that rushing-out agenda, it will fan the fires, and with more smoke in the air, we'll lose sight of the source once again.

> ## Problem-Solving Model
>
> Step One: Identify the problem.
> Step Two: Brainstorm solutions.
> Step Three: Choose the best option, and rehearse it.

What can we do instead? Dr. Myrna Shure, known as the "problem-solving psychologist" and the author of *Raising a Thinking Child*,[3] advocates that we let go of what we think might be the "right" answer or "our" answer (especially since our version of the question may not even be the same as the one our children are concerned about) and instead listen to our children's version of "what happened." And rather than getting to the end of the story quickly, you can take what I call "the scenic route." Don't go as the crow flies; don't rush to the finish line of how to fix things; it doesn't save time. Instead, walk along with them, getting all the nuances and hearing the story *as they experienced it.* The intervention isn't to change the story; it is to *ask*, at key points, questions that open up options so that your child rewrites the ending herself. Being stuck in a big emotion gets worse because of feeling stuck, and just the idea that there could be a different way of looking at the problem—a different tact she could take, and a different outcome, presented gently and neutrally—frees a child from being stuck in the corner of a closed room. Suddenly doors appear in her mind where there were none. So, the specific steps you can take are as follows:

Identify the Problem

Rather than assuming you know why your child is upset, ask her:

- What happened here?
- What part is upsetting you the most?
- When did you start to feel upset?
- Was there something different you were hoping would happen?
- What are the ways your mind is magnifying the bad? How?
- What are the ways your mind is minimizing the good? How?

Generate Solutions

Once you have defined the problem, begin to generate options. Young children may need your help with this, so you could start with an idea and then take turns back and forth. Even with older children, this strategy can be helpful, as they want to (and need to) be authors of the solution, but in general they don't like to feel as if they're doing all the work. Questions to ask include

- Can you think of a different way to do that?
- What are some ideas that might work to fix it?
- What would happen if that didn't work out?
- Is there something else you could do instead?

Choose the Best Option and Rehearse It

Once you generate ideas, you can role-play them to let your child *discover* what would happen if she went that route. Hold back from giving your opinion. If you think your child may be miscalculating a situation, you can say:

- That's possible, do you think something different might happen instead?
- Are you ready to try this? or, What part of this are you ready to try?
- What do you need to do to be ready?
- Do you want to practice with me?
- Do you want to write it down?

Establish a Cue to Signal the Start of Trouble

Consolidate your learning with your child. During the process of sorting through what happened, keep your ear out for a cue or catchphrase that your child may want to bookmark for the next time things start to heat up; for example, "The yikes alarm is going off," or "The give up button is being pushed," or "The everything, nothing, never, no feeling is starting," or a cue like "Do a walk-away." Younger children could make a picture or poster with those words; teenagers could give you permission to use those words the next time the situation comes up.

Remember that the real goal isn't getting to the best solution fastest. Instead, you want to help your child learn how to rally from the obstacles that she encounters and learn that managing feelings will lead to clearer thinking.

PART THREE: TOOLS FOR INCREASING EMOTIONAL REGULATION

As we know from our own experience, we can do certain things to help us cool down when our emotions start heating up; now the challenge is to help our kids do the same. In this section, we look at specific strategies to help our children befriend their emotions as an important part of themselves and learn how to work with them. The concepts here help to fill up your child's toolbox for managing his emotions.

Empathy: Accepting Feelings

"I shouldn't feel this way; I hate feeling this way; I'm a baby for feeling this way." No matter what the feeling—fear, anger, sadness, embarrassment—a voice inside often adds insult to injury by telling us that on top of everything else we've done wrong, we shouldn't be feeling the way we do. Just as our empathy and reflection of our children's feelings lets them know that they are accepted, adding a line to their own self-talk like "It's okay to feel this way; it's normal to feel this way; I am feeling angry, and that's just where I am right now," gives your child one less person to fight with when that fight will only fuel more emotion and distract from the issue at hand. Empathy with themselves redirects children back to where the problems can be solved. You can model the lessons of empathy by demonstrating them with your child. Rather than jump in and fix the problem, empathize with his feelings. You may be surprised that just giving him that support may help him locate the solution himself. You can model empathy with yourself when you say to your child things like "I feel angry right now that the kitchen is a mess," or "I felt really sad to hear that Granny was sick." Children not only learn that it is normal to have emotional reactions to situations, but they begin to learn what feelings match up with which situations, and also what the language is for expressing those feelings.

Our children are always listening, especially when we're *not* trying to get their attention. If your child hears you say, "I hate that Bill at work—what a jerk," he will learn one language. He'll learn something quite different if instead he hears, "I had a frustrating day today [temporary]. I got really mad at Bill because he didn't get the papers to me on time [specific]. I've got to talk to him about that tomorrow [action to fix it]." As parents, we can work diligently to temper our reactions in front of our children. Unprocessed, overwhelming emotion should be avoided as it can be frightening and confusing to children, but small displays of emotion like the one in this example are essential for children to learn how to be effective in the face of challenges.

The Pause That Refreshes: Cultivating Mindfulness in Children

Watching our children get swept up in emotion, we may wish they could pause—just for a second—and at that moment choose not to explode or fall apart. In fact, though it is not our instinct to do so, mindfulness—the practice of stepping back from the moment by being fully present in it, breathing and observing rather than rushing in and judging—can be cultivated into a habit that has great benefits beyond the moment. In the last decade, there has been much empirical support for the relationship between meditation techniques and improvements in attention, memory, and academic performance over all. Visualization and relaxation exercises known as "mindfulness exercises" have been introduced in classrooms as a technique for helping kids to stay calmer, have more self-control, and improve their focus at school. Aside from the fact that children and teens welcome the opportunity to "chill" during the school day, they are making use of their calm breathing when they really need it.

Mindfulness is about shifting perspective out of the immediacy of the moment—judging it and ourselves by it—and instead finding a point of stillness and quiet inside what is actually just one moment. Why do we need to find this place? It can become an internal orienting point for us, a virtual home base that is always there. Rather than the *absence* of control that we can experience when feelings bubble up, in that place we feel the *presence* of our calmness—like an internal all-clear signal. Finding that place to quiet ourselves and reset our baseline is a practice that can be very useful, especially to interrupt the escalation of a big emotional moment. In general, once we have cultivated the ability to press the Pause button, we have more choices than our automatic reactions. In addition, educators are beginning to recognize how mindfulness, when used as a regular practice, can help maintain a greater sense of calm and focus, and preliminary studies with anxious children suggest that young children truly can integrate and make use of these deceptively simple moments of being to improve their state of mind.[4]

Consult the resource guide at the end of this book for many excellent resources on mindfulness. For our purposes here, we look at a specific exercise that you can do with your young child or teenager to help her experience some distance and perspective on her emotions.

Mindfulness exercises often include visualizations—focusing on either a single object or a place to facilitate the slowing down of breathing and the filtering out of distractions. For a child who needs more to do (sitting still is hard), it can be fun to learn mindfulness by using sounds and keeping her attention focused on the sound throughout its length. One can purchase meditation bowls making sounds that start small, widen out, and then return to silence, but even the slow whistle one makes when imitating a bird song will suffice. Making and stretching the sound *ohmmmmm* with your own voice is how meditation is traditionally practiced. The trick is that the sound needs to stretch, so that your child's breathing and focus track along the beginning, middle, and end of the sound.

The following visualization exercises are meant specifically to help kids in "storms," or "big feelings" moments. You can say this script aloud to your preschooler or even teenager (in fact, try it yourself), and ask him to imagine this scene. It is best if your child closes his eyes for these exercises, but if he can't, he can choose one object to focus on (and not look at you). Afterward, he could draw or illustrate the story in frames; for example, before the storm, during the storm, and after the storm passes.

- Imagine that the feeling you are having now [name it: anger, sadness, worry] is a big storm cloud in the sky. What color is it? What color is the sky when the clouds are in it? Are there birds in the sky? Look at the clouds: They are moving. Look at the sky: It is still. The sky is always still. And the clouds are moving. What wind do you need to blow the clouds by? Can you picture in your mind a gentle wind blowing the clouds away? Do they go quickly? Do they go by slowly? What does the sky look like now? What color is the sky now that the clouds have passed?

- Can you imagine putting the feeling you are having on a stage or on a movie screen? Can you describe the feeling you are seeing? When you are close to it on the stage or screen, how does it look and feel? Is it very big? What color is it? Now imagine that you are stepping back from the feeling and are in the audience instead of near the action. What happens when you choose a seat way back in the theater? Does the feeling shrink? How does it make you feel to see that you are separate from the feeling? You can choose whether to get close to it or to hang back.

- What color is the feeling you are having? [Usually anger is red, sadness is brown or black, but there are no wrong answers.] Describe the feeling. Can you picture a canvas where you paint that color? Can you see it in a frame? What color is the frame? Do you want a plain frame or a fancy one? Can you now enlarge the frame and make the picture bigger? Is it as big as an elephant, a house, an airplane, a shoebox? [Sometimes it's easier to make it bigger first and then to shrink it.] Now can you shrink the frame as small as you want it? It could be as small as your hand. After the picture shrinks down and you are more comfortable with it, do you want to change the feeling? We can do that by changing the color. What color would make it feel better? [Often blue, sometimes green.] Do you want to paint the color, or would you like to shine a magic/healing/calming light on it? Notice how we can make feelings seem bigger or smaller just with our minds.

Now that you understand the basic concept, you can invite your child or teen to come up with his own images. Some children may see the emotion as a mountain they're climbing, and the mountain gets bigger or smaller. Sometimes it may be a wave that feels big like a tidal wave and then gets smaller. Then, besides using these concepts with your child, you may find yourself referring to this "hub" of acceptance and calmness when you are talking at dinner about something that came up at work, or about how you were stuck in traffic and were going to be late to your doctor's appointment. Instead of freaking out, you remembered your child's image of watching a kite drifting gently, gently through the sunny skies over the pink sand of your favorite beach, and then you became very calm inside. Not only will sharing your use of your child's image reinforce the idea that this is a useful technique, but he will also feel very proud to have been able to help you. For more information on mindfulness exercises for kids, mindfulness or other meditation apps for kids and teens, please see the resource guide at the end of this book.

Engaging in Active Activities. *Vive la différence.* We've just seen the power of stillness in anchoring our children when feelings are rocking their boat. On the other end of the spectrum, but not in opposition to mindfulness, another option to use after your child has gathered herself is to get moving. Often, trying to think her way out of what is going on is not as good a solution (not yet, anyway) as "picking up her brain" and getting involved in something else. Like bumping the needle on a skipping record to move it along, this switch in activity opens up new feelings and new stimuli. Rather than being stuck and repeating the same grooves in the record, she is now moving ahead and will begin to feel better. Much of the discomfort in anger and even sadness is not the situation itself but the physiological responses that the feelings create—surges that are too big to be taken sitting down—and there's a reason: We've pumped enough adrenaline into our systems to outrun a bear! In a calm moment, have your child make a list of things she really likes to do. You can pull out this list while she is waiting for the intense feelings to pass.

This strategy is suggested by Mary Fristad and Jill Goldberg Arnold in their book *Raising a Moody Child.*[5] They stress that children should be encouraged to brainstorm activities in each category, just to gain more flexibility. Rather than singling out one child, the whole family can truly benefit from this exercise, which can easily be done in a few minutes after dinner one evening. Give each member of the family a sheet of paper with the headings in the accompanying chart, but leave some boxes open: Perhaps your children will come up with their own categories. Share your answers as collective brainstorming. There aren't any right answers, only what's right for each person.

Deep Breathing. Proposing that someone "relax" when he's upset might be considered a hostile maneuver. But when the body is revved up with adrenaline and in an agitated state, a competing or opposite response such as relaxation can begin to reprogram the system and reset it to baseline. Rather than use the word *relax* (which despite your intentions may feel like a demand), ask your child just to breathe with you—a few breaths, slowly, deep into your abdomen—and to exhale thoroughly to help their body get into calmer mode. Phrasing it this way helps kids to feel (and rightly so) that they are in charge of their bodies, that they call the shots, rather than feeling that their body is doing something *wrong* that they need to fix. Thinking that we're doing something wrong will not facilitate the relaxation process! Young children can picture inflating their favorite-colored balloon or blowing out candles on a cake with their breath; older children can picture matching their breath to the ebb and flow of a gentle wave. If your child is not ready to do this with you, just begin to quiet down your own breathing; your child may be able to borrow calmness from you. Teens walk around with so much tension as part of their (un)natural state, they especially need a reminder to exhale. As one teen said to me when she finally did take a deep breath and exhaled and noticed how her shoulders let go of their rigid pose, "That feels great, I *never* do that."

CHART 3-1

Active/Physical	Resting and Relaxing	Social	Creative
Go for a walk	Read a book	Call a friend	Write in a journal
Ride my bike	Knit or crochet	Talk to Mom and Dad	Make cartoon pictures
Play with the dog	Do deep breathing	Play a game with my sister or brother	Draw or sketch
Walk the dog	Listen to music		Play with my toys
Dance to music	Take a bath		Bake something
Work in the garden	Play with my toys		
Go on the swing set	Have a snack		
Play catch			

Distraction/Humor/Element of Surprise. Sometimes children get lost in a mood and don't know how to get out. Especially if they've made a big scene, they feel as if calming down is admitting defeat (of course, you were never their opponent, but no need to split hairs). That may be a moment to help them save face with some humor. If your child needs help decelerating from a big emotion, a perfectly timed comic sneeze (or even a natural one) will catch a young child by surprise and break the tension—a deus ex machina descending from the sky to change the mood and save the day.

This kind of simple distraction is most flexibly applied with younger children, who are never very far from a mood change. Antics similar to a dramatic protest may help them settle down: "Please don't be upset, please, please. We need you. Our pet zebra is refusing to sing because you are upset. Listen to him try to sing—it sounds awful!!!" With older children, the right timing is crucial, along with striking the right tone, so that they never feel your levity is a sign of disrespect. Rather than humor, levity may be accomplished with empathy, peppered with a wry note of sarcasm and, especially with teenagers, a hint of loose language to appeal to their darker side, which they may find paradoxically cheering: "How many people do you think are having the same being-a-teenager-truly-sucks moment, right now?" or "These Guinness World Records moments of terribleness are so hard don't you think?" They may be surprised by your language and comforted by your getting it: They are feeling so bad that this is not a moment for decorum. If you are voicing how they feel, they may be freed from having to be the messenger.

A Word About "Venting." For decades, it seemed common knowledge that venting—in the form of punching pillows or hitting an inflatable Bobo doll—was a healthy way to manage anger or frustration, and many books, including my own, have advocated it. However, the research has not borne out this theory. Why? Because those venting activities are now recognized as *increasing* adrenaline, which as we saw earlier has already been released when we feel upset or threatened. So, when we get wildly physical, we are adding to the problem. If a child is overstimulated with anger and then goes at a punching bag for five minutes, he may be increasing the problem by releasing more adrenaline. Mediated or guided ventilation is an alternative to this free-form venting and does seem to help, for instance, using boss-back talk: "Here's Mr. Meany. He is really making you mad. What do you want to say to him?"

Looking for Triggers. If you are finding that your child is highly emotional, look for common triggers and see whether some behind-the-scenes planning could prevent the problem in the first place. Your child walks in from school and is miserable about her day, but you find that after eating a sandwich, she has transformed from her demon self back to your loving daughter. When this happens week after week, parents learn not to panic or to think, "Oh no, my child is miserable at school. What do I do?" Instead they hustle over to the fridge and make a healthy snack—or better yet, pack one for the school bus trip home. Similarly, if your child is having meltdowns every time you go on errands at a department store (and hunger isn't the cause), it may be that all the sights, sounds, and choices are overstimulating, and it is best to keep those trips to a minimum. If understimulation is a trigger, have your child generate an activity list for the fridge for "boring times," and/or have her assemble a bag of activities to keep in the car for meetings, waiting rooms, and other boring adult events. Common meltdown triggers:

- Hunger: need more frequent snacks
- Fatigue: need earlier bedtime
- Poor diet: too much junk food
- Overstimulation: too much noise and activity, too many choices
- Understimulation/boredom: not enough variety in things to do
- Excessive time on their own (TV, computer, video games)
- Stress: not enough unscheduled time
- Lack of structure: too many surprises, not enough predictable scheduling

It can be helpful to track your child's tough moments over a few weeks or the last few episodes you remember and see whether you can find a pattern. For example, if she always melts down on Wednesday, and Tuesday night is karate, this meltdown is likely to be fatigue-triggered. The answer is not to quit karate, but not to add any extra responsibilities on Wednesday, and to make sure that Wednesday is an early-to-bed night. You and she can discuss the important explanatory data: "I bet math homework feels harder tonight because last night was a late karate night and you're tired. Does that make sense?" You can use the accompanying chart for your own data collection and/or for a review with your child after the fact to look for two things: (a) Can she find a pattern to the triggers; and (b) with the benefit of time and distance, can she come up with different reactions that she would like to try? A word of caution: When you are angry with your child about her meltdowns, it is not the time to work on this project together. Instead, find a time when you can actually make it a learning experience. Kids can smell a rat, and if you have any agenda of making your child feel bad about the problem, she will make sure that this project will not be pleasant or productive for anyone concerned.

CHART 3-2

Date/Time	Antecedent (situation)	Behavior (your child's reaction)	Possible trigger?
Saturday 10 a.m.	Long line at the restaurant for brunch	Meltdown	Hungry? Waited too long to eat?
Monday 4 p.m.	Running errands after school	Meltdown in car	Tired and hungry after school? Too many stops?

PART FOUR: IN THE HEAT OF THE MOMENT

In the Heat of the Moment: Strategies to Cool It Down

Remember, essentially, when kids are in a negative spin they're getting picked on or bullied, and not necessarily by an outside source, but by their own thinking, accusations, misperceptions, and explanations for what is going on at that particular moment. So, if you get into a fight with your child at such times, you are increasing that meltdown exponentially, and you can feel the heat. You may not know that if you let up on the heat, even for a few seconds—while you pause, walk away, close your eyes, fast-forward, and picture the moment *after* the crisis has passed—those small but crucially significant steps will *decrease* dramatically the momentum of the meltdown. Remember the goal is to maintain safety, but not to stop the meltdown. Trying to stop it adds energy to it. Instead, you want to let it run out of steam.

What to say to your child:

- *I want to help you; let's work together.*
- *We need to slow this down; can you breathe with me?*
- *You are the boss of you; you are in control of yourself.*
- *This is a storm, but it will pass.*
- *You can decide how big you want the storm to be.*
- *We can keep it smaller by staying calm together.*

What to do:

- Walk away for a few minutes.

- Take deep breaths, in and out slowly and evenly through your nose and mouth, and with each breath, use your right hand to trace the hills and valleys of the fingers on your left hand.

- Do stop, pause, and give yourself a moment to consider your options; don't go with your first reaction.

- Do remember that whatever is going on is temporary and manageable; remember the end could be just minutes away.

- Do make sure that your child knows that you want to help. Try to work together with your child without blaming: "I know you don't like what's happening. I don't either. Let's work together. I want to help you."

- Do slow down the escalation by talking calmly and slowly, and state the obvious about what's going on: "You're really upset right now. You're really having a hard time right now. This isn't how you want things to be happening now."

- Focus on the immediate goal: reestablishing safety, both physical and emotional. Figuring out the whys of the situation needs to wait until you have two people who can think straight.

- If you find that you are getting very angry yourself, *tell, don't yell. Tell* your child that you are about to yell, or you're about to lose it, giving him a warning of where this is going. It will help you to blow off steam without actually losing control. If you are unable to work together, take yourself out for a few minutes' time-out, and explain that you'll return to talk when *you've* calmed down. If you do lose it, be sure that you apologize after, this models for your child how we all need to take responsibility for our own behavior, and helps kids feel secure that stability has been restored.

What not to do:

- Don't rush ahead to think about fixing the problem or punishing for it.

- Don't try to correct, criticize, or threaten consequences for your child being upset or angry. You will only add fuel to the fire.

- Don't try to reason with your child in the heat of the moment.

- Don't panic; remember this is temporary and manageable.

- Don't feel rushed. Your heart is pounding because you are upset, not because there is something you need to do quickly. Doing things carefully will have much more positive long-term effects.

After the Heat of the Moment. Many parents tell me that after a big scene or emotional eruption, they are so relieved that it's over and their child is better that they never discuss it; they don't want to make waves. But actually, after the heat of the moment (even if it is the next day), great learning can occur when you begin to sort through what happened. The goal is to rebuild and repair, not to repeat in slow motion the embarrassment or pain. Such a post-crisis discussion can be a mastery experience for your child, using her competence rather than her chaos. Together, you can go through the problem-solving steps above to see how things might have been settled differently.

Remember, the goal in what some may see as a rehashing is not to make your child feel bad; she probably feels bad enough already. So, for example, with a young child who got so frustrated that she kicked her brother, you can start nonjudgmentally: "Can you tell me what happened here?" Remember, don't ask, "Why did you do that?" If she had the presence of mind to know why, she probably wouldn't have done it. Give her the chance to say what she did wrong before you do, so she can get credit for getting it right: "Do you know why I was upset about this?" Then reinforce her answer—with a young child: "Yes, that's right we don't kick people. When we're mad, what can we do instead?" Or with a teenager, "Right, we can't just blow up on each other. The world will never have peace that way. Let's think of different ways that we can work this out." Give your child the opportunity to apologize, but don't force it; forced apologies are worse than none at all. Forced apologies don't help you feel vindicated or comforted, but they are also an affront to your child because she feels insulted by being forced to say something she doesn't feel yet. An apology, like a good wine, can't be rushed. But it will be truly savored at the right time.

Meanwhile, you can cue your child to move in that direction by letting her know how you feel: "This hurts my feelings" or "This took up a lot of time that I didn't have. Can you think of a way to make it better?" Whenever possible, rather than scrambling for consequences, focus on reparations. Remember that the goal of discipline is *learning* to be a good citizen, with behavior that we want to see repeated. The goal is not to frame your child for being a bad citizen; we don't want to see more of that behavior, so highlighting it is counterproductive. If you *break* something, even if it is the peace and sanctity of your household, the best reparation strategy is to *fix* something. Following our parent mantra of "work smarter, not harder," here's a smart-parent moment: Ask your child (even your preschooler) what would be a good consequence or way to fix what's gone wrong. You are not obliged to take the suggestions, but you will be exercising the "responsibility" neurons in the brain, which will make your child stronger for the next time.

When a Crisis Turns Dangerous

Following the guidelines in this chapter, you can decrease the chances that you will have a crisis in your house. If a younger child is physically out of control, typically passive restraint methods, such as a tight hug or wrapping your child in a blanket, will help you calm him down and to restore safety. If older children are prone to physical outbursts because of a psychiatric condition, such as a mood disorder, oppositional defiant disorder (ODD), disruptive mood dysregulation disorder (DMDD), or attention-deficit hyperactivity disorder (ADHD), it is essential to work with your child's mental health provider to devise a specific safety plan in advance, so that in a moment of crisis, you don't have the extra stress of trying to figure out what to do.

CONCLUSION

When it comes to our children's feelings, our most important maneuver is not to try to steer them away from them, but rather, by making the experience safe and knowable and even productive for them, to help them navigate their way through. Take a look back on what you have learned here, and choose one idea that you are going to use to react differently this week, for example, to listen more and fix less, to breathe with your child, to practice mindfulness, to think of being the sky instead of the storm. Any new move will not only make you more effective but, over time, will have a positive ripple effect on the rest of your family as you model for them what emotional intelligence looks like in action.

CHART 3-3

Ineffective Maneuvers		Confidence-Building Maneuvers	
Telling your child what to feel:	Don't feel this way; you're fine.	Empathizing with how your child feels:	This feels really bad right now; that's okay. It usually does at the beginning.
Minimizing your child's feelings:	It's not so bad; you'll be fine.	Normalizing your child's feelings:	I think anyone would feel upset who was in this situation.
Invalidating feelings (with positive intent):	You're not terrible; you're great. Don't say that about yourself!	Validating feelings:	You feel really bad about yourself right now. It seems as if right now, nothing you can do is right. That happens. I feel that way, too, sometimes.
Highlighting the size:	You are too upset; we can't talk if you are this upset.	Making it a manageable size:	How big does this feel to you? How big do you want it to be? Let's work on this when you're ready.
Solving for your child:	I'll take care of this. I can type your report for you. I'll call the school. You don't need to be friends with that person if she said that.	Invitation to problem-solve:	Are you ready to talk about this now? Can you tell me what happened? Is there a different way of looking at it? Can we think of what your choices are to fix this?
Moving your children on:	Come on, let's go do something else. You can't sit here and think about this all day.	Giving your children choices to help forward movement:	I know it feels bad now, but the feelings will fade after a while. We can help that happen faster by getting busy with an activity.
Making it stop:	That's enough now; you need to stop.	Encouraging a shift:	If we give this more time, I think it's just going to get harder. What else would you like to be doing right now if you weren't upset? Shall we try that? Or, what needs to happen so that you can do that?

4

SHINING THE LIGHT ON YOUR CHILD'S UNIQUE ABILITIES

Finding and Applying Your Child's Strengths

Every man has his own courage and is betrayed because he seeks in himself the courage of other persons.

—Ralph Waldo Emerson

You are your best thing.

—Toni Morrison

If resilience is about bouncing back from adversity, then strengths are what children push off from to set that bounce in motion. Often, kids who are pulled toward the negative feel empty-handed when it comes to strengths. How can they identify and value their strengths when they are cursed with the uncanny natural ability to find fault with anything—the closest target being themselves? These children are wired to *notice* what is wrong and twist that "wrongness" around to be their fault—from the bus driver who didn't say hello as they boarded in the morning, to the one word missing from their term paper, to the friend who abruptly stopped texting in the middle of a conversation. We could say that from a neurological point of view, these children aren't zoned for noticing what is *right*. Not yet, that is. It isn't that they are lacking in strengths by any means; the mere fact that kids with negative thinking withstand what they hear in their head—the grueling climb up and down mountains of disappointment and self-criticism on a daily basis that may be worse than anything others who are wired differently ever hear even on their worst day—proves that they have strength and courage in spades. But that's not how they see it. Their sense of what is right with them—how they are not only surviving, but often thriving—is artificially eclipsed by the surplus of observations they make of what is flawed. So, our children's strengths are always there, but they get trampled and lost in the shuffle, in the relentless stampede of negativity. To put the challenges in their lives in perspective, your children need to right-size their strengths without diminishing, devaluing, or overlooking them.

A second obstacle to children seeing their strengths is their misperception of how abilities do and don't work. We might overhear our children saying things like "I'm not smart; look how hard I have to study!" Kids are quick to disqualify accomplishments that require effort and fall into the belief that *true* accomplishments just happen—voilà! Overly impressed by the visible result—the grade, the trophy, the prize—they may lose sight of the invisible efforts that were crucial in bringing the accomplishment to fruition. Not only is their equation off—you can be "smart" and still have to study—but it overlooks the fact that "studying hard" in and of itself is replete with strengths. In her greatly influential book *Mindset: The New Psychology of Success*,[1] Stanford University psychologist Carol Dweck describes how children with a "fixed mind-set" think that intelligence and other abilities are finite assets that we just have or are born with, whereas children with a "growth mind-set" view abilities as increasing as we learn from experience. To growth-minded children, effort, failure, and making mistakes are not the telltale signs of limitations; they are the grist for the mill of increasing and expanding one's knowledge base. We will look more closely at Dr. Dweck's work in Strategy Six (page 109) and spend a whole chapter (Chapter 7) buffering our children against failure, but suffice it to say here, we need to be careful about not feeding into a fixed mind-set by just focusing our praise and attention on our children's grades or products rather than their efforts.

A third obstacle to children seeing their strengths is the unfortunate belief that knowing and showing your strengths is somehow the same as bragging or being conceited or is otherwise something that's just weird. This belief, ubiquitous especially among teenagers, only adds to their confusion about what is expected of them, given that their peers are saying, "Downplay those strengths; that's weird," and at the same time they are surrounded by adults focusing on how important those same strengths will be for their college applications. While being sensitive to our children's uneasiness about showing off their strengths, we need to help them sort out the differences between using a strength to put someone else down or to brag, and applying themselves because that is what is meaningful to them.

POSITIVE PSYCHOLOGY:
REFOCUSING ON WHAT'S WORKING FOR YOUR CHILD

Positive psychology is a cutting-edge movement in mental health whose starting point is that the role of psychology is as much finding what is *right* in a person as it is fixing what is *wrong*. Nowhere is this premise more important than in approaching children with a negatively biased mind whose warped lens magnifies what's wrong and distorts their self-image. While clearing distortions is one powerful way of correcting that warp, identifying strengths is another. In the generous spirit of a calm moment when they can step out of the marathon of lunches, homework, and laundry, parents can beam with delight at the uniqueness of their children, but bringing an appreciation of those strengths into their daily lives may be challenging. Expediency rules the day, and the search for quick solutions may not leave time to notice the sacred fingerprint of a child in his going about something very differently from what we would expect.

Once our children's strengths have been identified, they are infinitely portable. Our kids can move more fluidly through their lives knowing that they—like all kids—come well stocked with a wealth of resources at their fingertips for mobilizing in times of distress, for using every day to create a satisfying life for themselves, and also for sharing their continuously developing gifts with the world.

Strategy One: Building and
Broadening the Strength Vocabulary

There is a myth that Native Alaskans have one hundred different words to describe snow; in reality, it may be more like seven. When it comes to describing our children's strengths, we may find that our vocabulary could use some expansion and refinement as we are often drawn to just one word: *smart*. We may notice that the tendency to equate strength with intelligence is rampant in our daily conversations: "You got an A on your spelling—you're so smart"; "You built that block tower so tall— you're so smart." Everything comes back to smart.

Who will benefit from this expansion in our appreciation of strengths? Diversity strengthens a culture, so we all stand to gain. The straight-A students whose accomplishments are publicly valued feel pressure to maintain that one facet of their identity or all is lost, so recognizing other gifts broadens their base of security and satisfaction. Taking a broader view of children whose strengths don't fit into our culture's most obvious value categories opens doors to the recognition of their potential to contribute positively to the world. As Robert Brooks and Sam Goldstein, authors of *Nurturing Resilience in Our Children*,[2] write, "Every student possesses at least one skill or island of competence that can be highlighted or displayed in schools." When we all take a broad view of talents, we ensure that all children are being acknowledged, for children will believe and feel the satisfaction of their strengths only if they see them being valued by others.

One consequence of a narrow focus on certain areas of competence is leaving children who have other talents off the radar. Another consequence is that we may be missing the enduring personality qualities— ingenuity, creativity, loyalty, persistence—that will carry our children throughout their lives. These qualities are not registered on a child's school transcript. Goldstein and Brooks suggest that parents find these islands of competence by asking themselves what characteristics of their children bring them the most joy.

Another source for identifying these critical but intangible qualities in our children is to complete an online questionnaire developed by Martin Seligman and colleague Christopher Peterson. This profile of character strengths is based on exhaustive research culling strengths from such varied sources as religious and philosophical texts.[3] Some examples of the qualities identified are curiosity, perseverance, courage, genuineness, kindness, generosity, and self-control. The questionnaire for youth is available on the Web at www.viastrengths.org. I encourage you to set aside some one-on-one time with your child to complete the questionnaire, which takes about forty-five minutes; together you will be discovering the qualities that are most characteristic of your child, so that both of you can put a finger on what makes her who she is.

Whether you complete the survey or create a list from your own observations, share your findings with your child. See whether your child agrees with the results, and help her write down her top two or three strengths on a card that she can keep with her, on her desk, on the fridge, or in a poster she makes for her wall, so that her roster of strengths is the first thing she sees when she wakes up in the morning. You can then encourage her to notice how she applied these strengths in different ways during her day over the next few weeks. The whole family can get involved by generating their own lists of personal strengths; you may even find that your dinner conversations or car rides are enriched by talking with each other about everyone's respective strengths. A fourteen-year-old patient, Cecilia, was feeling down because she was new to her high school and was not getting the grades she was used to. Feeling despondent, she told me, "I have no talents, what's the point of going to school if I have nothing that I'm good at?" Actually, Cecilia had lots she was good at in school and was struggling with only two classes. She also had many strengths far beyond the categories of a particular class syllabus. Articulate, sensitive, loyal, creative, independent—all of these characteristics jump out within minutes of meeting her. We worked on the VIA Strengths Survey together, and she was excited to learn of the many strengths that were her signature, including love of learning, perspective, valor, and loving. As we made the list, her face brightened. "I guess I didn't realize how much of me there is that doesn't show up on a test at school," she said. The following week, as she was telling me about her surprise that a friend had reached out to her when she was really stressed out, she was able to recognize that even though she hadn't been aware of her strengths in that moment—loving and perspective—her friends knew them spot on. Discovering her list of strengths helped Cecilia to understand herself better, and it also organized the template through which she saw the world. Rather than just organizing her observations and connecting the dots around what had gone wrong, she began more and more to recognize the positive, unique constellation of abilities she brought to her day.

Strategy Two: Identifying the Behind-the-Scenes Strengths: The Way You Do the Things You Do

We can also start the search for our kid's strengths by taking their accomplishments ("what" they've done) and then rewinding to identify the intangibles that went into them ("how" they did it). So, for instance, when your son gives a great trumpet performance, is it just that he has an ear for music, or did he also prioritize and organize his time well to practice? Did he persevere when he was struggling to master a new section? Was he courageous in asking for help? Was he able to appreciate the beauty of the music? Did he allow himself to release himself into the flow of music, without just worrying about making it perfect? The result—the good performance—is one thing. But the qualities that made that moment possible are woven into the lasting fabric of his being. This should *not* be a secret—especially to him—but should be more like the specifications in an owner's manual. As we saw in the late Ms. Morrison's wise words, children need to know that *they* are their best thing. Even if a child has not yet hit his stride with his strengths—by which I mean that he hasn't found that niche that fully makes use of his unique strengths—his strengths are still of value. He doesn't have to search for that value in external validation. If this fact is held and recognized by the family, the rest (his niche) can wait.

This principle applies to other contexts, not just performance. Imagine that your child is having difficulties with a friend, and then things improve. Do a rewind with your child. Ask her, "How did things get better? What happened?" When something works, we don't want it to be a mystery to our child; we want her to see the steps *she took* to make a difficulty better, so that she can take credit for her efforts, repeat the steps when she's in a similar situation, and see herself overall as capable of greatly impacting the course of her life.

Strategy Three: All in the Family: Finding the Strengths of the Home Team

We live with them, we eat with them, and yet how our families actually work together often feels like a mystery. In any group—a team, a choir, a corporation—each group member is essential for what he or she brings to the whole. One way to tap into and bring out the unique qualities of your children is to ask each family member to imagine for a moment that the family is actually a business, and then to assign titles to each family member for what department they would run. Very interesting conversations and discoveries emerge, even around the dinner table, when each family member (including the parents) participates in this exercise and compares notes. Spotlighting what each person does best, you may find that one child is the head of the humor department because of the corny jokes he shares; another, the head of goodwill and compassion because of how she shows her concern for all people and is never disparaging about her friends. The information technology director is often the person in the family who actually knows how to get your digital calendar syncing with everyone in the family, or how to set up your Bluetooth speaker. The chief-of-organization title may go to the kid who never loses papers and is also the real-time family calendar because she can keep everyone's appointments in her head. The beautification committee head may bring home artwork, artfully fold napkins, bring in flowers from the garden, and notice the little things. Using a list of the job titles generated from the individual contributions of the group, together you can create a family organization chart. Let each member choose her or his favorite title, and then make a poster for your fridge: "Welcome to the Smith Family. On staff we have. . . . " Having articulated areas of strength for each family member, you can refer to these facets of each personality in casual conversation—"We need a technology consult"; "We need a beautification consultation"—reinforcing positive aspects of each child's personality in action. Although it may feel a little awkward at first, this exercise is really about stopping to recognize and cherish what we may unintentionally take for granted every day: the gifts of each person in the family. Because we are all a work in progress, repeat this activity a couple of times a year, or even once a year, and you may be surprised to see both what changes and what stays the same. Hold on to the old charts and stick them in the family photo album as another way of documenting the changes in your family over time.

A second dinner-table activity is for each family member to write down his or her favorite or most admired qualities about each person in the family; use a separate card for each family member. Then, you can mix up the cards, pull them out of a hat, read them, and see who can guess which person the card is describing. At the end of the activity, each person can take her or his card and keep it to refer to. It is especially touching to see how siblings—even those who often do battle with each other—describe what they value in one another.

Strategy Four: Separating the Enduring Strengths from the Temporary Struggles

What if your child is perpetually stationed in negativity land and, as a result, is often completely miserable with herself—and you feel as though you've been emotionally off-roading through treacherous terrain all day to help her feel better? The notion of finding strengths may seem so remote that you are probably thinking, "Are you kidding? I'm just glad we both survived the day!" Take the time to separate what you might consider your child's true nature from the struggles and challenges she faces because of her negative thinking style.

On one side of a sheet of paper, write down the first ten things you enjoy about your child. Think about proud moments and what qualities went into making them happen. Flip through the photo album and savor pictures of your child at different ages. What do you enjoy most? What do friends, family, teachers, or coaches comment on about your child? What is her essence that people are drawn to? On the other side of the page, write down your child's struggles or symptoms. From this activity, you can gain perspective on the struggles and see them as the temporary ripples set against the lasting qualities of your child. Make a mental note of these strengths and qualities, and recall them the next time your child is in a negative spiral. By keeping a more balanced picture of her strengths and struggles, you'll pave the way for her doing the same.

You can encourage your children to generate their own strengths list by using the following suggestions:

- Have your young child make a collage of pictures that are "all about me": things he loves to do, things that he is good at. When you talk to your child about the activities, look for ways that each activity is connected to various aspects of your child. For example, if your child says, "I love animals," after hearing what he loves about animals, you might say, "I notice that you are very sensitive to animals—you are very kind and want to make sure they have an owner. Animals like you because you are so gentle with them."

- Ask your older child to think back to two or three of her happiest or proudest moments: "What is the picture you have in your mind?" "What caption would you put on that picture?" "What is the belief that you have about yourself?" For example, if your child says something like "the canoe trip at camp," help her track back to what made that time special: "I was afraid to do it, but I was really proud I did." You can say, "That took courage." If she says, "I loved how we had to work together in teams," you can say, "That is a strength of yours, connecting and coordinating with others." Ask your child, "How do you want to remind yourself of that?" You can suggest that she keep a picture of that time on her bedside table or type up the caption and put it in her room.

- Ask your child to think about a teacher who really liked him: "What kind of comments or compliments did he or she give you? Think about a teacher you really liked. What did you like about that class? What does that say about you?" Write down the resulting adjectives.

- Ask your child, "What would your friends say they appreciate most about you?"

You can stop there, or ask a child who is feeling acutely that her struggles undermine her strengths to make a list of her favorite attributes and strengths on one side of a page and a quick list of her struggles on the other. Have her go through the list and identify which items are "temporary" and which are "permanent."

Sometimes distinguishing between what is a struggle and what is not is tricky. Kids often complain that a parent who has a problem in mind "overdiagnoses" it or sees it everywhere. Take Marianne, the vivacious and social mother of Natalie, a soft-spoken, self-directed girl who suffered from social fears and depressive thinking. Marianne was in some ways struggling more than her daughter: Natalie knew that even though she wanted to increase her comfort in being around her peers, and she was doing so step by step, she also felt very contented with her own company—and she needed it. Her downtime was sacred to her. She liked to practice violin for hours. She would get lost in the music, and it was a very important part of her life. To Marianne, Natalie's downtime was a symptom, a sign of being anxious or too depressed to socialize. The more her mom anguished about Natalie's not spending enough time with her peers and about how lonely Natalie must be, the more frustrated Natalie felt: Her mom didn't understand; it wasn't all depression! As we talked the problems through, we saw that some of the behaviors that her mother identified as problems were actually strengths for Natalie: her resourcefulness in being able to occupy herself, her being satisfied with her own company, her dedication to her music. Because these were not part of Marianne's repertoire, she was seeing Natalie's time alone as the *absence* of something, as opposed to the *presence* of other important aspects that Marianne could be proud of.

Strategy Five: Finding Strengths Even (Especially) in the Presence of Adversity

The anxious children with whom I work come to me doubting their courage. They are afraid of everything. How can they be brave? they wonder. I explain that courage doesn't come from the easy life; it comes from facing and overcoming their fears. The parents of sensitive, negative-minded kids may doubt their children's strengths because they, too, feel they have so many weak points: They may cry more, get angry more, and be more affected by things. How can they be proud of themselves? As we saw in Chapter 2, part of the problem is that they are misattributing a no-fault negative mind-set as a personal failure. Although negative thinking can affect the whole person, it is not due to a flaw in the whole person; rather, it is a thinking habit, which, above all, can be changed. It is important for both children and their parents to understand that strengths are often shown through adversity—whether actual traumatic events or the fallout from a mind magnifying problems that are manageable. Children who are working on overcoming a negatively tuned mind are heroic, strong, and accomplishing an important neurological coup, with limitless benefits for their health, satisfaction, and well-being.

Strategy Six: Minding Your Mind-Set

> I am the only child of parents who weighed, measured, and priced everything; for whom what could not be weighed, measured, and priced, had no existence.
>
> —Charles Dickens, *Little Dorrit*

None of us want to be that family. None of us wants our children to feel weighed and measured like this character in *Little Dorrit*, and yet, if parents at times feel like ATM machines for their teenager's money needs, teenagers often feel like grade machines, their parents always looking for "A's." In fact, pasting together sound bites of our conversations with our older children might reveal a sort of absurd rap song: "What did you get? What did you get? Why just a B? Why not an A?" Numbers, grades, and rankings are a very compelling bottom-line way that our culture keeps score, but keeping our eye on the big picture, we want our children to have lasting satisfaction and contentedness in life, and as we saw in Chapter 1, that happiness does not come from increased income; it isn't guaranteed by a great transcript or a great SAT score, either. In fact, children face great burnout when their self-worth is transitory and only as good as their *next* good grade.

We may find ourselves fighting an uphill battle to send the right messages in our homes. We also may be doing battle with ourselves because as much as we would never want our children's worth reduced to a number, we know that the system, however flawed and slow to change, operates on this principle. Focusing solely on grades or SAT scores is a sure way of missing out on the unique strengths that each child possesses. But what are the "right" things to pay attention to? As we saw earlier, psychologist Carol Dweck, author of *Mindset*, answers that question with one word: *effort*. Focus on your child's *efforts*—what they bring to and put into their work rather than grades. Dweck argues that focusing on grades as the unit of value of our children not only causes us to miss out on our children's strengths, but also, by basing their worth on something that is not under their control, makes kids afraid to take chances. When product (grade) becomes more important than process (learning), children may believe that they are inadequate unless they are able to meet the very specific goals they think define one's success, and they will want to quit. I have worked with many talented students who "underachieve" because they'd rather not try at all (or not try their best) if they sense that failure is possible. Recall that as we saw above, Dweck differentiates between a fixed mind-set, "believing that your qualities are carved in stone," and a growth mind-set, "a belief that your basic qualities are things you can cultivate through your efforts."[4] Although we may have a combination of these mind-sets, it will be beneficial to call out our "fixed mind-set" thinking and do a pivot to growth rather than endure the incalculable pressure of approaching the world in a fixed mind-set. Consider this, children with a fixed mind-set proceed like a gambler who has put all her chips on the table at every move: Rather than knowing that making mistakes or learning would be an acceptable outcome (you win some, you lose some, and you learn from all), and that they would still hold onto their identity and their smarts (the bulk of their chips) even if they missed an answer or a grade, they feel that every interaction is either an opportunity to prove they're smart or a humiliation that proves they're dumb (they'd lose all of their chips).

Kids prone to negative spins may come with a lot of resources or a few, but they have so much riding on their bet—their intelligence, their reputation, their sense of self—that they are going to want to stay out of the game because they have so much to lose. Also, as Dweck points out, if you have a fixed mind-set about intelligence, you are going to feel an "urgency [either] to prove yourself over and over"[5] or to hide and not be found out. Further, kids are going to mistakenly interpret their need for help or their hard work as a sign, a validation, that they aren't smart because smart is, to them, something effortless.

A growth mind-set helps children to feel free to focus on improving rather than proving themselves. They can identify their own strengths, including those that don't match up with what someone else has in mind and work on improving those strengths by comparing themselves to *themselves*, rather than comparing themselves to others. We don't want to inadvertently force our kids to hide the truth about themselves because it doesn't match up with our interpretation of them and of what success is and what their future should look like. If kids have to pretend to be someone else, devalue their interests and talents, and act as if they are interested in business when what they love is science, not only will they feel alienated from themselves, but they won't benefit from your wisdom and guidance (and we benefit from their gifts) because they've had to go underground with their plans.

Mind-Set Dos and Don'ts

- Don't overemphasize your child's "potential"; this makes kids feel pressured because their current accomplishments are not valued, and their worth is conditional and will remain on hold until they have reached some future action, deed, or endeavor.

- Don't focus solely on *outcome*, such as grades or global characteristics: "You got an A. You're smart." The inadvertent message is that when they get a B, they're not smart. A younger child who is told, "You read that word—you're smart," may be afraid to try another word because if he struggles, it will prove he's *not* smart.

- Do focus on process: "You really pushed yourself"; "You worked hard"; "You really synthesized the information well"; "You used your creativity on that essay"; "You really took risks and stretched your comfort zone with that presentation." Focus on younger children's effort: "You are really working on your sounding-out skills"; "You're really attacking those new words"; "It's exciting to figure out a new word!"

- Do focus on effort and perseverance: "This was a hard chapter to learn, but you really stuck with it."

- Do focus on learning: "What did you learn from the test? From the chapter?" "What did you find most interesting?"

- Do encourage reasonable risk-taking, for instance encouraging your child to not just play it safe by taking the class that's easiest, but to take on greater challenges.

- Do quell your own anxiety about your child's future; just observe what your child prefers and connects with without racing ahead to a future goal. If your child is a good baker and your mind says, "Okay, he can be a chef," try to keep your calculations to yourself. Focus on enjoying his gifts for what they are now in the moment.

- Do keep an open mind about your child's direction. If we are too focused on looking for one thing for our children, we lose sight of what matters to them.

- Do notice and track how your child is expressing abilities all the time—in the present moment—by following observations, discoveries, and interests and encouraging curiosity.

Strategy Seven: Effort and Showing the Seams: Success: The Backstory

> I have not failed. I've just found 10,000 ways that won't work.
>
> —Thomas Alva Edison

How does success work? Look at any social media feed and kids see those snapshot moments (airbrushed, beautiful, happy) and connect the dots: Success and happiness are effortless and constant factors of the very lucky and attractive. The fact that those feeds have been carefully curated aside, kids don't see the outtakes of that picture-perfect public persona: the hard work, the bad hair days, the rejections, the blemishes, the disappointments, the loneliness. It's as if life is an HGTV television program: in the course of an hour, an old wreck is restored to an architectural gem; or a cooking show, where in thirty minutes, we go from breaking eggs to a five-course gourmet meal; or more to the point: the YouTubers whose apparent meteoric rise belies the months of followers in the double digits, the hours of effort that ensued to make that meteor look as if it came out of nowhere. Fortunately, with some explanations about how learning really works, kids can understand the link between knowledge and effort and can benefit from the freedom afforded by that understanding.

So much of kids' frustration and negativity stems from two factors: how they think *they* should work ("If I can't do this puzzle or geometry equation, then I am stupid") and how they think the *world* should work ("If I'm good, things will go right; if I'm smart, things should go easily"). So set are these ideas that when things don't work out as children anticipated, of course they don't think, "Oops, wrong prediction," or "Some things worked out and others didn't," or "Everything's hard at first. Keep trying." Instead, their sense of self gets washed out, and they conclude, "That didn't work. It's my fault. I am a failure. Don't try again." There is much in our culture that feeds the illusion that instant or effortless success is the rule. As an antidote to this culture of instant gratification, parents must teach children how things *really* work, so the children can value their own strengths and efforts.

How can we do this? Parents can show their seams. Children revere their parents even while treating them on occasion like chauffeurs, maids, or worse. But when you share details about your life, come out from behind the curtain of the "perfect person" that your child may imagine (but will never admit to), and talk about your own struggles, kids are astonished. Tell them how a project isn't working out, and how you are rethinking it. Show them the bookshelf you're building (invite them to help) and let them see it develop in phases. Tell them that you didn't get the deal you were pitching, and you're analyzing how much the reason it fell through was "about me" and how much was "about them." This doesn't mean venting raw, unprocessed emotion to your children, or burdening them with your problems; rather, once the situation is somewhat cleaned up and understood, you can role-model for them how things "going wrong" doesn't mean being stupid or a failure and isn't a sign that they shouldn't have tried. It is what happens in life and demonstrates that it is survivable.

Showing the seams also means developing a safety net for trial and error. If you draw a small circle around yourself and what defines success, you won't be willing to take a step; your safe zone for taking chances is very small. Don't just say that mistakes are part of life and then, when you or someone in your life makes a mistake, be unforgiving; your child sees you crying over spilled milk and that picture negates a thousand reassuring words. So, make sure that your child sees by your example that people make mistakes and may get mad, but then they get over it and they fix the problem.

If you need some more glamorous models than the trials and tribulations of your own life, share with them some "famous failures." Like Mr. Edison's quote about the road to successfully inventing the lightbulb, history gives us countless examples of the not-so-linear route from obscurity to success. Many websites and books have compiled lists of celebrity or famous failures; read through the list with your child, and have everyone in the family choose a "new hero" from the group who can admit that they failed first. Some colorful facts that my patients have enjoyed include discoveries made by accident, such as Silly Putty and penicillin, as well as the surprising facts that Albert Einstein didn't talk until age four or read until age seven, Walt Disney was apparently fired from a newspaper job for lacking creativity, Charles Schulz of Charlie Brown and *Peanuts* fame had every cartoon he submitted rejected by his high school yearbook, and the Beatles were rejected by two record companies before Apple Records picked them up.[6] You could ask your child to guess which companies started in a (inventor's parent's) garage. The answer? Apple, Google, Amazon, Harley-Davidson, Disney, and Mattel! The road to glory is a long one and starts with risk and tenacity, not with a meteoric rise! (For more ideas and fun facts, see the resource guide at the end of this book. For more information about handling failures, disappointments, and losses, see Chapter 8.)

Strategy Eight: Global Failure or Specific Glitch: What Does a Lack of Self-Esteem Really Mean?

Many children come into my office for the first time, plunk down on the couch, and reel off all the things that are bothering them: "I'm afraid to take chances; I get nervous on tests; I don't have enough friends." Then, they will add, "Oh, and I have no 'self-esteem.'" When I hear those words, I get a certain feeling of uneasiness. First of all, there is the contradiction: In the very same moment that these children are saying they have no self-esteem, they are in the process of articulating their needs and advocating for themselves—not a likely activity for someone who feels no self-worth. But more than that, I hear them echoing a generalized, global label—no self-esteem—that they have heard used to describe, erroneously, their frustration with a very specific situation, for instance, struggling with math. Even if it's a series of situations, rather than seeing themselves as essentially whole but having trouble with one or two specifics, children are burdened with the unwieldy, broad label of "lacking self-esteem." It is not a case of missing self-esteem, but misattributing a specific problem to the whole child. Or, more to the point, their thinking is not letting them see the value they intrinsically have as a person.

When parents say that their child or teen has low self-esteem, they are mislabeling something *limited* as something *lasting*. Your child doesn't need to think *better* of himself, necessarily; he needs to think more *accurately* about himself. Rather than using this global label, help your child step out of the big box of trouble he *thinks* he's in and find the smaller, more accurate one he can manage. A child who says, "I have no self-esteem—I don't feel as if I can do anything," needs help to understand that this moment's frustration or disappointment is making him *feel* that way, which is contrary to the truth in general. Children may be pleasantly surprised to be "allowed" to feel good about some things, even if they don't feel good about other things. Help your child not to let the "all-or-none" error get in their way. It's best to wait until the most acute phase of feeling upset is over before they decide about what they can and can't do.

Strategy Nine: To Be of Use: Practicing Strengths, Playing to Strengths

> The main constraint in achieving expertise is not some fixed prior level of capacity, but purposeful engagement involving direct instruction, active participation, role modeling and reward.
>
> —Robert Sternberg[7]

Dr. Robert Sternberg, an esteemed scholar on theories of intelligence, has proposed a three-part theory of intelligence, which in addition to the conventional dimensions of analysis and problem solving, includes creative intelligence (being able to solve novel situations) and practical intelligence (the ability to respond and adapt to everyday life). To Sternberg, intelligence is about purposeful engagement. Following up on this definition, Strategy Nine gives our children opportunities to apply themselves, to experience at an age-appropriate level the sense that they are contributing members of their world. Too often, against all our intentions, our children feel disenfranchised in various aspects of their lives, either because there is one right way to do things and it is not their way, or because they get used to simply following directions and turning off their innovative side. Encouraging children's input and participation— from soliciting opinions for dinner menus, to finding chores that are not *too* horrible and that they can take pride in, to letting them creatively set the table—doesn't just make kids *feel* important; they *are* important. Such tasks give them a real, valuable role to play in the family.

If family life is a microcosm or training ground for experiences that children will have in the larger world, then it is clear we need to provide opportunities for children to be active participants rather than bystanders. The belief about oneself as being capable—what psychologist Albert Bandura referred to as "self-efficacy" is bolstered by mastery experiences: setting out to do something and seeing that you can get it done—whether it is building a block tower, resolving a fight with a friend, writing a term paper, or climbing a mountain.

Parents will always need to set reasonable parameters for their children, but children should be given as much leeway as possible within those parameters. If your child *wants* to do his social studies homework before his math, but you want him to do his math first, let him do his social studies first. Don't miss the big picture here: He actually *wants* to do his homework, but he wants to do it his own way! You can share with him why you think math should come first, but he may need to learn for himself. Let your younger child choose his own clothes, and tolerate a few discordant color days, so your child will learn that, within reason, he can make a plan and execute it. When our older daughter, Meredith, was about three, she would choose her socks in what we saw as mismatched pairs, but Meredith insisted that they did match. "They are neighbors," she explained. Her principle of neighboring socks not only saved us many a shopping trip for matching pairs but, more important, provided her confidence in her own judgment. If through our comments and expectations we are inadvertently training our children to wait for our instructions and approval, we can't fault them for not taking initiative and embarking on a project without our permission.

As any overworked parent knows (and we're all overworked), our kids have no shortage of opportunities for firsthand experience. You would be amazed what our children can do when we stop overdoing for our kids." The next time you are about to lose your cool over one more demand by your child, take a deep breath, exhale, smile, and then ask her: "What part of this can you do yourself?" Can't cut up the apple? Not a problem; she can get it from the fridge and wash it for you. Your daughter needs her new jeans washed by tomorrow? Hey, she can bring down the whole load of laundry and maybe even get it started. It's a win-win situation: Your child is building more self-reliance, and you, aside from facilitating it, are getting some good collaborative help.

In addition to the day-to-day chores, you can involve your children in bigger projects in the family. Taking a vacation but don't have time to compare hotel prices? Looking for some free concerts in your area? Hire your teen to find the best deals online. Their participation in the planning will likely invest them more in making the time enjoyable. Overwhelmed with decorating for a holiday? Let your creative grade school or even preschool child roll up his sleeves and propose a decorating scheme. Can't find your favorite David Bowie song in your collection, hire your middle schooler to search for it online. Although these examples may be a little homey, consider the research findings that tell us how simply allowing children to choose their pen color makes them more prolific writers than children who don't get to choose. It is clear that finding reasonable opportunities—from the mundane to the exotic—to let children know that their say counts puts them on the pathway to making their mark on the world.

Strategy Ten: Encouraging Resilience:
Out of Struggle Comes Strength

> If we want to raise resilient kids we must avoid expending
> all of our energy on attempting to change the world; rather
> we must begin by changing what we do with our children.
> We can no longer afford to assume that if our children don't
> face significant stress they will be unburdened as they transi-
> tion in adult life.
>
> —Robert Brooks and Sam Goldstein[8]

Our last strategy may seem antithetical to the notion of strengths. But allowing kids to fall gently—losing a homework paper, or getting a bad grade on a test and not intervening to fix it for them—is a way of en- suring that they will build enough resilience to successfully leave us one day. Having received a balanced diet of protection and exposure, chil- dren will have the skills and the confidence in their abilities to tackle the inevitable hurdles in life. So, while there is much we do to ensure our children's safety, one paradoxical thing we must do is *not* do it all.

The challenge of encouraging resilience that I see in my practice and even in my own home every day is having the courage as a parent to let a child struggle—not excessively or uncompassionately, but waiting, bear- ing witness to the pain that our children suffer when a friend leaves them out, a girlfriend breaks up with them, a rule is broken and a consequence follows. Rather than thinking about stopping yourself from solving a problem for your child, think instead of "sharing the job." First, see what part of the problem your child can tackle herself, and then accommodate or fill in.

Sometimes it's not a matter of our letting our kids struggle because adversities such as death, illness, and injury do occur. Even then, we can instill the belief that our children can overcome, that their lives aren't ruined, that these events are part of life and in fact, though perhaps not immediately, the overcoming itself will reveal many previously unrecog- nized strengths.

Family Activity: Constructing a Strengths Synonym List

There was one year when everything was "annoying" to our older daughter Meredith. Well, not everything, but if anything bothered her, it was "annoying." Finally, we told her that we'd be happy to listen to her observations if she'd just use a different word. Her vocabulary increased greatly that year. To help your family expand its vocabulary of strengths beyond *smart*, *strong*, or *pretty*, have each family member write down ten positive attributes on a piece of paper; keep the list nearby, and when anyone reverts to the old standbys of *smart* or *gifted*, pull out the list and find the words (or add them) that may better describe the attribute. This activity will enable children to deepen their appreciation of those they are describing, broaden their perspective on what constitutes a strength, and—as a bonus—increase their vocabulary.

CONCLUSION

In this chapter, we've looked at many avenues for identifying and making use of our children's unique strengths. As we turn now to the master plan, make a short list of your child's top two or three strengths—the attributes you most admire right now in your child that make them uniquely themselves. We will draw on these in the next chapter as we encourage children to look at their negative thoughts through a different lens—summoning the perspective of, for example, their "mature" self, their "patient" self, or their "determined" self.

5

GOING FROM THE "NO" TO THE "KNOW"

The Master Plan for Overcoming Negative Thinking

When Tia has a bad day, first I listen and really want to help; then I get frustrated that she seems to want to feel worse instead of better; then I get mad at her; and then, the icing on the cake, I give myself a guilt trip because I've just made my daughter, who is already upset, have one more reason to feel that way. If I'm trying to make it better, how come it always gets worse?

—mother of a ten-year-old

One's destination is never a place but rather a new way of looking at things.

—Henry Miller

CHANGING WHAT YOU CAN: FREEING OURSELVES FROM THE STORIES OUR NEGATIVE BRAIN TELLS US

Attention-deficit hyperactivity disorder (ADHD) is often described as a condition in which children's brains are wired *without* the speed bumps to slow them down from being impulsive. If we stay with the traffic analogy, children with negative thinking habits can be seen as having a brain wired to find, fall in, and personalize the potholes that we call here "negative think holes," which are part and parcel of the road of life. Optimistic children isolate problems and, though not pleased about them, narrow their scope and broaden the array of solutions. In contrast, kids with pessimistic thinking, by no fault of their own, broaden and deepen the problem, adding all sorts of unrelated factors and narrowing the scope for solutions. A simple forgotten yogurt becomes "Great, my lunch is ruined, and wouldn't you know it would happen on the same day I have this huge math test? I'll probably fail. Nothing ever works for me [permanent]. There goes my day [pervasive]. I always have bad luck [personal]." Instead of being a slip, a stumble, a small misstep, the negative event becomes a magnet drawing all other possible misfortunes and disappointments, past, present, and future.

Our goal is to help our children see the distinction between *events* (stuff that happens to us) and our *commentary* about those events (the story we tell ourselves about those events—why they happened, what they mean about us and about life). Although we can't change the adversities—the forgotten yogurts—we can change the commentary. How we see it and what we do about it are entirely up to us. Our goal in working with our children is to help them see that an event is not locked into any particular interpretation or commentary, and that they get to choose the story they want. When they choose to stick with that first draft, automatic "everything is bad, nothing is good, life is miserable" story, they're going to feel defeated before they start anything else. When they enlist our inner editor and choose the "today was a bad day" or—even more to the point—"today's chemistry test was brutal" story and keep the narrative to an isolated event, they are deflecting a meteor and instead keeping the problem small.

Pulling together the lessons thus far, in this chapter we present an action plan to use when your child is stuck in negative thinking, so she can jump off the pessimistic track and access many more accurate, adaptive, and even inviting ways to understand her situation and what she can do about it. Initially you may want to jot down all the steps of the master plan, to ensure that you are heading in the right direction. Over time and depending on your child's needs, you may find that to best help her pivot out of the place she's stuck comes down to two ideas: *empathizing* with her perspective and then helping her through compassionate and colorful reminders to be her own editor and *shrink* that unwieldy, overwhelmingly distorted view of the problem created by the negative brain, so that it feels more manageable and she is able to see options for moving forward that were previously not on her radar.

GETTING OFF THE NEGATIVE TRACK: SEEING THAT YOU HAVE OTHER PLACES TO GO

When your child or teen is miserable, helping her feel better is one of the challenges and privileges of parenthood. The solution isn't to remove our kids from the miserable situation, but to remove the distortions and amplifications from their thinking that created the misery in the first place. Every situation can be read lots of different ways; our goal is to teach our kids just that: don't go with the first (automatic) story about something that happened to us. Instead, we need to teach kids to pause, notice their reaction, rather than running with it, and exercise their flexibility by seeking out other more accurate interpretations (as Henry Miller's comment that opens this chapter suggests). How do we get our kids heading down that path? We don't do it alone: No need to drag an unwilling passenger. It's not that children in a negative spin don't want to be happy; it's that they don't see any alternatives to their unhappiness. These steps will show your child how to rewire his thinking from the dark and hopeless situation it *feels* like into the realistic, manageably sized challenge it *is*. The difference between being in the "no" ("Nothing is working, and nothing will change") and being in the "know" ("This *one* thing isn't working, and here are my options to change it or learn from it") will feel instantly liberating for your child. With practice, the brain makes new connections and learns to look for all the possible options—especially the ones that feel better, and over time, switching out of pessimism will become more automatic.

The key is recognizing the difference between distorted negative thoughts and realistic accurate thoughts, like two different ring tones on a cell phone. Kids can train their ears to distinguish the familiar negative-thinking ring of *always, never, nothing* from the *sometimes, soon, in time* ring of possible thinking. Children are able to limit the impact of their thoughts when they can say, "Oh, that's just Blamo [or Mr. Perfect]. He always shows up and makes me feel worse when I'm already feeling bad. I don't have to pick up that call, I'm going to let that go to voicemail." Or, for older kids: "This feels bad, but it's probably not as bad as I'm thinking it is; let me pause and really think this through."

Don't Stop the Thoughts, Stop the Attention to the Thoughts: Click Over to More Accurate Thinking

- Unfortunately we can't just go in there and change our thoughts, but by changing our reaction to the thoughts, we train the brain to filter out these distorted, intrusive assessments of our life and over time we have fewer negative thoughts. Just relabeling negative thoughts—using their invisible thought stamper that says: Exaggerated! Irrelevant! Wrong! enables some kids to immediately move over from negative thinking to accurate thinking and be on their way. It's as if their smart brain was put on "hold" when the negative brain interrupted the call. By relabeling the negative interpretations as unreliable and unfounded, these kids are immediately able to click back to clearer thinking. For other kids, the negative thoughts are more sticky; these children need to interact with those thoughts more to understand *why* it is okay not to give them authority; they will need to generate proof. Ultimately, all children can learn that the smartest thing to do is "think in twos": their "first thoughts" (the negative thoughts) are the one that are automatic—fast but not accurate—and they need to cultivate the essential habit of pairing those with their "second thoughts" the ones that take some investigation, before settling on their final assessment of the risk, consequence, or meaning of a situation.

EASING INTO THE LESSONS: LONG-DISTANCE LEARNING AND LEVITY

While in the end, we all like to learn how to do things that are "better" for us, getting there is often better served by using what I call the "long-distance learning" approach: first use the example of someone else to teach a principle, before a child tries to apply it to herself. It's kind of a cousin of the asking advice "for a friend," idea, we don't like to be in the hot seat and neither do our kids. So, rather than making these lessons about your child, ask about their friend, or an imaginary person or character who is in a situation similar to how they're processing it, but different in content. If your young child gets upset when math homework is hard, but responds resiliently when she meets disappointment building Legos—teach the lesson about a Lego builder first; your child will see the error of that builder's ways and then apply it to herself. Teens never want to be the focus of anything remotely critical, so even though you want to help them when they are saying how "stupid" they are in physics, give them some room and walk them through the thinking process you'd like them to adopt in the context of something they don't struggle with: writing English papers. Have them put themselves in the mind-set of a friend who can't write a paper easily: What should they think? That they're stupid? or that they need help with the specific challenge of outlining? From a more distant vantage point (that of a friend who is upset about not scoring a goal in soccer, or even of you yourself, when you are upset about burning dinner), kids can analyze and be critical of others' thinking errors without having to be critical of their *own* reactions (and you aren't being critical either). When children see that Disaster Man thinking is widely shared and not unique to them, they will feel freer to apply the strategies to themselves.

On the question of levity: Sometimes speaking in serious tones about a heavy topic is the only respectful thing to do, and most of us sense that. At other times, your instincts may tell you that you have a little more room to lighten things up. Just because the problem feels heavy doesn't mean the solution has to be, too. Remember that the levity is about the subject, not about your child. You are not making light of his situation; you are helping him see the situation in a different light. So, use carefully chosen words at a carefully chosen moment, and do look for opportunities to use exaggeration and absurdity to bring some comic relief into the mix. For example, when your teenager says, "I am the biggest freak to walk the planet," rather than trying to talk him out of it directly by listing all the ways he's great—using a tone of urgency that keeps everyone in emergency mode, you might say, "Yes, I think I read that in the newspaper earlier today. Or was it the six o'clock news? I thought that was actually about me . . . " Or "Biggest freak, well, you know we are proud of you, whatever the distinction is." This unexpected and perhaps absurd response helps to break the ice in the conversation in your child's head and change the mood. Nota bene: Your tone should be compassionate, and definitely on your child or teen's side, never in a mocking or teasing way. You are showcasing that the negative thinking is absurd, not that your child is. When your young child says, "I'm a bad girl, I made a mistake!" you can turn to an imaginary audience and say warmly, "Okay, everyone who has ever made a mistake, raise your hand! Wait—it's not just Suzy? Meany brain, stop bugging Suzy; everyone makes mistakes!" Although there are moments when comments like these would be insensitive, in other moments they will be the icebreaker not only between you and your child but, most important, between your child and her negative thoughts. We saw in Chapter 3 that empathy is a way of bringing your child back to herself; some well-timed humor is occasionally the vehicle that will provide that ride. Not surprisingly, as we will see, empathy is the first step in the master plan.

PART ONE: ESTABLISHING THE FRAMEWORK: SCRIPTS FOR EXPLAINING NEGATIVE THINKING TO YOUR CHILD

To begin the conversation about negative thinking, you can explain to your child of any age that when something happens—a disappointment or bad news—it's as if we begin to fall into a hole: The bigger the hole, the more work it is to climb out. You have to use all your muscles, and you get tired, and it takes a long time to feel better, but we can catch ourselves. What makes the hole deeper is the story you tell yourself about it. The more you say things like "This is impossible," or "It's always like this," the deeper you go. When you think accurately—recognizing that a situation is temporary and there are specific reasons that things went wrong—your thinking becomes a ladder to help you climb out. We can make this concept more accessible for young children by giving them a visual aid: "It could be a big, big, big hole, like for a what? A whale? Or a medium hole, for a what? A horse? Or a small hole, for a what? A mouse or a groundhog? What can you say to yourself to make the hole smaller? How deep do you want it to be? Do you want someone to come in with you to help you out? The Try It Tiger? Your Mojo Brain?"

A second way to help your child understand the "stuckness" of negative thinking is through the brain nets illustration. You can explain, "Everyone has negative thoughts, but some people's brains get stuck longer

The Negative Think Hole

Gets deeper and wider

"I Goofed"

"It's always like this"

"It'll never change—nothing ever works"

with negative thoughts. Their brain gets in the habit of holding onto the thoughts in a net. But just because the thoughts are stuck in the net doesn't mean you have to keep thinking about them. The negative brain catches disappointments, mistakes, accidents, regrets, and old news and keeps them in that net. The more you sort through and question or get upset about the stuff in that net, the more your brain will keep those thoughts around because they *seem* important. Things get stuck not because they are really more important, but because getting upset about

Brain Nets

Thoughts fall through   Thoughts get stuck

the thoughts makes them seem more important and stick in our mind. You can, in fact, shake out the nets and clear out all the debris."

A Script for Explaining Negative Thinking to Your Young Child

For young kids you can invent a story about a funny animal, say, a squirrel; make sure to include your child as much as possible in the process of telling the story: *"What do squirrels like to collect?" "Nuts." "Right, squirrels collect nuts. Well, one day there was a squirrel named—hmmm, what is a good squirrel name?" "Nutty?" "Okay, Nutty. Well, one day Nutty was feeling kind of sad. Do you know why? He was having trouble collecting nuts. Well, actually, he was doing fine collecting nuts, but his friends named— hmm, more names?" "Chippy and Jumpy." "Okay, Chippy and Jumpy were counting their nuts and they had twenty nuts, and Nutty had only ten. What do you think Nutty was feeling?" "Sad." "Right, he was feeling sad. He wanted more nuts. But do you know what he was thinking to himself? He had a Mr. Grumpy in his head saying, 'You are a bad squirrel. You can't find nuts. You'll never find as many nuts as Chippy and Jumpy.' And the more he listened to Mr. Grumpy, how do you think he felt?" "Sad." "Right. Wait a second, poor Nutty is going to be so sad that he won't keep looking for nuts. Winter is coming, and he's going to be hungry. Quick, let's help him. Maybe there is someone else who could tell him something different. If Mr. Grumpy is being sneaky and saying mean things, what would Mr. Smarty tell him? Or who else could give him advice, Mr. Nicey? Could he tell him some different advice? Mr. Smarty could say, 'You're a clever squirrel. Don't worry about your friends. You found all those nuts yourself. How did you do it? By following your squirrel nose. You can do it, Nutty. Use your nose and find five more nuts.' How do you think Nutty felt when he listened to Mr. Smarty?" "Better." "Yes! And whenever Mr. Grumpy tried to sneak back in, do you know what Nutty said?" "'Good-bye, I'm not listening to you. I can collect nuts!'" "Very good. I bet Nutty wasn't hungry that winter at all!"*

Another strategy to explain negative thinking is to use the analogy of a story: *"I know you're upset that you lost your airplane, and it feels like life is going to be terrible forever. Let's say that is the sad story. Let's put that book down and pick up a different story. What would that story be called? The happy story? The good story? The true story? What does it say there? Let's read:*

So Winston lost his favorite toy in the backyard, and then he was sad, and then, he decided to—buy a new one, play something else, get some neighbors to help him find it. Hmm, that sounds like a very interesting story. Should we keep reading it, or do you want to go do it?"

A Script for Explaining Negative Thinking to Your School-Aged Child

"Disappointments, mistakes, embarrassing moments, they happen to all of us. Do you remember the other day, I told you how I said hi to your gym teacher and called her the wrong name? So, we know that those things happen, nobody is perfect, but sometimes our brain holds on tight to those mistakes and doesn't let us forget. It's not that we need to remember them because they're so important. It's just as if it's stuck in the net, or the person who was supposed to take out the trash forgot to, so it hangs around. We need to shake it out! But another thing happens when it hangs around: It starts to grow, and rather than just being upset about the mistake itself, we get upset about ten more things that we think will happen because of that mistake. Or we start thinking about times in the past when we've messed up. So, remember when you were upset that you got a B on your poster for the science project—because you forgot the references? Well, it was understandable to be disappointed about that because you had worked really hard on it. But then, some tricky magician came along and turned that one disappointment into two, three, and four. So, now instead of just being upset about one thing, the science grade, you're also thinking two, that your teacher is mad at you, and three, that you're going to fail science, and four, that you're going to flunk out of school, and then five and six, you'll never get a job and you'll be homeless. What you need to do when that happens is to recognize the magician's trick and shrink the problem back to where it started because the original problem—the grade—is something that you can manage. You know that you can learn from it, you know you're human, and we all make mistakes every day."

A Script for Explaining Negative Thinking to Your Teenager

"We all feel at times as if our brain is beating up on us—as if it's our own worst enemy. Let's say you forgot to bring in one of the props you needed for

a presentation you were giving. You already feel bad about that, but then your brain starts making it way worse by saying things that aren't about that moment at all but are more general: You're a jerk, how could you do that, you blew it, it's all your fault, you'll probably get a bad grade, you never do anything right, you'll never get a good job if you make stupid mistakes like that. Sometimes we can tell when our mind is being really negative and going overboard, but other times, we believe what the negative thinking is telling us. It's like walking into the wrong room that we didn't realize was the "all bad" room. We assume that the person at the information desk knows what he is talking about and has authority. If only that room were labeled! If the guard stepped aside, you could read the sign on the door that said, 'Office of Impossibility, Pessimism, Helplessness, and Failure.' But you didn't even know what you were walking into. You just stumbled in there by accident, out of negative habit. You don't have to stay—the door isn't locked. Your instincts would tell you to get out—in the mind it is harder, but you are allowed to do an about-face and say, "I don't need (or want) to be in here." Go to another room, a room with the lights on. Once you start to understand this, you can recognize when you're in that room, and sign or no sign, you can decide to go across the hall to—I don't know, what would we call it? 'The Office of Possibility, Optimism, Truth'?" [Encourage your child to choose a name for herself.]

What Are You Walking Into?

For teens who prefer the technical over the metaphorical, you can offer the following: *"The brain was built to last. We are born with the capacity to protect ourselves: The brain has systems for readiness, for scanning for trouble, for warning us of danger. Because survival is also contingent on our ability to adapt and grow, the brain is also equipped with another department, which enables us to explore, to experiment, to learn new ways, to develop. Scientists have found that some people are born with presets programmed to use their problem brain more (the right front part of the brain), and others more easily use the adapting side (the left front part of the brain). It's not anybody's fault. Genes have something to do with it, but what is most important is that the brain is very flexible and changeable and gets good at whatever it does a lot of, so when we are programmed to find the flaws or see what's wrong in us or a given situation, we do it so often that it becomes effortless, or automatic. Without even trying to be negative, we find ourselves getting totally bummed out by seeing ten steps ahead and how nothing will work out. It may be that the brain is overprotecting us by overmobilizing the give-up-and-hibernate response. But that response is premature. Sure, something didn't go our way, but it doesn't mean we have to give up. We can't overdo it; the negative brain is in overdrive trying to protect us. Sometimes it seems like giving up is the only way to not look like a fool (that we cared or something), but this is a temporary stop only. Really giving up would be the big mistake. And actually when we begin to notice when our mind is 'making a right turn' to the negative side and develop the habit of looking at situations from the other side of the brain—the side that scans for possibilities and problem solving—we find that this new habit gets more and more automatic and easy."*

Going from the "No" to the "Know" 131

The Master Plan

Empathize with Your Child: Meet your child where she is; accept and reflect what your child is feeling.

Relabel and Get Specific: Figure out what really went wrong; help your child shrink the problem back to the specific issue at hand.

Optimize and Receive: Help your child to generate different perspectives on and narratives about the situation and choose the one that is most accurate, optimistic, and opens up possibilities.

Mobilize: Encourage your child to pick up her brain and get busy, taking action to fix the problem, not dwelling on it.

PART TWO: THE MASTER PLAN

Step One: Empathize with Your Children's Experience: Start from Where They Are

As much as the end result of the master plan is to help your child embrace a different point of view on her situation, your first goal is not to lose your audience by coming on too strong with the agenda of change. Instead, start from where she is: What emotion is she expressing? Reflect that with your words or a hug, a gesture. Squatting down to her level or a step forward in her direction may be all it takes. Thoroughly accepting how she feels doesn't mean that you agree with her or see the situation the same way, but it does release her from having to show you how bad they feel. So, if your child says, "I feel like I'm in jail," resist the urge to say in so many words, "Are you crazy?" Don't try to steer her off her course. Go in the direction of her swerve, and you will be able to redirect her back to herself. The key is to normalize her experience without minimizing it, and to reflect it back and by adding a "right now" at the end of whatever feeling she is having, there is a light suggestion of the temporariness of feelings. "I hear you—you are really feeling trapped right now. I feel that way sometimes, too." Rather than saying, "But you're fine, everything's great in your life!" go for connection because if you're too cheerful, she has no choice but to be grumpier to get her point across. As the popular bumper sticker says, "If you are not outraged, you are not paying attention." You don't want to oppressively correct your child or go in with the *right* answer. If you immediately launch into all the reasons why this view isn't right, your child will either feel bad for feeling the *wrong* feeling, or, will have to repeat herself going more deeply into that feeling to get you to understand, and may even over time stop turning to you because you just "don't get it." Instead, introduce the idea of choice: "Your thoughts are making you feel really bad, right now. I want to understand. Something's going on for sure, there's a lot of different ways to look at it, can we unpack it to see what's happening? Let's figure out together what you think is really true and what just *feels* true right now."

Ways to express empathy:

- *This feels really bad, right now.*
- *This is a really hard time, right now.*
- *I know this is so upsetting to you, right now.*
- *I know this makes you feel very sad, right now.*

Ways to transition to strategies:

- *I know you don't want to be feeling this way.*
- *I wonder if there is a different way to see this.*
- *Things look really bad to you right now. I'd like to help you.*
- *It's hard to feel this way. Something is bothering you, I want to help you figure out what it is.*

Step Two: Relabel and Get Specific: Figuring Out What Went Wrong

Relabeling: Know Who Is Calling Before You Pick up the Phone. If only our automatic negative thoughts came with a disclaimer—"The message you are about to hear is notoriously unreliable, distorted, and out of proportion"—what anguish we could prevent. Instead of being led down a thorny path lined with terrible impossibilities, accusations, and more, we might steel ourselves, get some distance, or get ready to take our thoughts with a grain of salt. Relabeling is about noticing the familiar "ring" to children's thoughts and distress: the *everything, always* ring tone, or the *ding-dong of doom and gloom.* Kids can learn to recognize it immediately, and just as we prepare ourselves when we look at our phone's caller ID, when children know that it is Mr. Negative calling, or you suggest it to them, they know where that conversation is going, and they can come into the conversation prepared rather than being taken off guard. Interestingly, even though hearing a litany of negative thoughts could make anyone feel bad, over time, when we *hear* that same old story, like a broken record, and can predict, "Yep, I knew my negative thinking was going to jump to that conclusion," we can decide not to *listen,* and that decision leaves us free to choose other interpretations.

An essential advantage of relabeling is that it establishes a "third party," to defuse the tension between parent and child. Rather than saying things like "You're so negative," or "Your thinking is so pessimistic," parents can say to young children, "Mr. Meany seems to be bugging you again. Do you hear how he is telling you all those terrible things?" Or with a teenager: "You're getting hit with a negativity shower; all the circuits are going to the negativity brain," or "It sounds as if the inner-pessimists have taken over the microphone. That's got to be hard. Is there anyone else on the panel who wants to offer an opinion?" With this

DO YOU KNOW WHO'S TALKING TO YOU?

approach, your child doesn't feel cornered or blamed or required to go with the first thought that comes to his mind. After all, it is not his *choice* to be thinking this way, and together you can critique or poke fun at, or simply correct the assumptions and judgments of the negative brain.

Ways to Relabel with Young Children. To make the distinction between an attack of I-can'ts and your child's own thoughts, you can use stuffed animals to play different parts. Refer back to the portrait gallery exercise in Chapter 2, and enlist your child's creativity to distinguish the voices and get a conversation going between the two sides of the story, for example, Magnifier Man and Right Answer Gal.

Ways to Relabel with School-Aged Children. *"We know that part of the brain tends to exaggerate a problem and makes it seem as if everything went wrong. It's not true; it's your brain overreacting. Something might have gone wrong, but it's manageable. It may not feel that way because Magnifier Man, or Permanent-Marker Man, or Give-Up Girl is telling you it's impossible. What do you want to call your negative brain, so that you won't confuse it with your other side, your smart, optimistic, possible, competent side? We can have a debate. Whose story do you believe more—the Give-Up Girl story or the Yes-You-Can Man story? Do you want to draw a picture of your two characters? We can hang them up on the wall and give them 'user names,' so when you get a message, you'll know who it's from, and you'll be ready."*

Ways to Relabel with Teenagers. Teenagers are introspective and spend much time trying to understand themselves. They are very prone to thinking, "Why am I thinking this? What's wrong with me?" They may think they are "crazy" or just "a loser," but either way, teens aren't kind to themselves when it comes to very common and expected *first* responses in situations of disappointment. Help save them from hours of going down the rabbit hole with their thoughts and teach them the secret shortcut, namely that thinking "What's wrong with me? I can't do anything" is not a sign of their incompetence by any means; it is an impersonal universal knee-jerk reaction and they can nip it in the bud and say, "There's that 'I'm doing everything wrong' thought again," or "I'm having that 'I'm such a loser, why would anyone want to hang out with me' thought again," or "this 'remembering and cringing thing' about everything that I've done wrong in the past is because I'm tired, not because it's really important or true." If your teen is not so analytical, another way of thinking about negative thoughts is that they are sort of like pop-up windows in the mind: "*We don't ask for these thoughts to be there; they just pop up, but we learn quickly to ignore them and not get pulled in by the hype—we don't really believe that we'll win a free computer by clicking on the dancing monkey. Similarly, when we learn that negative thoughts are automatic and unreliable brain messages, we can get savvy and not get pulled into believing them more than other sources of information. So, whether you think of negative thoughts as a pop-up window, spam in your inbox, or a telemarketer calling your house, you do have a choice about how you handle the thoughts. They may be 'pushy' because they're trying to sell you something, but they don't really know you and what you need. They are just automatic reactions that everyone has. They only have the authority and power we give them.*"

Getting Specific: What Went Wrong: Finding the Straw That Broke the Camel's Back

Don't be tempted to try to solve the huge problem that your child initially presents you with: "I hate my life, everything is terrible, I can't do anything right." The target is actually much smaller, so teach your child to shrink it by narrowing it down from its global form to the specific offending thought or situation that needs to be addressed. With young children, you can frame this approach as doing "detective work" to locate the source of the problem; with older children, you can explain that it's usually a triggering event that makes us feel really bad—a straw that broke the camel's back. Evaluating the thoughts about that specific situation holds the key to helping us know what to do to feel better.

Questions to narrow the problem down:

- *When did you first feel that way?*
- *What is making you feel that way the most?*
- *What is your brain telling you about this situation?*
- *Is everything feeling this way in your life or just some things?*

- *Do you always feel that way or just sometimes?*
- *Why do you think that happened? Was it something you could control, or does it have to do with other people or situations?*

Ask your child to try to narrow the problem down to the bull's-eye:

- *When did you think that first, or the most? (In gym class.)*
- *Name the one thing that happened or that you thought that really made you feel that way (the straw that broke the camel's back). (Couldn't do the rope climb.)*
- *Use the rule-outs of the 3 P's to narrow the problem down.*

Have your child read the *first thoughts* and *second thoughts* in Chart 5-1, and ask how she feels about each—and which she would prefer to hear. Hearing these stories side by side in the child's own voice is a powerful tool to reinforce the idea that *she* gets to choose how she talks to herself about her life.

You and your child can use the neutralizer machine in the following illustration to turn her distorted first thought into a more accurate, neutral second thought. Modeled after a stereo amplifier, this drawing highlights the idea that our children have the power to change how their thoughts impact them—and even how they hear them—by modulating the controls. Children's first thoughts come in sounding harsh, global, permanent, their fault, and too serious. By toning down the hype of the negative through the many errors and distortions that amplify it, children can hear the information accurately and then be the judge of what they want to do with it. So, for example, if your child is thinking, "I'm the worst girl ever because my teacher got mad at me," she can adjust the tone to "calm," the size to "specific," the length to "temporary," and the fault to "shared" ("I was the one who misbehaved, but my teacher was the one who yelled"). Your child can copy this illustration or personalize it by filling in her own neutralizer buttons.

CHART 5-1

First thought		Second thought	
Permanent: Forever thing	I hate school. I'm doomed.	Temporary: Right now	Today was not a good day.
Pervasive: Everything	Nothing is working out.	Specific: This one thing	Gym class was tough.
Personal: My fault	I am such a wimp.	Not personal: Because of someone else	I am not a rope climber— at least not yet.

When Your Child Needs Stepping-Stones to Cross Over to the "Know." Just remembering to relabel and narrow it down is enough to get some children moving. For those children who need "proof" that it doesn't make sense to stay on the negative track, we need to get quickly to a more accurate picture. In their book *The Resilience Factor*,[1] Karen Reivich and Andrew Schatté present three fast-acting taglines for efficiently snapping back to reality, using what they call "real-time resilience." Take for example the thought: *This is the worst weekend vacation I've ever had*:

- That's not true because—*It's not awful; it's just disappointing.*
- A more accurate way of seeing this is—*This wasn't my first choice for vacation, and I am really tired, so everything seems worse.*

The Neutralizer
Get the information without the hype

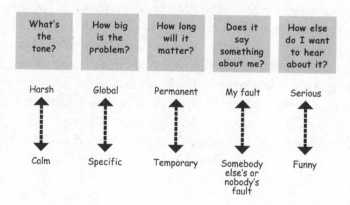

- A more likely outcome is—*I need to get some sleep and figure out some fun things to do.* And I can—*try some new activities; maybe they'll be fun.*

Your child can write down the words to complete these questions, or you can be the interviewer, reading the sentence starters to your child and then handing the microphone over to him to complete the sentences. Your child can rephrase the taglines in his own words, write them on an index card, and keep the card in his pocket to refer to when needed.

Parents should also refer back to the list they made of strategies in Chapter 2 to do some "fact-checking" and narrow down the big problem to the specific problem at hand. For instance, review the following:

- The facts-versus-feelings pie charts, which will help your child see that even though he's feeling totally upset, the facts are in his favor.

- The trunk, branch, leaves exercise, which distinguishes the problem leaf from the otherwise healthy and successful tree.

- The look up, look down exercise, which is a variation on the fortunately, unfortunately strategy. Have your child first look "down" to make the situation worse ("I could have gotten food poisoning on vacation, it could have rained, or I could have stayed home and done chores all weekend") and then look "up" to see how the situation could be even better ("I could try to bring a friend so I wouldn't be bored"). The goal is not to feel grateful, in the guilt-inducing sense, but to turn up the intensity of how disastrous things feel to discover that they aren't as bad as they could be.

Take some index cards and write a strategy on each one. Put the cards in a hat, and when your child is struggling, you can pull a card out of the hat and try the strategy to get things moving. Better yet, your child can choose his own top five strategies from Chapter 2 and this chapter, and when he is struggling, you can remind him to "take out the big five" and choose which strategy to start with. Remember that we do better in a crisis when we are prepared, so make copies of those strategy cards, and keep them accessible. Rather than fumbling in the crisis, having the ideas written down will give your child the steps and the hope that he can feel better soon.

Step Three: Optimize and Rewire:
Generating New Versions of the Story

Optimizing a system means making modifications or trying different settings to make it run more efficiently, use resources more wisely, and conserve energy. When a child is in negative-thinking mode, her thinking is stalled, her strengths and resources are locked up, and her energy, motivation, and hopefulness are being drained. The optimizing step is about trying out different settings or perspectives on the specific problem that your child has identified—"I'm not going to have any friends at camp"—and choosing the version or interpretation that works best for your child, the one that is the least damaging, is the most accurate, and gets her system moving in a new direction. Like a teacher who needs to "call on other kids" when one persnickety child is dominating the class, children can be encouraged to step into their rightful place of authority and tell Permanent-Marker Man or Disaster Guy to give it a rest and let other voices be heard. Note that we are not leading with the "why" questions here, as in: "Why would you think that?!" Kids will just need to defend their reasoning instead of questioning it themselves. We're also not leading with, "What's the worst that could happen?" question because kids are already thinking in worst case scenarios, we don't want to prime that pump, instead we want them to get in the habit of challenging and editing those extreme and unlikely predictions with options that are more accurate and likely.

Questions for optimizing:

- *That's one way that you feel. Do other parts of you see it differently?*
- *That's what you're feeling now about yourself; before this happened, how were you feeling?*
- *If you could win a million dollars by guessing right if these conclusions are true or false, what would you say?*
- *You may decide that this is impossible, but let's get some more data first before drawing that conclusion. Can you tell me step-by-step what is going on?*

- *If you gave Mr. No's thoughts a true/false test what would the right answer be?*

- *Is that Mr. No's version of the story? Let's see how someone else would write it. What about your optimistic self, or your driven self? What would Try-It Guy say?*

- *Let's look at this situation through a different pair of glasses. How about your smart glasses?*

- *Where does that version of the story lead? How is it going to end? Is that going to be good for you? What would be ideal? What would be realistic?*

- *That makes sense from the pessimist's point of view. Can we try a different operating system?*

- *Tomorrow morning how do you think you'll see this situation? Let's borrow that perspective now.*

- *Negative thinking is giving you no credit for anything good in this narrative, can you balance out the picture and give yourself credit where credit is due?*

Loosening the Grip of the Negative Thought: Playing with Power. If your child is having trouble shifting gears because the negative perspective is too strong, you can help him free up energy in a number of ways. One is to break up the tyranny of the negative by having him "boss it back." Another way to demote the power of the negative grip is through playful means, saying phrases like "I am a terrible person," "I suck," and "I am a failure" in a funny, rather than serious, voice or accent.

Bossing Back the Negative Brain. Have your child tap into the same righteous indignation she would if her sibling or a bully were interfering with her happiness, taking a toy from her, or in some other way trying to control her life:

- *I'm the boss of me! I decide what to think! I'm not listening to you!*

- *Disaster Man, you're toast! I'm in charge!*

- *I'm shaking out the net. These thoughts are clogging the system!*

- *I'm hitting the reject button! I refuse to accept what you're saying!*

In a Different Voice. Imagine if Daffy Duck were broadcasting the evening news, or Sponge Bob were issuing you a speeding violation. A serious message becomes less so when delivered in a silly voice. Because negative thoughts do not deserve the authority we initially grant them, children can feel free to play with that authority by saying the thoughts with a funny accent or in pig latin or even singing them to a silly song. By shining the goofy light on these otherwise heavy thoughts—just for a split second—the levity shifts them to a new vantage point:

- Say the thought in a different voice—try different accents or imitate different characters saying the thought. Instant levity occurs when you hear an exaggerated accent that is different from your own. Perhaps Groucho Marx or Johnny Cash gives a rendition (even if your child doesn't know who Groucho Marx or Johnny Cash is, the message will get through!).

- Sing the thought—make up lyrics to "Row, Row, Row Your Boat" using your negative thoughts, for example, "I am a terrible person; I'm the very worst; I make so many mistakes every day; it makes me want to burst." Perspective springs from exaggeration and humor. Although it's a campy strategy, even a teenager may remember these silly songs when he is in the midst of beating up on himself, and smile.

Rewriting the Story: The More Interpretations, the Merrier. Now that your child is ready, the following exercises will help her generate a variety of points of view on her situation. Tap into your young child's imagination to accomplish this step, doing role-plays with stuffed animals representing different points of view, for example, "Mr. Grumpy is bossing you around. Are you ready to boss him back? What do you want to say?" Emphasize with older children that through drawings, debates, and consultations with imagined others or even competitions, *they* get to decide which answer or interpretation rings truest and is best for them.

Invite the Possibility Panel. This is a favorite strategy for kids and adults alike. If your child is locked into one way of looking at the situation, bring in some other opinions. Have your child or teen choose the friends, experts, or wise mentors (even if he doesn't know them personally) to

Whose perspective would you like to invite?

The Possibility Panel—Your Internal Board of Directors

"weigh in," such as his best friend, his coach, his hero, or Oprah. Have him write the names on a card or sticky note and keep at his desk, or on his phone. When he is upset about a situation he encounters (bad day at sports, not getting a lead in the musical, having writer's block for college applications), he can imagine his inner board of directors and how these other voices (who likely have had many, many moments like these!) would advise him. Completing the exercise (or even just contemplating it) will loosen up the gridlock that negative thinking has on his brain, and in the end, he will have many different perspectives and, as a result, many different options for how to proceed.

Switch Glasses: All Wrong to All Right. Another way of getting a different perspective is to switch from the "what's wrong here" to the "what's right here" glasses. For example, ask your child who is feeling terrible about a test grade to look closely for what she actually did that worked out well, or what circumstances worked out in her favor in addition to identifying what didn't work.

From Here to Eternity Versus From Here to Absurdity. Although we want to help children move from negative thinking, which can be characterized as the worst-case scenario, to the more likely scenario (what they really think will happen), sometimes it helps to take a slight detour and make a quick stop at the very best-case scenario. Make a chart with three columns on the page. Title one "Worst-Case Scenario," the next "Ridiculously Best-Case Scenario," and the third "Most Likely Scenario." After your child writes the negative story ("I'll go to school and fail the test"), have her stretch over to the ridiculously best: "Aliens will come and abduct my teacher, and there will be no test." Then it will be easier to find the middle ground or the most likely scenario: "I'll go and probably do okay on the test." Stretching to the absurd in either direction will help loosen up your child's thinking to see that there are many alternative viewpoints in between.

Doing the Time Warp. What feels like the end of the world today may be barely a memory tomorrow. Ask your child to consider the following questions: What does this mean to you right now? What will it mean tomorrow, next week, a month, or a year from now? If it is going to be forgotten soon, how important could it be now?

Step Four: Mobilize: Be the Change You Want to See!

There is a certain point where you can't *think* your way out of your mood anymore, but you can *move* yourself out of it. What we know about brain rewiring is that actions can speak louder than words. If you sit still dwelling on a situation, it is harder to shake it off than if you get up and do something active. Like picking up the needle on a skipping record and putting it down elsewhere, doing something active helps your brain get engaged in something enjoyable and pass the time until your nervous system recovers from what felt like a near miss. It's not that you necessarily need to forget about what you were thinking before, but you may be like a windup toy that spins its wheels when it gets wedged against a wall: No matter how much it spins, it can't get moving. It needs to be picked up and headed in a new direction.

Sometimes children will be ready to mobilize by acting on their new solutions: making the call to a friend that they were dreading or tackling the project they thought was impossible. At other times, kids just need an active activity to let the brain reboot out of negative mode.

These pick-me-ups don't need to take long; sometimes, just two minutes of playing catch is all a child needs to feel revived, clear, and ready to restart. For teens who tend to retreat to their room, their version of "getting active" may consist of just getting a change of scenery, such as having a snack (not in their bed), or watching five minutes of a favorite comedian or kitten video (with someone to laugh or oooh and aww with) to facilitate a shift in perspective and mood.

Brain pick-me-ups:

- Playing a fast game of catch with a nerf ball or balled-up pair of socks
- Playing a quick game of laundry-basket basketball
- Dancing or singing to favorite music
- Listening to an energizing playlist on your phone
- Doing Sudoku or other puzzles
- Going for a walk
- Playing with the dog
- Playing Simon Says
- Going for a bike ride

It is important to note that "picking up" is entirely different from *distracting* oneself from negative thoughts. Distracting yourself is like playing a game of hide-and-seek with your negativity. Even if you pretend it's not there for a while by doing something else, eventually it will find you because you still think it's valuable information. The master plan is about training yourself to recognize those unreliable, knee-jerk, exaggerated first reactions in the face of disappointment or frustration and *underreact* to them because you understand that they are not personal or accurate assessments about you or the situation in that moment, and therefore do not warrant your attention. When you devalue and downgrade the authority of the thoughts, and get busy with the things that matter to you more, you're not distracting; you're dismissing the thoughts. You've established who's the boss; you've made it clear in your mind that these thoughts are not worth your time, and only have the power you give them. You are ready to either let them float on by or to amend, correct, or replace them. The more kids do this pivot, the more their brain learns to filter out these unhelpful thoughts from the get-go.

Making Mobilization a Habit. Kids with negative thinking get into negative feedback loops and they can't get out. Their negative thoughts about themselves or events lead to negative feelings, which in turn leads to the conclusion that they should just avoid situations (because people will be mean, or think they're weird, or it just won't be fun). The more kids stay at home withdrawing and isolating, the more convinced they are that these perceptions are true because they don't get to test them out to see a different reality—Oh! some kids *were* nice, some things *were* fun!—further paving the path to depression. For kids who are walking this path regularly by avoiding and retreating, it's best to work some regular activities into their schedule that they find meaningful (social, educational, spiritual). This is a form of behavior therapy called behavioral activation and it is a very effective element of treatment. The key is to schedule ahead on the calendar, or have your teen schedule on his phone—small but frequent antidotes to avoidance so your child gets in the habit and doesn't have to muster the motivation or inspiration for what to do—it's already on the schedule: playing with pets, texting a friend to see what she's up to, going for a run, watering the plants, writing a note to grandparents, learning something new, gathering clothes to donate. Yes, working that "other-focus" over their "self-focus" can be even more effective in shifting out of negative mode, but doing nice things for themselves is great, too. Over time, these pick-me-ups become their own habit and your child might not even need a schedule because he is initiating these types of fulfilling activities on his own.

When Thoughts Get Stuck at Night. Many parents have asked, "What do you do when these thoughts are happening at bedtime? It's hardly the moment to be running around playing catch." If you have followed all the steps and your child or teen has fact-checked the negative thoughts, no longer feels overpowered by them, but still can't switch gears and settle down to sleep, here's a different version of four doors that we saw earlier in the chapter. Have your child draw four doors and then on each door ask her to name a topic she *loves* to think about: for young kids,

The Four Doors
To help with sleep

cupcakes, fairies, birthday parties, their dog, their toys; for older kids and teens, celebrities they'd like to spend the day with, their dog, vacations they'd like to take, clothes they'd like to design, proud moments. The idea is to help give your child a framework and a starting point and then let her imagination do the rest of the work.

Another wind-down exercise is for your child to describe in detail five things she is grateful for; these could be moments that went well, accomplishments during the day, or people she is grateful are in her life. As we'll see later in Chapter 12, gratitude is not a platitude; it creates a powerful sense of inner well-being and connectedness that is an effective buffer against depression.

Reinforcing Your Child's New Way of Thinking. You can praise your child for standing his ground when it comes to the negative think traps—when he slips in and pulls himself out, or when he's able to circumvent them altogether. Be specific: "You really thought your way through that one"; "That was a tug of war, and you really held on and didn't let yourself slip too far"; "This was a tough situation, and you didn't let the commentary take over."

With younger children, you can use stickers as reinforcers for "bossing back" Mr. No, or for catching themselves telling the always, never, everything story and switching over to the sometimes and some things story instead. Tangible reinforcers, such as special activities or small prizes, may be appropriate for children for whom struggles with negative thinking are very frequent. In these cases, shaping new behaviors is more urgently needed, and there are opportunities to practice every day. You are reinforcing your child's efforts at being flexible, trying something new, or working on thinking patterns.

Dos and don'ts:

- Do let your child know that you accept her negative thoughts and feelings.
- Do be patient; realize that this is a process that takes time.
- Even if your child starts out negative, she still gets "credit" for turning it around.
- Do engage your child in the process; let her tell you how and when she wants to talk about these topics.
- Do remember that everyone has bad days; they are temporary! If your child doesn't want to work on this one day or seems to have forgotten all the lessons, remember that tomorrow is another day!
- Don't expect your child to want to work on this all the time.

CONCLUSION

A journey of a thousand neurons begins with a single rewire. Knowing that there is another destination greatly increases the chances that you will head in that new direction. The neural relandscaping is happening in the form of healthy growth of new circuits in the prefrontal cortex that transport your child from right-brain negative thinking to left-brain possible thinking. Over time, these new circuits will develop into brightly lit pathways flashing the clear message: "Right this way; it's okay, you've got this; this you can manage."

Negative Meets World

Navigating the Glitches of Life

6

WHEN NEGATIVITY TAKES HOLD

Does My Child Need Professional Help?

I know what sad is; it comes and goes. When I'm depressed, it doesn't feel like it will ever go away.

—fifteen-year-old boy

I really started to panic when Ari woke up saying, "I can't take it anymore." We knew that he was having a lot of anxiety about school: tests, girls, gym class. He was really hard on himself, but it seemed as if we were helping him, getting through to him. Every night we would talk it out and make a plan. But then something changed. He didn't have the "fight" in him anymore, and that scared me more than anything. I could deal with whatever he was going through if we were working on it, but then he dropped out of the deal. He said there was no point in trying; it was just going to be more problems the next day and the next day. That morning I knew we needed to do something different. He was slipping off the radar, and we were watching it happen before our eyes. There was no way we were going to let him fall. It was the beginning of a lot of unknowns for us, but one thing was absolutely clear: We needed help.

—mother of a thirteen-year-old

HOW MUCH NEGATIVITY IS NORMAL?

There is nothing more consuming and debilitating for parents than worrying about whether their child is okay. When we are looking at our kids under a microscope, searching for the ups and especially the downs of their day, and we're seeing lots of downs, it is hard to know how much is too much. And yet, as with Ari's mother, our instinct that something isn't right and needs attention can be as important as any other diagnostic criteria. The key questions we must ask ourselves over the course of days or weeks (not just during the worst moments of our child's day) are

- Is my child or teen acting like his normal self (temporary fluctuations in mood, energy, sleep, appetite in response to specific circumstances) or is his negative, irritable, or sad mood the pervasive or default mode even in the absence of triggering events?
- Do we have a communication system? Are we able to talk about and work on the issues that arise, or does my child consistently refuse to discuss them?
- Is my child making progress? Is he experiencing less distress, is he making use of the strategies we've talked about even when I don't initiate them? Is he still wanting to feel better? Is he participating more fully in his life? Does he seem less troubled more of the time?

When we find that our kid's suffering operates independently of life circumstances (in intensity and duration), and that the methods we've been using are no longer having an impact, it's time to reassess our strategy and seek professional help.

Because frustrations are part of anyone's life, we would expect to hear negative thoughts and reactions interspersed with other more positive or neutral themes in the soundtrack of all young people moving along in their development. When the negative notes dominate, the soundtrack strikes the ear as discordant. In this chapter, we look at the typical developmental challenges for preschoolers, school-aged children, and adolescents and at the ways in which negative thinking may be an expected though temporary reaction to situational factors. Sometimes, however, children have difficulty getting a solid foothold in the downward spiral of negative thinking, and they slip into depression.

What we will see in each developmental stage is that it is normal to react to disappointing events by having a bad day here or there, or even a bad couple of days, but our antennae should go up when we notice a change in our child's behavior or personality. If children begin to respond differently than we would expect, to be irritable or withdrawn without a trigger, or to begin planning ahead to opt out of activities they would normally enjoy, the negative mood, rather than just being a reaction to life, is becoming a way of life. A list of the signs of depression across age groups follows. If these and/or the specific red flags for each age group are present consistently for two weeks, and the strategies you are using are not helping your child move out of that phase, it is time to seek professional help.

General Red Flags for Depression

- Change in mood: more withdrawn, more irritable, angry, apathetic, unmotivated, or sad
- Lack of interest in activities previously enjoyed, refusal to participate in usual activities
- Crying easily or excessively
- Increased clinginess or separation anxiety
- Physical complaints: headaches, stomachaches
- Change in attitude toward life: things are exhausting, boring, too hard
- Persistent symptoms, consistently being present for at least two weeks
- Symptoms interfere with your child's ability to function or cause significant distress

NORMAL DEVELOPMENT, NEGATIVE MOODS, AND RED FLAGS

Preschoolers

Fluctuations in Mood: A Moment-to-Moment Venture. To preschoolers, the world is their oyster. You will be hard-pressed to find better company for almost any activity, from washing the car to cooking to raking leaves, because life is an adventure and they want to get their pudgy little hands all over it. But the frustrations of a preschooler are just as characteristic. When he is trying to reach a light switch that's too high or zip a jacket or make a goal in soccer, his distress is poignant and may manifest itself in tantrums, but just as remarkable is his ability to switch gears and moods when the next good thing comes along, such as a yummy snack or an airplane passing overhead. Another pathway to frustration is the attempt to detect rules or predict behavior (the preschooler who doesn't understand why you are still saying no to the chocolate ice cream even when she said, "Please"). However, when a young child is at risk for depression, his distress is prolonged, may interfere with his engagement in other activities, and may result in disruptive behavior. Normally exciting opportunities don't interest him, and he may seem tired and irritable, may have physical complaints, may express anxiety about being away from his parents, and may look sad and cry easily. There is no spark, and his reactions are very flat.

Normal Negativity in Preschoolers.

- They are easily frustrated when plans don't go their way, or things feel unfair.
- They may fight, tantrum, and get extremely discouraged, but this reaction is brief. In part, it is due to their developmental plight of being greatly impacted by whatever is happening in the present because they don't have a sense of the future.
- Distress does not interfere with their enjoyment of things.
- They are easily talked out of or distracted by another activity—even if dramatic, the moods last minutes but not hours or days.

Red Flags for Depression in Preschoolers. While we may think, how could a preschooler have such profound, grownup experiences as depression, a recent study that replicates earlier work found that approximately 2 percent of preschoolers meet the criteria for depression:[1]

- Their appearance and outlook are sad; they have difficulty smiling, their gaze is downcast, and they describe other people or situations as sad or hopeless.

- Their activity level changes for them. They may be overactive (restless, needing to be occupied and moving all the time) or underactive (lethargic and tired).

- They are uninterested in previously pleasurable activities; old favorites are met with apathy.

- Their frustration tolerance decreases, and there is a marked increase in tantrums or unusual behavior such as hitting, biting, and screaming.

- They may exhibit separation anxiety, protesting being apart from parents in situations in which they were previously independent.

- They show frequent physical symptoms of feeling uneasy such as headaches or stomachaches.

School-Aged Children

The Age of Big Thoughts. Leaving behind the years of experiencing life through "full body contact," school-aged children are thinkers. They are beginning to shift from surveying the territory and learning everything they can about how the world "out there" works. Instead, they spend increasing amounts of time turning inward and contemplating the what-ifs of life.

One of the great signals of this stage is plasticity of thinking. Children at this age think ahead, and they think behind. Thinking becomes an activity in itself. The result may be more daydreaming, more anxious thinking, and more negative thinking resulting in some difficulties shutting down the mind at night.

With this ability to analyze often comes discouragement. These children aren't necessarily satisfied by reassurance. They need to make their own decisions and draw their own conclusions. They may get more anxious at night as they think ahead to the challenges of the next day. Because they can make predictions, they get into patterns of predicting what can go wrong. As they become more aware of their own behavior, they may exaggerate or magnify its impact or use their thinking ability to selectively find confirmatory evidence: "I got the answer wrong on the board and now everyone thinks I'm stupid." Because of the normal "busyness" of the brain in middle childhood, you may spend more time processing the fallout from these misperceptions. Although there may be brief dramatic scenes, typically these concerns do not interfere with these children's ability to enjoy life. A negative mood may last a matter of hours or a day, but rarely longer. Stressful themes or ideas may stay bookmarked in a child's mind, and she will need to return to them and keep processing them at quiet times until the issues are settled. In contrast, children who are vulnerable to depression can't put their burdens aside; instead, they carry their doubts and negative views into new situations. They may become irritable or withdrawn and not want to participate in previously preferred activities. While not actively rejected by their peers, they may assume incorrectly that how bad they are feeling about themselves is directly correlated with how others view them. Their motivation to do homework and extracurricular activities may drop as their discouragement broadens.

Normal negativity in school-aged children:

- Overthinking and overanalyzing may lead to inaccurate (generalized) conclusions.
- Greater awareness of social standing may lead to unfavorable comparisons and performance anxiety.
- The ability to think ahead may lead to anxious anticipation and what-iffing.
- These thinking patterns may be consistently present in negative situations but do not carry over in general and do not interfere with a child's ability to engage in and enjoy life.

Red flags for depression in school-aged children:

- Negative self-image: "I'm stupid"; "No one likes me"; "I'm a loser."
- Sad, irritable, or angry mood and behavior; feelings of defeat about the future; impatience; easily frustrated; at times, hostility or aggressiveness.
- School avoidance.
- Frequent physical complaints and trips to the school nurse.

- Weight loss or failure to thrive: loss of appetite, indecisiveness about or lack of interest in food.

- Having difficulty making decisions, overwhelmed by formerly manageable responsibilities, overthinking options to the point of paralysis.

- Frequently on the edge of tears.

- Excessive worries: Children may feel sudden separation anxiety or hesitate to go to a friend's house even though these were previously comfortable activities.

- Decreased energy: lethargic, too tired to move, trouble getting up in the morning and getting going at school.

- Changes in sleep patterns: difficulty awakening, difficulty falling asleep, napping during the day.

Adolescence

Identity Is Everything. Adolescence has long been characterized as a dark and stormy phase that includes managing hormone havoc and changes in appearance, feeling the intensification of the importance of social standing, looking for a core identity, and facing questions about college and the future looming ahead. However, anyone who has been around a gaggle of teenage girls at a sleepover, or with a group of teenage boys playing sports or video games, knows that the storminess is often the temporary letdown between periods of total engagement. With greater freedom comes greater frustration when teens are forced back into the mundane and less entertaining life of home chores, homework, and lame family humor. Teenagers need to go through this growth and separation—being critical of their families, making their own decisions, establishing their own values and priorities, inspired by their parents but not carbon copies—so they can eventually launch, separate, and be their unique selves in the world.

As in the life of celebrities, but without the fringe benefits, the pressure is on teenagers to be the coolest, but to act as if coolness takes no effort whatsoever: to give the impression that you have an enviable life that is always fun, even though, in truth, you spend a lot of time with your friends just trying to figure out what everyone else is doing;

standing hours in front of the mirror in order to look as if you spent no time at the mirror at all; claiming you've made no effort with your wardrobe, though you have meticulously made it ragged in just the right ways. The struggle to be "without struggle" is all-consuming. This sentiment is captured in the popular film *Juno*, when the hip, smart-mouthed sixteen-year-old Juno says to her boyfriend, "You're, like, the coolest person I ever met and you don't even have to try." Her earnest, self-effacing boyfriend, Bleeker, can't take the compliment and confesses, "I try really hard, actually." The process of true identity formation may be seen as gradually shedding the pretending and posing and getting comfortable with who you are.

It is common for teenagers to lose perspective on the scale of events—getting a bad grade, a break up, not being chosen for the performance band. With their inchoate identity, that one thing that didn't work out can feel like a total loss in how they define themselves. Kids can be expected to be in a funk for a day or two after a disappointment like this, but the funk also motivates an escape from pressure into a submersion in pleasure—not wanting to do homework, and instead wanting to play video games, eat junk food, watch television, or talk to friends endlessly. In contrast, a child who is vulnerable to depression doesn't retreat to pleasurable activities or connection with friends but isolates himself, not wanting contact with others, and instead surrounding himself with destructive influences or simply total distraction.

Normal negativity in teenagers:

- Has extremes in moods, ambivalence about commitments; can be as critical and cynical about things as she can get excited and invested in them (sometimes the same things at different times)
- Rejects parental opinions (at least temporarily)
- Retreats and isolates herself for brief periods of time
- Feels frustrated by pressures about the future
- Temporarily questions the importance of routine activities: "What is the point of algebra? When will I need it in my life?"

Red flags for depression in adolescents:

- Shows a change in character: is irritable, snappy, belligerent, passive, or sad for extended periods of time
- Has feelings of sadness, hopelessness, helplessness
- Is preoccupied with himself, withdrawn; spends increasing time alone
- Shows deterioration of self-care: isn't concerned about his appearance, appears unkempt, may be unable to brush his teeth or hair
- Shows a decline in schoolwork; doesn't participate in class
- Loses interest and pleasure in friends, hobbies, family, sports
- Abandons previously enjoyable activities
- Changes in energy: noticeably lethargic, sluggish, slower to respond; or jittery, restless, agitated
- Changes his sleep patterns: sleeps all the time; or is restless, unable to sleep
- Shows changes in appetite: emotional overeating or decreased appetite
- Shows self-destructive behavior, such as cutting himself, thinking and/or talking about death and suicide

DIAGNOSING DEPRESSION

According to a recent study, at any given time nearly 2 million children under the age of seventeen have a current depressive disorder.[2] The consequences of childhood depression are devastating and truly affect every aspect of children's functioning and development. Their attendance and ability to perform academically are impaired, social withdrawal only increases their sense of isolation, family conflict can be both a contributing factor and a consequence of childhood depression, and they are at increased risk of suicide. Depression is diagnosed when symptoms

- Are long-lasting (two weeks or more)
- Are causing distress and/or interference in daily activities

Types of Mood Disorder Diagnoses

Several different diagnoses, summarized as follows, include depressive symptoms. It is important to emphasize that depression can be a "co-morbid" diagnosis; that is, a child may have a diagnosis of, for example, attention deficit disorder and depression, or of panic disorder or obsessive-compulsive disorder and depression. Approximately three out of four children with a diagnosis of major depressive disorder are also diagnosed with an anxiety disorder, and one in two with a behavioral disorder.[3] Often, but not always, this duality results when a child has received insufficient treatment for a condition, such as an anxiety disorder and, after months of struggle, may develop hopelessness and discouragement, simply feeling exhausted by the strain of being worried all the time. In such situations, the depression may need to be treated first so that the child can shift his thinking patterns and see that improvement is possible.

CHART 6-1

	Adult	Child	Adolescent
Depressed Mood	Sad, blue, down	Irritable, aggressive, crying, whining; may be accompanied by anxiety about separation or being in new situations	Irritable, aggressive, sensitive, belligerent, argumentative
Diminished Interest	Lack of interest	Apathy, less curious, less responsive, less playful, no enthusiasm for previously enjoyed activities, withdrawal	Everything is boring, not important, no point; stops typical activities; shows no initiative; nothing to look forward to
Significant Weight Loss	Loses weight	Failure to thrive, not interested in eating, decreased appetite	Weight changes; may overeat or skip meals, or not be hungry

	Adult	Child	Adolescent
Insomnia or Hypersomnia	Trouble falling or staying asleep	Disturbed sleep, difficulty falling asleep, waking up easily, or unusual napping	Unable to sleep, staying up all night, napping right after school
Psychomotor Agitation or Retardation	Feeling uncomfortably revved, unable to sit still, unable to summon the motivation to move, moving noticeably slowly	Always moving, like a motor speeding up or slowed down, responding slowly, moving slowly	Pacing, moving a lot, slow to respond, staying on the couch or in bed, moving slowly when doing ordinary activities
Fatigue or Loss of Energy	Feel exhausted, unable to move	Lying down a lot, playing sick	Excessive sleeping, lethargic
Feeling of Worthlessness	Blaming self, intrusive negative thoughts about self	Saying, "I'm stupid," "I hate myself," "I'm a bad girl or boy"	Feeling guilty, feeling as if I do everything wrong, everybody hates me, poor self-esteem, negative comments about self: "I'm stupid, I'm ugly, I hate myself, I don't care"
Diminished Ability to Think or Concentrate	Can't focus on work	Overwhelmed by choices, can't make decisions, can't sit still	Can't focus on schoolwork, unproductive, frustrated because can't read or retain information
Recurrent Thoughts of Death	Intrusive thoughts about dying	Asking about death, saying "I want to die"	Thinking about death, thoughts about suicide, saying "I want to die, no point in living"

Depression. According to the fifth edition of the American Psychiatric Association's *Diagnostic and Statistical Manual of Mental Disorders*, or *DSM-V*, a major depressive episode is defined as consisting of five of the symptoms in the following list during the same two-week period, every day. One of the symptoms must be either depressed or irritable mood or loss or interest or pleasure in activities. The symptoms must mark a change from the child's typical functioning, without being due to a medical condition, such as hypothyroidism (see page 163):

1. Depressed or irritable mood most of the day, nearly every day, as indicated by either subjective report (e.g., feels sad, angry, empty, hopeless) or observation made by others (e.g., appears tearful)

2. Markedly diminished interest or pleasure in all, or almost all, activities most of the day, nearly every day (as indicated by either subjective account or observation made by others)

3. Significant weight loss when not dieting or weight gain (e.g., a change of more than 5% of body weight in a month), or decrease or increase in appetite nearly every day. Note: In children, consider failure to make expected weight gains.

4. Insomnia or hypersomnia nearly every day

5. Psychomotor agitation or retardation nearly every day (observable by others, not merely subjective feelings of restlessness or being slowed down)

6. Fatigue or loss of energy nearly every day

7. Feelings of worthlessness or excessive or inappropriate guilt (which may be delusional) nearly every day (not merely self-reproach or guilt about being sick)

8. Diminished ability to think or concentrate, or indecisiveness, nearly every day (either by subjective account or as observed by others)

9. Recurrent thoughts of death (not just fear of dying), recurrent suicidal ideation without a specific plan, or a suicide attempt or a specific plan for committing suicide.[4]

Persistent Depressive Disorder (Dysthymia). Whereas major depression is incapacitating for children, persistent depressive disorder, previously referred to as dysthymia, is a milder form of depression, with fewer symptoms but a more chronic course. Because it is more persistent, it is especially likely to interfere with a child's functioning. The following are key *DSM-V* criteria for persistent depressive disorder in children and adolescents:

A. Depressed or irritable mood for most of the day, for more days than not as indicated either by subjective account or observation for at least 1 year.

B. Presence, while depressed, of two (or more) of the following:
   1. poor appetite or overeating
   2. insomnia or hypersomnia
   3. low energy or fatigue
   4. low self-esteem
   5. poor concentration or difficulty making decisions
   6. feelings of hopelessness

C. During 1 year for children or adolescents of the disturbance, the person has never been without the symptoms in Criteria A and B for more than 2 months at a time.[5]

Abnormal Thyroid Functioning. The thyroid, a gland located in the neck below the voice box, releases hormones that regulate energy, growth, and metabolism. Changes in thyroid functioning can mimic psychological symptoms such as anxiety or depression. For example, people with an overactive thyroid may seem speeded up. They may exhibit marked anxiety and tension, emotional lability, impatience and irritability, distractibility, and overactivity, may be more sensitive to noise, and may have issues with sadness, depression, and fluctuations in sleep and appetite. In contrast, people with an underactive thyroid may seem slowed down. They may have a loss of interest and initiative, generally a slowing of response time and other mental processes, poor memory functioning, and an overall damping down of the vivacity of personality. Because of the overlap in symptoms, before diagnosing depression, often a psychiatrist or physician will test thyroid levels to rule out a physiological cause of the target symptoms. Parents can request a thyroid test if the doctor does not routinely do one.

TREATMENTS FOR DEPRESSION

If your child is exhibiting the symptoms of a depressive disorder as described here, professional help is indicated.

Cognitive Behavior Therapy

Cognitive behavioral therapy (CBT) had its start in the 1950s with the pioneering work of such visionaries as Albert Ellis and Aaron Beck. The prevailing view at the time was that being depressed or anxious altered our thinking: Nothing could change how we felt until we weren't anxious or depressed anymore. In contrast, CBT offered the very hopeful and, for the time, radical idea that our distorted thoughts *create* feelings of depression, not the reverse. This was a welcome shift in approach, as it let individuals know that they didn't have a disease they were passively stuck with; rather, they could directly influence how they felt by challenging distortions and intentionally practicing new, healthier, and more accurate ways of thinking. CBT was readily embraced by the psychological community and patients looking for relief, and some four hundred outcome trials later, CBT has been shown to be effective for a wide range of disorders. Many specific studies have supported the efficacy of CBT in treating depression in youth.[6] Recent and past meta-analyses of cognitive behavioral therapy have shown that it is successful in the short run in changing the negative thinking that characterizes depression, but more than that, it is extremely effective in preventing another depressive episode. This is the case with studies of adult depression as well. In CBT, children and teens will learn:

1. Psychoeducation: Behind-the-scenes explanations of why they are thinking and feeling the way they do and the scientific explanations for how they can change those thoughts and feelings.

2. Cognitive restructuring: Identifying the thinking errors associated with depression, through logical challenges, learning and identifying cognitive errors, and devising a system for distinguishing distorted thinking patterns from accurate thinking.

3. Relaxation or mindfulness exercises: Addressing the role the body can play in either ramping up or calming down; children and teens

are encouraged to practice brief "unplugging" exercises to establish quiet, to help them make choices about how to think and feel rather than being controlled and limited by instant first reactions.

4. Behavioral activation: Working from the outside in. Exercises target mobilizing activities for children and teens who are withdrawn or not motivated. Identifying and scheduling activities to counter the inertia of depression can spur motivation and positive affect.

5. Relapse prevention: Reviewing the key strategies, phrases, and ideas that have worked best to stabilize and overcome negative thoughts; identifying potential stressful situations that could trigger a setback; establishing the best mind-set for preventing relapse: "Don't be upset if it happens; take action."

CBT: An Active Treatment, a Collaborative Effort. In contrast to less directive therapies, in CBT there is no mystery about what is going on in the sessions. Skills and strategies are reinforced at each meeting by being applied directly to whatever thoughts, feelings, and situations occurred in the past week. The child, the therapist, and the parent together devise exercises to complete between sessions to monitor mood, reinforce skills, and generalize their application beyond the therapy hour. Although sometimes children fear that "homework" from therapy will be unpleasant or will be graded, the goal is to make the work creative and satisfying as well as effective for the child. CBT works best when children are equal partners in the collaboration process: The therapist gives the ideas, and the child is encouraged to speak up about how to personalize those ideas to best fit her needs. Parents need to be part of the collaboration, too. Because parents are the front line for children, treatment will be more effective and the benefits more lasting when therapists empower the parents to learn the skills right along with their child. Then they know how to understand the language of depression, answer questions when their child is upset, encourage their child creatively to do the cognitive reframing, and help her pick up her brain and get busy when she's stuck. If you are feeling in the dark because the therapist is not sharing feedback, make your feelings known, not only because it is your right as the consumer, but, more important, because of the benefit for your child.

CBT for Teens. Although all teens want to feel better and get relief from their depressive symptoms, it's complicated. Some may want medication rather than having what feels like an overwhelming experience to talk through their feelings with a therapist. Other teens are concerned about side effects of medications, and do not want to risk gaining weight. CBT has consistently shown to be effective in treating depression. In a recent study, teens who participated in CBT recovered seven weeks faster than did those in supportive counseling and were less likely to require hospitalization. After six months, the majority (70%) of teens receiving CBT had recovered versus 43 percent of teens who were not in the program.[7]

Where Do I Find a Qualified Therapist Who Practices CBT? CBT is fast becoming the treatment of choice for therapists who want to offer effective, time-limited treatments to their patients. Psychologists, social workers, and certified counselors can receive training in CBT. When looking for a referral, start with a trusted source such as your child's pediatrician or your school counselor. In addition, many professional organizations keep lists of qualified therapists by geographical area. Please see the resource list at the end of this book for many such organizations.

Finding the right therapist for your family is typically based on two equally weighted factors: the first is training and competence; the second is chemistry. Even a most highly regarded therapist may not click for your child, and the treatment will not be productive. Likewise, the most delightfully warm therapist may lack the specific expertise you need, and the treatment, however pleasant, will be ineffective. Parents interviewing prospective therapists should feel free to ask open-ended questions. For example, rather than say, "You do use CBT, right?" ask, "What treatment approach do you use with children with depression?" Instead of asking, "You've treated a lot of kids and they've gotten better, right?" ask, "Approximately how many children have you treated, and how have they fared?" Other important areas to cover include how parents are included in treatment and how, if at all, the school is involved. I have had many parents tell me that with a previous therapist, they just dropped their child off, picked her up, and paid and really had no idea what was going on in treatment because it was "private." It is my firm belief that while the specifics of your child's treatment may be private if that is his preference, including his parents in the process—so that they understand what their child is experiencing and his needs—is an essential component of the child's recovery. Children include their parents either directly or indirectly in their symptoms. No one else has more potential to influence their child in the small but crucial moments of the day, where the way that a parent fields a question can either strengthen a child's resolve or inadvertently reinforce his negative voice.

As to chemistry: When you are asking therapists questions about experience and competence, you will get a sense of your comfort with them: Are you learning from them? Do you understand their explanations, or are they too technical? Do they make you feel comfortable? Are they comfortable with themselves? Chances are that if you feel comfortable with the therapist, your child will, too.

Sample questions for a prospective therapist:

- What is your orientation in treatment? (Rather than saying, "Do you do CBT?" let her tell you.)
- What kinds of strategies do you use to work with depressed children?
- How do you engage children in the treatment?
- How many children have you seen with this issue?
- Are parents included in the treatment? In what ways?
- Do you have contact with the school?
- What is the best way to contact you in a crisis?
- Do you accept insurance?
- How long is a typical treatment?

Can Young Children Participate in CBT? Parents and even professionals often wonder whether young children who aren't able to sit and write out thought lists or reflect on their thoughts and feelings can successfully participate in CBT. A growing body of literature supports the effectiveness and appropriateness of CBT with children as young as age eight. However, in my own practice and in practices around the world, clinicians are confident that their young patients, even four- and five-year-olds, can learn techniques for recognizing and "bossing back" their negative thoughts, with the assistance of their parents as coaches. Young children may lack the ability to spell, but their abundant creativity and desire to be happy and in charge of themselves more than make up for these deficiencies. When given the opportunity to do relaxed breathing, or to role-play teaching Mr. Meany how to be nice, young children are some of the quickest learners to be found. Parents do need to be involved to sustain the lessons, so make sure that if you are taking your young child to treatment, it is to someone who works closely with parents.

Should Medication Be Considered?

Parents want to do what is best for their children. Sometimes they feel that since depression is a serious condition, its treatment requires medication. This is not necessarily the case. Discuss with your child's therapist or pediatrician whether a consultation with a psychiatrist is indicated. While some psychologists have earned the license to prescribe medications, the overwhelming majority of psychologists and all social workers are not able to prescribe. Psychiatrists are medical doctors who have received additional specialized training in the treatment of mental disorders such as depression and anxiety.

Any medication, even an over-the-counter pain reliever, carries both risks and benefits. The medications most commonly prescribed for depression are called selective serotonin reuptake inhibitors (SSRIs). These include the popular brands Prozac, Paxil, Zoloft, Celexa, Effexor, and Lexapro. The Food and Drug Administration (FDA) is responsible for monitoring the safety of the medications available, and only one SSRI, Prozac (generic name: fluoxetine), has been approved for use in children with depression. That other medications have not been approved for use in children does not mean they are less safe or less effective; it simply means the manufacturers have not submitted research for approval specifically for children.

Limitations of Medications: Although rates of depression are increasing in children and teens, and medications prescribed regularly, a 2016 meta-analysis of thirty-four treatment studies involving over five thousand subjects, medication treatment studies for children and teens found weak evidence in support of medication treatment for children and teens, the most significant benefit was for Prozac in terms of effectiveness, and only Prozac was statistically significant over placebo treatment.[8]

Benefits of Medication. The benefits of SSRIs have been demonstrated in a recent multisite study called the Treatment of Adolescent Depression Study, or TADS. In this study, led by Dr. John March at Duke University, and funded by the National Institute of Mental Health (NIMH), moderately to severely depressed teens at twelve additional medical facilities around the country were randomly assigned to receive either Prozac, a placebo (an inactive sugar pill), CBT, or a combination of CBT and Prozac. After twelve weeks of treatment, the researchers found that 71 percent of teens who received fluoxetine and CBT improved with treatment, compared with 60.6 percent who received fluoxetine alone, 43.2 percent who received CBT alone, and 34.8 percent who received a placebo.

There were some interesting differences in how adolescents responded to the treatments. There was a "speed effect" in that medication appeared to work faster (twelve weeks) in reducing depressive symptoms, whereas by twenty-four and thirty-six weeks CBT and medication alone were equally effective. There was a slight increase in rates of suicidal ideation and gestures among youth receiving fluoxetine, but CBT appeared to ameliorate this risk. The combination of CBT and medication appeared to have a more favorable safety profile than fluoxetine alone and appeared to offer the best balance of risk and benefit. If a depressed adolescent is experiencing suicidal thoughts, CBT is strongly recommended in addition to medication.[9]

The take-home message from this large-scale study is that treatment with fluoxetine may speed recovery, and adding CBT offers a longevity effect, provides additional safeguards for those vulnerable to suicide, and teaches children a lifetime of skills to manage their depressive thoughts, an essential safeguard against a relapse into depression in the future.

In a recent follow-up to this large-scale study, researchers concluded that "functioning generally improves among most adolescents who have received empirically supported treatments."[10] One multisite study found that among kids who are not responding to medication, switching to another medication plus CBT was more effective than a medication switch alone (54.8% vs. 40.5%).[11]

In teenagers with moderate to severe depression, medication appears to be an important component of the treatment plan. The data are not sufficient to suggest this conclusion for younger children, or for children with a mild depression.

Risks of Medications. In June 2003, in response to concerns about increased suicidal behavior caused by SSRIs, the British Department of Health warned physicians to avoid using SSRIs in treating depression in children under eighteen. In October 2004, the FDA required manufacturers to include a black-box warning—similar to the Surgeon General's warning on cigarette packages—to inform the public about the increased risk of suicidal behavior with SSRIs. This FDA requirement has launched a heated debate among professionals, who are both polarized on the nature of their concerns and united in their cause: making sure children stay safe. Doctors on one side of the debate argue that these black-box warnings may keep children off medications that could save their lives; on the other side, the concern is that these medications are potentially life-threatening.

If you and your doctor decide that an SSRI is indicated for your child, the FDA recommends that your physician evaluate the child once a week for the first month of the new medication; the first month appears to be the time when children are most at risk of becoming "activated"—a stage of agitation that may be associated with increased risk of suicide when a child is starting or increasing an SSRI. FDA guidelines suggest that children and adolescents taking an SSRI medication should have close monitoring for any worsening of depression, or activation: sleeplessness, agitation, or emergence of suicidal thinking during the first few weeks on a medication. Unfortunately, compliance with these guidelines is not monitored. If your child is starting a medication, please discuss your concerns about monitoring his symptoms with your doctor.

It is important that children who are on medication should not stop, increase, or decrease medication without consulting a child psychiatrist. An abrupt cutting off of the drug may cause adverse side effects or a relapse of depressive symptoms. Parents who are concerned about the risks of medication should discuss them with their child's psychiatrist.

Suggested questions to ask your doctor about medications:

- What are the known immediate or long-term side effects of the medication?
- What is known about the effectiveness of the medication?
- How soon should I expect to see improvement?
- What are the signs of an adverse reaction?
- How do I contact you in an emergency?
- How often will you see my child after the medication is started?
- How do I handle a missed dose?
- What is the target dose for this medication? How quickly will my child get there?
- What lab work is required before or during the course of the medication?
- What is the anticipated course of treatment? How long will my child stay on medication?

Medication or Therapy or Both?

All parents want to do the right thing for their child, especially when their child is suffering. They may think that medication is a necessary component of their child's treatment. In fact, across hundreds of studies, CBT has been found as effective as medication in treating depression, and it has been found to be twice as effective in preventing a relapse of depressive symptoms. If both treatments are ostensibly impacting the brain, why would one be better in preventing depression from coming back? A study conducted by researchers in 2004 compared brain scans of depressed patients being treated with medication with those of patients being treated with cognitive therapy. What the researchers found is that the two treatments target different areas of the brain. Antidepressants work by calming activity in the brain stem—the limbic system—calming down our emotional reactions to things. This tamping down can be essential to counteracting the overwhelmed feelings in depression that keep people limited. Cognitive behavior therapy works on the cortex, the seat of higher reasoning, helping us think and solve problems differently.[12] This difference is likely why CBT has a protective effect in reducing relapses into depression. If negative emotions return, those who have learned to handle them will be prepared to interpret and process them adaptively, preventing them from multiplying.

Integrative Health: Alternative Strategies

What of alternative or integrative treatments for depression? Some parents are relieved to know that alternatives to medication exist; other parents are skeptical: "How can a vitamin help my child, and how do I know the vitamin is safe?" Researchers have begun to identify key substances that may improve or compensate for the compromised brain functioning associated with depression. This is a fast-growing area of interest for researchers, and given the vastness of the subject and our focus on psychological treatments, it is beyond the scope of our investigation here to present a comprehensive discussion, but two promising findings in the area of integrative treatments for depression may lead you to consult the resource guide at the end of the book for further information. As with any health decision, consult your physician before starting any treatment.

Omega-3 Fatty Acids. Everything old is new again. The dreaded cod liver oil that our parents reluctantly drank is making a comeback; not only is it better-tasting now, but researchers are beginning to identify the benefits for a variety of health conditions, including depression. We need these particular types of fatty acids to build brain cells that promote better cognitive functioning. We can get them either from taking fish oil, or from eating foods rich in omega-3s, such as salmon, flaxseeds, walnuts, and soybeans. Health experts suggest a ratio ranging from of one to two, to one to four omega-3s to omega-6s, but in our high-saturated-fat diet, our intake of omega-6s is typically ten times more than our intake of omega-3s.[13] Experimental studies have found a higher rate of omega-6 in meats and vegetable oils in depressed animals, and they suggest that an increased intake of omega–3s may lower the levels of omega-6 fatty acids.[14] A recent study found highly significant reductions in depressive symptoms in children (ages six through twelve) who took omega-3 fatty acids for at least one month.[15] A recent review found similar results in adults: a reduction of depressive symptoms that were not responsive to medication.[16]

Vitamin B$_{12}$. According to the National Institute of Health Fact Sheet, vitamin B$_{12}$ helps maintain healthy nerve cells, for nerve growth and for the maintenance of healthy red blood cells. Depression, among other symptoms, such as fatigue, weakness, and loss of appetite, can be a health problem associated with a vitamin B$_{12}$ deficiency.[17] B vitamins are essential for motivation, mood, experience of pleasure, and cognitive functioning. The highest amounts are found in clams, liver, fortified cereal, and fish. A promising study from Finland found that depressed patients with higher levels of B$_{12}$ at six-month follow-up fared better in their treatment of depression than did their counterparts with lower levels of B$_{12}$.[18] Because vitamin B$_{12}$ is found in meats and fish, children who are vegetarian may be particularly at risk for B$_{12}$ deficiency. A recent study found that patients who were treated with vitamin B$_{12}$ supplements along with antidepressants showed significantly greater improvements in depressive symptoms than those treated with antidepressants alone.[19]

Let the Light Shine In. Some kids show a greater risk for depressive symptoms during the winter months when there is less natural light; this is referred to as seasonal affective disorder (SAD), the phenomenon named for increased depression in areas with the darkest winters: Alaska and Nordic countries. Bright light therapy (BLT) has been shown to be effective in reducing depressive symptoms in SAD, but its efficacy has also been demonstrated with depression that doesn't have a seasonal pattern.[20] There are many theories as to why this intense light exposure improves our functioning, which are still being researched, but nonetheless, sitting under a special light box that has bright light (about 100 times as bright as usual lighting inside, but a fifth of the light of a sunny day) for thirty minutes a day, as soon upon waking as possible, while reading, eating breakfast, and so on, has been found to reduce depressive symptoms and improve mood and sleep.

The Protective Power of Sleep, and Exercise. Who Knew? Lack of sleep in children and especially teens greatly increases their risk of having cognitive deficits, such as memory problems, executive functioning, and organization, but lack of sleep also puts kids and teens at risk for mental health problems, specifically it increases their risk of depression, and even suicidal thoughts.[21] Teens who go to bed at ten were much less likely to suffer from depression than were their counterparts who set their own bedtime after midnight. An essential part of any treatment approach with kids and teens is looking at sleep habits and making sure that routines support turning off the technology well before bed and winding down (see Chapter 12 for specifics). Another staple of good health that our great grandmothers would likely have encouraged—get off the couch, and move! Exercise—specifically high-intensity exercise three times a week—appears to be an effective treatment for depression, improving depressive symptoms to a comparable extent as pharmacotherapy and psychotherapy.[22] The reasons for this are many, first: high-intensity exercise releases endorphins (the feel-good hormones), so kids will feel much better after exercising, that offer an on-the-spot benefit. A more lasting reason, aside from all the health systems (cardiac, pulmonary, immune functioning, stress reduction) that benefit from our getting up and moving, is that in depressive mode, the body downshifts; we don't move much and so the system adjusts to this lower gear; as a result, mustering energy to do things is a task unto itself. In contrast, when we make a regular practice of exercising, it resets the body's systems to the active range: it will actually take less pushing on our part to get things done because the body will be warmed up instead of stalled out.

CONCLUSION

Although many children with negative thinking do not develop depression, parents need to know how to recognize the first signs that their child's negative thinking has got the upper hand and become debilitating, so they can immediately intervene to prevent a descent into depression.

7

PREVENTING THE WORST:
TALKING TO KIDS ABOUT SUICIDE

Ryan was a well-liked junior in high school, an athlete, and a great student. He had a big heart and was at the center of social life in his grade. On the outside, he looked like a typical high school student. On the inside, he may have been, too. His last post on his Facebook page read: "This is too hard, there's too much pressure. I can't do this anymore." And before anyone, the hundreds of people who would have done anything, could save him, tragically, he was gone.

It's every parent's worst nightmare. The unimaginable tragedy of losing their child to this irreversible decision he or she makes—alone—in their most vulnerable moment—is the reality that more and more families and communities live and relive for the rest of their lives. Alarmingly, suicide is the second leading cause of death in young people aged fifteen to twenty-four, according to a recent CDC National Center for Health Statistics study, and suicide rates among teens, which had previously dropped by 15 percent from 1999 to 2007, recently rose by 56 percent between 2007 and 2016.[1]

Suicide is a permanent solution to a temporary problem. Seeing the big picture, seeing past the struggles of the day, can feel impossible to some teens. But if they were able to step away from the impossibility and get engaged with something—that moment would pass and they would be okay again, maybe even great. Until the next time. It is difficult living moment to moment like this, but over time, with treatment and support, the vicissitudes of life become more manage-able, and kids become resilient. Kids want a solution to give relief from the pain that they are experiencing, but the finality of suicide is something they cannot comprehend. Although many risk factors have been identified, which we will look at closely, talking about suicide with your child is *not* a risk factor; in fact, being able to "go there" can provide a lifesaving buffer because the number one protective factor against suicidal behavior is social connectedness. If you are cultivating a space in your relationship with your kids to discuss even the most difficult of topics—you are creating a place where they can feel safe and supported.

TO TALK ABOUT IT OR NOT TO TALK ABOUT IT . . .

Parents may be reluctant to discuss suicide with their children, fearing that this may cause more harm than good, that they are somehow sug-gesting the behavior. The opposite is true. If kids do not have those thoughts, it won't cause them to become suicidal, any more than talking about smoking, drugs, reckless driving, or unintended pregnancy causes those behaviors. The fact is, if your child is suicidal, it will be a great relief for him to be able to tell you, and it could be lifesaving. You are opening up the door to these types of conversations with him so that he knows, whether he needs it now or not, that you are open and not afraid to talk about this very difficult topic—that you won't judge him, you won't get mad at him—on the contrary, you are grateful that he is coming to you for help. You're teaching him that those feelings and thoughts are a sign of a problem, and when your child has them, he needs to tell someone (preferably an adult) and get help. Consider the alternatives: Children or teens who are not talking to their parents are likely either turning to their unprepared peers for advice, or worse, to no one.

Even if kids have not had suicidal thoughts themselves, or don't know someone who has talked about or committed suicide, it's likely that they have had exposure through television programs and other me-dia. Professionals cite several concerns about featuring suicide in certain media—it glorifies suicide, shows graphic details, romanticizes the act, and overall can reinforce the idea that those who contemplate suicide should believe the distortions they are thinking about depression and hopelessness. Many parents won't permit their kids to watch programs where suicide is a primary plot point, and that is a reasonable decision. Alternatively, you can engage in conversation with them—offer to watch the program with them so you can discuss—as a way of ensuring that their take-aways are accurate and that they are safe. (Sample questions follow.)

Whether your family has a history of mental illness or not, all parents should talk to their children about suicide. Helping kids understand that while feeling hopeless, unhappy, even having the frustrated thought, "I wish I were dead" can pass through their mind—they should still talk to their parents about even those experiences to get direction on how to manage those thoughts so they don't multiply. But if this is how a child is feeling a lot of the time, wakes up feeling that way, and immediately returns to those thoughts when not occupied with something else, this is called depression and it is essential to seek professional help.

PROCESSING NEWS OF CELEBRITY SUICIDES OR IN YOUR COMMUNITY AS A WAY OF TALKING ABOUT SUICIDE

Although not in your child's immediate circle, high-profile/celebrity suicides can foster a sense of vulnerability for kids. The incongruity that someone whom your child admires, looks up to, sees as successful and happy—invincible—could also be so unhappy that she takes her own life, sets off waves of vulnerability and confusion. When a young person in your child's community takes his life, these feelings hit even closer to home and the interplay between identification and uncertainty ripples out. "If someone who *is like me* decides to take his life, could it happen to me? I've been unhappy at times—how am I different?" They may also question the meaning of life in the face of loss. When it affects their immediate lives, children are sad and thrown off balance, their world no longer makes sense in the face of suicide. Take these opportunities to talk with your children about the importance of not hiding feelings of depression or discouragement.

While we may struggle to find the right words to talk about difficult topics, what is most important is your stance and your tone. If we are using the "emergency tone" or are afraid, kids will see this and may struggle to absorb the important information that we want to convey. It will help to strike a caring, but matter-of-fact tone about suicide. Ask whether your child has had these thoughts and help her know what to do with them if they come. Not everyone has these thoughts, but it's not uncommon. Let your child know that there is always help.

GUIDELINES FOR TALKING TO KIDS ABOUT SUICIDE

When talking to young children about suicide, keep the message very concrete and simple: The person died and we are very sad. If they ask how, you can say that the individual had a disease (better than saying she was "sick," because your child may fear that being sick, as in common colds, means you die) and it took over and she died.

Start Open-Ended: Start with What They Know

When talking to older children about suicide—they may have heard about a celebrity suicide or suicide of someone at school and likely other children have shared information—it is best to start by asking what they already know. As with younger children, be clear that the person had a disease. Make sure they understand he had thoughts that are what we call distortions: at certain times, we don't see things as they really are, we see things as much worse, or bigger, or insurmountable and we feel hopeless, even though the things we are upset about are usually temporary and later we don't feel that way at all. This is why we need to get help and tell people when we're having those thoughts and feelings so that we can be safe until those thoughts pass.

Opening up a conversation with your teenager about suicide may be sparked by an item in the news, but the conversation needs to happen with all teens. It's always helpful with teens to start at a distance and not to get personal right away. Ask open-ended questions about whether they know kids who have talked about suicide, and what that was like for them, how did they respond, what did they feel, were they worried, and so on. Then, you can bring the conversation closer to home and ask whether they have ever had that experience themselves, or what they would do if they were having those thoughts.

Teach How Strong Feelings Come and Go

Your goal in conversations about suicide is to be proactive. Normalize in a sense "the abnormal," conveying that while it is very common for teens to have negative, depressive thoughts that can spiral into thoughts of suicide. But because they are distortions, it is important to teach children how those feelings come and go. Walk through another time in your teen's life when she felt very bad about something, perhaps even suicidal, and ask her how she felt a few days later. Help create that teachable moment when you say—exactly—this is why we need to talk to someone when we have those thoughts and feelings because as intensely as she felt at one time, she will feel quite differently about them another time.

They are a kind of trick of the mind. When we've had a bad experience, it feels as though our upset will never go away. What that person who committed suicide didn't have in mind and close at hand was someone to talk to and find the help she needed. But as we know—there is always someone who cares if we teach our kids to reach out. Whether it is to a suicide hotline, a friend, a parent, making the decision to ask for help puts a safety net under us that we simply, none of us, can have on our own.

Teaching Kids What to Do with Suicidal Thoughts and Feelings

> Sometimes I just want to curl up in a ball and die.
>
> —teen with negative thinking

When parents hear a statement like that from their child, before they can even think it through, the panic button is hit and they could find themselves saying, "Don't say things like that, you don't mean that. Do you know what that would do to us?" This reaction is understandable. But it is important to not shut the conversation down with your fears because teens may be overloaded with their own. In this most difficult of moments, it is essential to keep in perspective that the most important piece of information is that your child is telling you how she is feeling. No matter how difficult it is to hear, communication is always better than the alternative of silence.

Although all of us could feel understandably afraid, in this particular example, when the parent responded, "I'm glad you told me. Sometimes I have those thoughts, too. When I'm feeling overwhelmed, I tell someone I'm feeling overwhelmed, or just start to think what is it I really need to do now, and I start to feel more in charge." The teen replied, "That makes me feel so much better. I was so scared. I thought that meant I was going to kill myself or that there was something wrong with me." We see in this instance that having suicidal thoughts is distinct and different from having a wish to die. Although for kids most at-risk for suicide, there isn't that difference, many kids who have intrusive suicidal thoughts are often frightened by the meaning of the thoughts because they *don't* want to die. They wonder whether maybe they do want to *because* they are having these thoughts. From there, your conversation can open up. What makes you feel overwhelmed? What can you do when you feel that way? How long does it usually last? Opening up a space to talk about suicide and suicidal thoughts and feelings reduces kids' and teens' loneliness, gives a sense of being understood and hopeful that people can feel what they feel and survive, and protects them from following through with suicidal thoughts. The national suicide hotline, 1-800-273-TALK, and 911 are important resources that parents can share with teens to call at moments like this. Both can be accessed anywhere, any time in the United States. Seeking professional guidance in these matters will ensure for all involved that your child or teen is getting whatever help she needs to be safe.

In general, parents will do best to respond with a sandwich: support and empathy first—"You are really feeling bad, I see that. I want to help you and understand what's making you have these feelings right now." Then, add the "meat": "Moments can feel really out of control and bad. Can you tell me what you've been thinking and feeling lately because if we talk it through, it will probably feel different? That's how human beings work. Usually when we voice things aloud, perspective comes into focus, and simply having the support of sharing those hard thoughts can lift the heaviness from us." Talk to your child and use whatever steps from the Master Plan in Chapter 5 feel right. End on a note of support and encouraging communication: "I'm really glad that you told me about how you were feeling. I'm going to check in about this—what do you think is the best way for that to happen? Do you want me to say, 'How've you been feeling?' or would you rather have me say, 'Let's do a check-in?' But please, if I am not asking—please reach out to me. If you say, 'I need to talk,' nothing is more important to me than talking to you."

There are many cognitive strategies to help that perspective arrive more quickly. Like any negative thought—"I'm stupid; I'm worthless; I hate myself"—thoughts of suicide can reflect a habit of thinking, a default cognitive reaction or reflex that kicks in when a child is upset. Even if these thoughts are not your child's wishes, they can grow stronger through repetition. The goal is to help your child recognize such thoughts and rather than react with more negative thoughts, respond by using techniques that create distance and perspective by relabeling them as coming from their "negative" brain.

Red-pen editing sounds like this: "I'm having a thought right now about suicide. These thoughts won't help me. I don't want to do that, I want to feel better." Or relabeling: "That is not me or how I really feel; that is my perfectionism talking, or that is my depression talking." Parents can use similar ideas for helping their children manage the strong feelings that they may be having: by understanding that those feelings are coming from the thoughts they are having, they can see they have choices about the meaning they give to those thoughts. As we discussed in Chapter 3, the mindfulness strategies of acknowledging the thought without endorsing it—like a cloud moving through the sky, or a leaf down a stream—kids can acknowledge the presence of the thought and let it go: "I'm having a thought, right now, because I am feeling sad, but that's not really how I am feeling."

Ask your child to remember a big disappointment—remember how it felt so bad that day, and then that feeling somehow went away, it shifted— she lived through it and she wasn't so upset about it, maybe she even figured out that things were better than she thought. It's not that the situation is actually worse or actually hopeless, it's just that that trick is playing hard on her mind and not letting her see that things will always change and usually for the better. Parents need to convey the following messages:

- You should always talk to people if you are having these thoughts. I am here no matter how hard it might be, I want you to tell me if you are struggling with thoughts of depression, suicide, or hopelessness.

- It's always important to see that whatever is happening now, however much pain you are enduring is truly temporary—even though it doesn't feel that way. You know that if someone called with good news for you or maybe even invited you to come over, that would change things. There's always something that can change a situation. The page turns. It's a new chapter. This is why reaching out is so important.

- Your future self needs you to protect it. There is life on the other side of these feelings. Great opportunities, fun, love, connection, even if you don't think that now, or see that now, it's okay. Even if we can't see that far ahead, it doesn't mean it isn't possible. I will help you.

- When you're feeling down, it's hard to remember times when things were different, so, create a crisis kit: Think about the things that matter to you. Write down all the people who matter to you, your wishes and hopes for the future, your proudest moments; positive things that people have said to you; positive memories you've had; a list of favorite movies, favorite jokes, puzzles—put them in a box or type out your answers and put them in a folder on your phone or computer and look at them often, whenever you need to.

- One call, one conversation can make all the difference in the world—your world—but if you don't have that conversation, it's too late. There is always someone who wants to help you. So, let's make sure that even if you don't reach out to me, or to another adult whom you trust cares about you—though I hope you will, that you have the suicide hotline number: 1-800-273-TALK.

Finally, it is important to convey to your child that suicide, is always, always a tragedy. There is nothing good about suicide. All the attention that the person is getting comes after he's gone. The news will move on. The family and community will always be devastated.

If you suspect that your child is suicidal, get help immediately. Sometimes it is hard to know if there's an acute risk. Let the crisis center or emergency room decide. Until you can secure an appointment with a therapist, giving your child a suicide prevention hotline number can empower him to reach out even if he feels he can't reach out to you.

WHEN IT'S REALLY FRUSTRATION, NOT SUICIDAL INTENTIONS

Sometimes children, even young children, do, in a moment of frustration or upset, say that they want to die. Although these are not words a parent ever wants to hear, these single or infrequent reflexive, impulsive statements by a frustrated child may signal a need to work on distress tolerance, emotional regulation skills, or even assertiveness. On the other hand, they could suggest that the child is at risk for depression. It is important to note the context: If this is an isolated event and happens when a child feels cornered by a social situation she feels she can't manage, or is part of a dynamic with a teacher she can't see her way out of, or assignments or expectations that she doesn't feel she can meet, she is really saying, "I don't like what is going on here, I don't know what to do—I need help!" These moments need to be taken seriously in several ways—but don't panic. Your panic will frighten your child rather than help her fix the problem. Instead, calmly, use the problem-solving format in Chapter 3, and find out what was going on when your child said that. Then ask, "Did you really want to die, or were you upset and didn't know what to do?" You might hear answers like "I did so many bad things today"; "I was so embarrassed in gym class when I missed the shot"; "Nobody was listening to me at recess—I wanted to die," "I got cut from Varsity, I'm a total failure, I can't show my face." Make clear the distinction between wanting to die—to go away and never, ever come back—and being upset or overwhelmed and wanting the situation to go away or get fixed. Make sure that your child knows exactly what to say to get the help she actually needs. Role-play or act out various scenarios so that your child can practice her new one-liner: "I need help!" or "I'm frustrated, and I don't know what to do!" or simply, "I'm sad!"

Children must understand clearly that they need to use their words carefully because if they say they "want to die," even if they don't mean it, doctors will need to talk with them to make sure they are safe. Because of the serious risk of suicide, schools will take seriously even one suicidal threat or statement, and many will require that a child's safety be determined by a psychiatrist or psychologist before the child can return to school. Not only will having a more accurate "one-liner" help the adults around your child know how to best intervene, it will help your child. Saying or hearing over and over in your head "I want to die" negatively influences your child's mood. If instead she uses the red-pen editor (as discussed earlier) and said, "I'm feeling sad, right now," or even "I'm having those I want to die thoughts right now, but I know it's because I'm tired and overwhelmed," she would be learning how to be resilient and manage difficult moments, making those moments feel much more manageable.

IS YOUR CHILD AT RISK?

Discussing the risk of suicide in children is a daunting and tragic subject. The following statistics reveal a heartbreaking and alarmingly worsening situation. The purpose of this book is to identify the thought patterns that could potentially lead a child to depression and increase their risk of suicide, so as you read on, please keep well in mind that prevention is possible, and these sobering statistics are presented here to give you a sense of the scope of the problem to which we must collectively dedicate our resources. According to the Centers for Disease Control and Prevention, the number of teenaged girls who committed suicide doubled between 2007 and 2015; the number for teenaged boys increased 30 percent in that time period. Suicide claims nearly five times as many young men's lives as young women's. African American teens commit suicide at twice the rate of their non–African American counterparts. LGBTQ teens are three times as likely to attempt as their heterosexual peers; transgender teens are six times more likely to attempt than their heterosexual peers. Native American teens have the highest percentage of suicide of any ethnic group, 3.5 times that of any other group. A history of previous attempts, alcohol and/or drug use, depression, family history of suicide, and access to firearms are all risk factors. In many instances, there is what may be considered a "last-straw event," such as a breakup in a relationship, seeing this as the only way to escape a hopeless, difficult situation, or having constant depressive suicidal thoughts.[2]

When chronic risk factors (see the following list) combine with an acute event—getting a bad grade or report card, breaking up a relationship, suffering a public humiliation, being the target of pranks or teasing, getting in trouble with the law—vulnerable teens don't see the problems as solvable or temporary, and the solution they choose can be permanent. The red flags for suicidal behavior are listed on page 186; if your child is exhibiting any of them for days or weeks, or you see a drastic change in behavior over a shorter period of time, immediately seek professional consultation through a suicide hotline, your pediatrician, physician, or a school counselor. For referral information, please see the resource guide at the end of this book.

In addition to chronic risk factors, relentless negative thinking is associated with suicidal thinking—criticizing every move, shutting down any possibility of a good outcome, amplifying life's ordinary disappointments and challenges into a forever, set in stone narrative of impossibility and hopelessness. Researchers have identified that the cognitive distortion most highly associated with suicide attempts is "fortune-telling"—predicting negative events in one's life.

Risk factors for suicidality:

- Depression or trauma-related disorder
- A recent loss: relationship, pet, parent, divorce, loss of home or job
- Previous suicide attempt
- Public humiliation
- Stigma or other barriers to getting help
- High emotional sensitivity
- Highly extreme reactions
- Slower return to baseline after emotional reactions
- Substance abuse
- Bullying
- Lack of social support
- Chronic pain or medical condition
- Family history of suicide

- Presence of firearm in home
- Struggling with sexual orientation or gender identity

Red flags for heightened suicide risk in teens:

- Writing (poems, journal) or drawing about death or suicide
- Talking about previous or future suicide attempts
- Talking repeatedly about how she would be better off dead, how people would be happier if she were dead
- Repeatedly expressing hopelessness, worthlessness, loneliness, or feelings of extreme guilt or regret
- Showing a drastic change in behavior: appearance, eating, or sleeping habits
- Exhibiting extreme mood swings: going from very depressed to very happy without explanation
- Showing a severe drop in school performance, not caring about other responsibilities
- Engaging in high-risk behavior: taking drugs, pursuing physically dangerous activities
- Getting her affairs in order: making plans for giving away belongings, pets
- Acting recklessly or impulsively
- Withdrawing from friends, family, and previously meaningful activities

TREATMENT FOR SUICIDALITY

Dialectical Behavior Therapy

A specific type of cognitive-behavior therapy focuses on cultivating and reinforcing strategies for tolerating in-the-moment distressing thoughts, urges, feelings, and experiences to protect children from acting on their extreme reactions and emotions in a way that is harmful to them, including self-harm and suicidal behavior. Kids may feel like they need to try so hard to *not* feel the feeling that they do things that hurt themselves

more. Teens often feel that being frustrated, or depressed, or sad is unbearable, thus multiplying their distress: They are sad and they are angry
or upset about being sad, and they believe those feelings will never go
away. The idea here is that it's okay to feel feelings (see Chapter 3 for
more about managing intense feelings); even though they are uncomfortable, they are temporary and manageable. There is much overlap between CBT (the exercises described in this book) and dialectal behavior
therapy (DBT), but specifically DBT treatment combines an acceptance
of circumstances, factors, or simply the existence of feelings with the
skills to make changes. Several studies have documented the effectiveness of DBT in reducing anger, self-injury, and suicide attempts in teen
populations.

A few highlights of DBT exercises include

**Toning Down the Intensity: Rephrasing Judgmental Thinking into
Nonjudgmental Thinking.** What fuels our negative thinking is the narrative of judgment either of others—"He's so *mean!*"—or the judgment
of ourselves—"I'm such an *idiot!*"—stoking the fire of our distress. As we
saw in our Flexible Thinking exercises in Chapter 2 that described an un-
favorite vegetable neutrally, we can transform judgmental statements with
nonjudgmental ones and bring the emotional temperature down. "He's so
mean!" becomes "I don't like how he is talking to me; I want to do something about it." Or "I'm such an *idiot!*" becomes "I felt uncomfortable
when I gave that presentation, but it's okay and it probably didn't show."

Accepting Rather Than Fighting What "Is." When things don't go the
way kids want—the movie sold out, the Lego piece is missing, they
weren't invited to the party—much negative energy gets worked up
from getting angry at the parts that *can't* change, rather than focusing on
the parts that can and it makes everything feel much worse. Just being
aware that your child is fighting *what is* can be helpful; he may be able
to incorporate the self-talk, "I'm having that *fighting what is* thought
again; I'm going to focus on what I can do instead." So, "I'm frustrated
that I missed the train" becomes "I need help reading the schedule; I'm
going to ask for help so I don't miss another train." Or "I'm so mad that
I avoided the cafeteria all last year; now I don't have friends!" becomes
"I did avoid the cafeteria; that was what I thought was best; now I know

that if I want friends, I have to show up." Switching over to this kind of thinking helps kids not dwell on unpleasantness that only worsens their mood, and instead gets us feeling freer to see other options and spend our time more effectively.

Soothing skills: Instead of the counterproductive or harmful steps that kids take if they are very upset (pinching or cutting themselves, destroying belongings), children can identify things that work for them: petting their dog, asking for a hug, using aromatherapy (e.g., lavender oil), reading a poem they like, hugging a stuffed animal, listening to their favorite songs.

Behavioral Activation (BA)

As we saw in Chapter 5, the Master Plan, behavioral activation—is a very effective approach for treating depression. By asking your child to find *meaningful* activities—volunteering, taking care of a beloved pet, watching TED Talks, you circumvent the obstacle of finding *enjoyable* activities that can feel nearly impossible when feeling depressed. Essentially, BA counteracts the maladaptive closed loop of negative thoughts → isolation/avoidance → more negative thoughts ("I'm so unhappy; I hate everything; everyone hates me") → isolation/avoidance. BA is an opportunity to prove negative thoughts wrong by mobilizing children to orchestrate changes in their environment, for example, scheduling social contracts or exercise. These positive experience result in more positive thoughts and feelings, which increase the likelihood that kids would seek out more fulfilling experiences rather than avoiding them; it will bring them out of that closed room, out of the self-fulfilling prophecy of depression. Rather than having to muster the motivation in the moment, kids can set an alarm or reminder on their phone for activities that counter their detachment with engagement and are therefore positively reinforcing; for example, "Play fetch with the dog," "Talk to my cat," "Text Dwayne or Sunny to get frozen yogurt," "Time to sketch!," "Go outside and say hi to the next five people you see."

CONCLUSION

While no parent wants to talk about suicide with their child, initiating straightforward conversations with your kids could be lifesaving. Kids are unequipped to handle the big, overwhelming feelings they have— whether that is a reaction to the news of a high-profile suicide, or their own suicidal thoughts. Making clear to your kids that you are a safe place for an open dialogue that can even include *those kinds of thoughts* ensures that they will seek help if they need it. In general, braving the turbulent waters of talking about upsetting topics such as these sends a clear message to your child that they don't have to protect you. You are here for them and they needn't keep important thoughts secret or seek out the advice of their similarly ill-equipped peers. Help your child know that there are powerful and effective responses to these types of thoughts they can learn to get perspective, reset, and stay safe.

8

LOSING, FAILURE, PERFECTIONISM, AND JEALOUSY (OH MY!)

*Walking Your Child Compassionately
Through the Less Than Pleasant "Givens" of Life*

Mistakes are a fact of life. It is the response to the error that counts.

—Nikki Giovanni

You can't always get what you want.

—The Rolling Stones

Many years ago, we were cleaning up after our older daughter's fifth birthday party. The last two of our young guests were still sitting at the kitchen table in heated debate. Katherine, curly-haired and free-spirited, was happily singing the lyrics to the popular Rolling Stones song quoted above, but every time she sang the line "You can't always get what you want," her more serious five-year-old counterpart, Adrianna, interjected angrily, "Yes, you can!" Back and forth they went, over and over, until finally the parents had to intervene to break up this battle brewing over a clash in worldviews. Out of the mouths of babes. We've all sung those lyrics like happy Katherine, but when push comes to shove and things don't go our way, we feel Adrianna's indignation. We thought we *could* get what we wanted, and in that moment, we were sorely wrong. If we have trouble riding out these moments of disappointment, how can we help our children fare any better?

Fortunately, we don't have to be experts in these experiences to be good coaches for our children, but we may need to rethink our game plan: It's not about urgently talking our kids out of disappointments or preventing them from expressing frustration. Instead, it's doing a mind-set makeover, to realize that disappointments in appropriate dosages—like inoculations at the doctor—are actually good for our children. Rather than seeing these moments as obstacles to our children's happiness, we can set the right tone for our kids when we ourselves picture these moments as temporary detours. Remember how many things are *not* the emergency or disaster that they seem to be at first. We need to take the patient, compassionate, scenic route to help our kids figure that out with our support. When you're out of your young child's favorite cereal, or your middle schooler's class trip is canceled because of rain, or your teen misses the pool party that was going to be the most important social event of the year because he's sick, not only does he learn that these glitches aren't the end of the world, but he also learns how to manage the fact that they *feel* like the end of the world to him. Just as two children's experiences of receiving a shot at the doctor depends on what they're telling themselves about it ("Help! Get me out of here!" or "Is it over yet?"), the way children talk themselves through disappointments can either curtail or prolong the pain. In time, kids learn that it's risky to rest their entire happiness and reason for being on that one thing working out, and they even get savvy in how to breathe life into the mantra "Even when it doesn't work out, it works out." At first, tackling the project of managing disappointment may hardly sound inviting, but in fact, you will find that working through these adversities with your child can be a profoundly positive experience that deepens your trust and closeness because he has let you into his world when he was most vulnerable.

Life will naturally present our kids with these challenges if we don't get in the way. Warning: This will be a messy process. We are not expecting our children to immediately look adversity in the face and greet it with a wink and a smile. There will be some fallout, and they will need to make some noise about it, but with your help, they can also sort through and find what's salvageable—even if it's just that they survived. From those broken toys to those broken hearts, kids come to know that while they can't always get what they want, by doing the inner rethink, asking for help when needed, and advocating for themselves they can, in fact, get what they need.

PART ONE: ADVERSITY 101:
WHY NEGATIVE-MINDED CHILDREN NEED THE LESSONS MOST

If you get tired, learn to rest, not to quit.

—Banksy

Children and adolescents with a negative bias live a high-stakes existence because so much is riding on things going right for them. They characteristically put all their chips on the table with every interaction, so when they lose, in their mind, they lose it all. When they're crying that they lost a game, or they got a C on a pop quiz, the event is not a superficial scratch on their sense of self; it has made a deep impression. They haven't just lost that one thing; they feel as if they've lost their identity. Their reaction isn't in line with reality, but it is in line with how they are *perceiving* reality. A child sees a strike out in baseball as a total and irrevocable loss of her ability as a player, a teen sees his self-worth and future crumble with one unwanted grade. Given how devastating loss is to these kids, it is understandable that parents may swoop down Superman-style to protect them. But as with any vicious circle, when our secret mission is to keep them from experiencing failure—or more accurately, frustration or disappointment—children hear loud and clear the inadvertent message that failure is a really bad thing. If we want our children to be more resilient in the face of failure, we can't play "keep away." Our kids will benefit much more in the long run from our showing them that they can still win by facing these struggles head-on. Otherwise, they will burn themselves out overachieving to try to make sure they never fail, or at the other end of the spectrum, underachieve so they never have to feel the sting of failure: They drop out and don't try. If kids have choreographed their life around avoiding failure and loss, or we have done the choreography for them, they are novices rather than experts in failing successfully.

Rather than being damaging, so-called failure experiences in the right quantities are often the very experiences from which they not only rally, but often also learn the most. Sometimes they even decide that what initially registered as a failure was actually not. Separating the lasting value of what was learned in the process, from the likely fleeting meaning of the outcome, kids can learn that their efforts weren't a waste; they can glean something useful from the experience even if it wasn't what they thought. Paradoxically, the more comfortable our kids can become navigating through failure and disappointment, the more likely they are to take reasonable risks and succeed. So, into failure we go.

With these lessons you will develop X-ray vision to understand the anatomy of how your child internalizes negative events. With this vision, you can confidently guide your child out of the spin of failure and build a new hub, a new destination, which revolves around new ideas: effort, partial successes, the notion of a learning curve, and being in good company when the going gets tough. No longer stuck in a blind alley with their thoughts, kids will instantly lessen the depth of their disappointment, just by anticipating and foreseeing that there are alternate routes out of the maze.

Where Have All the Molehills Gone?
Lowering the Stakes in Our Expectations

"I can't fail this test—I'll never get into college"; "I totally have to beat my time in the mile—I'm a loser if I don't"; "I have to do a perfect job on my presentation—it's a quarter of my grade." Where does all this pressure come from? Parents who are laid back about success and comfortable with their own mistakes are baffled. But even parents who are a tad too success-oriented stare in disbelief at the monster they fear they've created and their child's urgency for things to be right, good, and perfect. The irrational equation of "I have to or else" is apparently woven into the woof and warp of our psyche. Albert Ellis, known as the grandfather of cognitive therapy, described twelve irrational beliefs—insidious, secret agents of distress that have the power to supersize or transform an ordinary disappointment into a major disaster. A subset from Ellis's catalog of the irrational includes:

- "I must be outstandingly competent, or I am worthless."
- "Others must treat me considerately, or they are absolutely rotten."
- "The world should always give me happiness, or I will die."

These beliefs may sound overly dramatic, but the next time you are feeling disappointed by your performance at your job or hurt by a comment from a coworker, you may find that these irrational beliefs capture your feelings alarmingly well. At least at first. And that's the point.

How do we reverse our kids' mountains back to molehills? Not by trying to convince them that the loss isn't so bad. At that moment, it is to them. You can teach kids to do the "perspective thing" when the absolutes of "everything is terrible" show up. The key is to backtrack: Identify their expectations in a situation, the picture they had in mind, so they can start to revamp these trouble-making beliefs and expectations into more adaptive ones. The reason kids fall so hard, typically, is that they started at a much higher altitude, with very high stakes. If your child is thinking, "If I can't get this math problem, I'm the dumbest person in the world," it's going to really hurt when she plummets from that height. If instead her expectation was "Geometry is new to me; the ride up the learning curve can be slow, but it will get easier eventually if I keep working at it; it always does," if she misses a problem it's not the end of the world. It's the beginning of a new world, in a sense. The sign that she is about to learn something. And shifting to this growth mind-set (see Chapter 4) will help these moments not be a surprise to her: her expectations prepared her for a likely scenario rather than one of absolutes. It is important to note here that this approach is not about lowering *standards*. It doesn't mean our kids should "settle for less and not care." On the contrary, it is about lowering the *stakes*, about their being *accurate* in their interpretations of *why* things go their way or don't, and assessing the actual consequences of those events (so different from their imagined catastrophic view). So, it's okay for our children to want to do well, want everyone to love them, want to have fun. Those beginning goals are fine; it's the inaccurate conclusions our children reach when those things don't happen that are the problem. Instead of the "or else" catastrophic construction, we can teach our children that the consequences of disappointments are temporary and changeable; in fact, our children get to interpret those consequences for themselves.

Falling Slowly and Getting Back Up Again: What Part of This Problem Can My Child Handle?

As well-meaning parents, we often find ourselves in the position of cheating—overprotecting, overindulging, overcompensating, or overdoing for our kids what we know they should do themselves. For instance, we rush out at ten at night to buy poster board for that forgotten project for our middle schooler (and either give a knowing glance to the other guilt-ridden, bleary-eyed parents in line or, depending on the absurdity of the errand, avert our gaze altogether) or stay up till the wee hours assembling the nine-hundred-sugar-cube replica of an Alaskan igloo. We might think, "Do we let them get the B because they didn't have the poster board, or do we buy it for them, knowing they're not learning to do things for themselves?" Or we do the "concierge" parent for our high school students, foregoing chores (naturally!), but practically becoming personal assistants packing their sports bags, bringing them their food in bed when they're too tired every day from their truly grueling schedules, doing their laundry even if we didn't grow up with such amenities. Why do we do all of this? Because: college. Everything counts for college. We all have our own versions of these scenarios because we don't want our children to fail. But deep down we know that if our children can't tolerate the distress of not even *failing*, but just slipping up a bit, they won't be able to succeed in life. Our cheating (when it becomes a way of life) cheats them, too.

What is the alternative? You are not going to throw your child to the lions to help him learn how to get over things, you're not going to stop helping your child cold-turkey, nor are you going to keep him away from the zoo. Rather than asking, "Do I let him fall, or do I catch him?" ask yourself, "What part of this can he handle? How can I share the task with him?" Look at your child's or adolescent's starting point—how he is reacting to disappointments or frustrations now—and help him stretch just outside his comfort zone. Here are some questions to guide you:

- *Can he stretch to take care of some of this task himself?*
- *Can I share the job with him? What part can he do? What part can I do?*
- *Will he grow from this experience, or will it be too hard and cause a setback?*

Moving Through Feelings: Fast or Slow?

As we'll see, for each of the following "givens-of-life" situations there are ways to move your child to a better place. Kids are going to need to vent first, and you may need to redirect them if after ten or fifteen minutes, their venting is lathering them up rather than cooling them down. Sometimes the only way to get to the heart of what really matters to your child is to jump in—not have them dabble with their frustration, loss, jealousy, or disappointment but get drenched. You can use the formula that follows to cut to the chase with your kids.

I wanted _____, but I got _____, and now I'm _____, because now I can't _____!

By completing these sentence starters, your child can generate all the material she needs to start working through what happened. Then, by filling in the blanks in the following, she can use her energy to think of what she can do next rather than use up all her steam (and yours) on what is already said and done.

The part I can fix or control is _____. The part that I can't control is _____. What I can do next time is _____.

Remember you don't want to coerce your child to *stop* thinking the *wrong* way, and *start* thinking the *right* way. Instead, step into your child's shoes and put yourself on the path with her. Misery does love company and it is easier to learn the territory in someone else's shoes first, so share your own messy experiences of slipups, disappointments, and downright failures—you'll be surprised by how textbook-rational your child can be when it comes to someone else's irrational beliefs. Eventually you will witness your child connecting the dots to her own life.

PART TWO: THE TROUBLE WITH TROUBLES: MANAGING THE GIVENS OF LIFE

Trouble Number One: Failure:
Cozying Up to a Necessary Stop on the Road to Success

If J. K. Rowling, creator of the Harry Potter series, had let failure stop her, we would never know of the escapades of Harry and his Hogwarts pals. As a single mother on welfare, Rowling wrote the first manuscript on napkins at a café because she couldn't afford paper. The manuscript was *rejected* by many publishers before it was finally bought.

Another famed author, Susan Eloise Hinton, published her first novel at the age of seventeen—*The Outsiders*—inspired by her horrified reaction to the gang behavior in her hometown, Tulsa, Oklahoma. Many middle school–aged children know about this book, but what they may not know is that S. E. Hinton earned a D in her creative writing class the same year that she started writing that book. Imagine if she had decided that D meant she couldn't write: Generations of children would have been deprived of the benefit of her insights.

As a culture, we haven't made it easy for ourselves to accept one of the most basic experiences of life: struggle. We stigmatize failure—it's for losers. And yet, *trying*, which is the part of losing that we can actually control—in a soccer game, a debate, a test, a college application—is the same necessary ingredient that ultimately allows us to succeed. The new construct we can lovingly and responsibly build for our children is that losing is not for "losers"; it's really for everyone because behind every great success there are lots of examples of things that didn't go so well.

Anatomy of Failure: Balancing on the Head of a Pin. Children who are focused on failing typically have a very specific definition of success, and the narrower the bull's-eye, statistically speaking, the greater the chance of missing it. With an all-or-none orientation, children get frustrated and give up easily. Given how hard it is to succeed in their system, it's that much easier to fail and there is no in-between. Their narrow definition of success creates opportunities for failure that you would never expect. Big things, small things—if they can use it as evidence that they've failed, they will. Children respond to this pressure in one of two ways. Either they crack under it, baffling their parents with why their otherwise strong child is disproportionately upset by an insignificant loss, or they protect themselves by reading between the lines: "If failure is at all a possibility, I'm not trying."

This fear of failure may be especially poignant in children who, through no fault of their own (and only to their credit), tend to do very well in most endeavors and don't often experience things not going their way. When things go off the track, their world *does* fall apart because their past experience told them that things would go very well. Finding themselves in unfamiliar territory leads to gross exaggerations, distortions, and mislabelings of why things happened the way they did. Isolated errors become generalized traits. With help, they can learn that one or even a few less-than-perfect grades don't in any way spoil their reputation as a student.

The Goal: Learning How to "Fail" Accurately

> Anyone who has never made a mistake has never tried anything new.
>
> —Albert Einstein

How to Talk Your Child or Adolescent Through Failure: Posing the Questions, Rather Than Having the Answers

When the going gets tough, the tough don't quit; they learn to broaden the criteria of what constitutes a success. Help your child analyze how he is deciding that he failed. Redirect him to define his goals: What did he want to get out of the project or challenge? Shine the spotlight with him on the mixed picture of good and bad; then, he will be able to see partial successes, or he will see that what his mind had decided was a big deal won't seem that way in a couple of hours or days. By shifting away from all-or-none thinking, and giving some thought to his own purpose, your child will feel less controlled by outside forces. In the same way that kids are more careful when they're spending their own money than when they're spending yours, if children are evaluating their own goals, rather than someone else's, they are more motivated to hunt for successes and may feel more satisfied by the process.

- Accept and empathize: *You're really upset right now. I know how disappointing this is for you. When you're ready, I'd like to understand what your mind is telling you about what happened and what it means to you.*

- Identify the goal: *What were you hoping would happen? What did accomplishing that mean to you?*

- Identify and learn from the failure: *What specifically was the failure? Was it really everything or just one thing? What do you know now that you didn't know before? Is there something else you would want to do differently as a result?*

- Identify your child's location on the learning curve: *When did you start learning this material? What will let you know that you mastered it? Where are you now in that process?* Ask your child to draw the curve and make an *X* to denote his current position. Next, have him estimate how long he thinks it will take to master or improve.

- Reframe: *Is there a silver lining? Is there some opportunity that this change of plans creates? Is there a strength that this failure highlights?* The child who may not do well on standardized tests can come to understand that his strength of looking deeply into the complexities of questions may work against him on a true-or-false test but will serve him well when writing essays.

- True versus imagined consequences: *What is your negative brain telling you is the worst possible consequence of this situation? What do you really, truly believe is the consequence of this situation? We can't fast-forward, or flip ahead the pages, but just like in a book or movie, we can't really know where this will lead, and that's a good thing.*

- Find the partial success: *What's the good part? What's the hard part? Are there aspects of this experience that did work, in addition to those that didn't?*

- No name-calling: Out of frustration children add insult to injury by saying "I hate myself," or calling themselves "stupid," "jerk," or "idiot" when they didn't do something right or don't know how to do something *yet*. It's hard to not get upset about this, but remember it's just a default reaction on their part when they're confusing the small thing that happened with the whole thing of who they are. Be matter-of-fact: *I know you're upset, but bad names only make it worse. Protect yourself! When we make a mistake or mess up, we can say, "Oops, I forgot," or "I don't know how to do this yet," or "Things didn't work out this time."* Or if you need to get mad, aim *away* from people; get mad at the situation.

- What part of this belongs to your child or teen? Your child can use the neutralizer machine from Chapter 5 and adjust the dials to see whether, instead of the outcome being all her fault, some was her contribution, and some not. Ask: *We can't change what's in the past, but we can find new ideas there for how to move forward. Now that it is over, looking back, is there any part of yours that contributed to the situation turning out this way? Is there anything that you would want to do differently next time? Are there things that you want to take credit for that you are pleased about?*

- Grade the grader: *Do you agree with the grade? What parts were interesting or challenging? Are there things you would have done differently if you were the teacher?*

- Contain the spill: *It feels like this changes your whole life, I know that feeling. Nothing can do that. This isn't a time to judge your whole life. I know you're feeling really upset now, but that is temporary. It's not a good time to make permanent assessments about yourself when you're upset, these things aren't permanent; they just feel that way.*

- Separate public from private: *How would you like people to react to this? What would that look like? Are there things you can do to lead them in that direction?* Kids who are known to do well in sports or academics, or even socially, may be minicelebrities in their school and feel that all eyes are on them when things go wrong and everybody knows. Especially with a teenager, you can encourage her to realize that while people may have their judgments about her situation, it's really her business how she wants to take it: *You actually set the tone for others. If you can take this in stride, others are more likely to follow your lead. Bigger than that, though, if you put this in perspective, it really doesn't matter what it means to someone else.*

- Give failure a more accurate name: *Now that we see it isn't really a failure, do you want to call it a fluke, a blip, a learning opportunity? What if every time you hear the word "failure" in your head you substitute that word instead? Imagine how that might help you get back on your feet sooner.*

- Reorient your attention: look for the good. For some children, failure lights up like bulbs on a Christmas tree. Like frogs wired to respond to little black dots (flies) in their visual field, children with a negative bent are wired to home in on what didn't work. The one B on a report card of A's will jump off the page; the one classmate who looks bored during your child's book report will torment him (even though this same classmate looked bored during *everyone's* book report); the one neutral comment amid the flurry of accolades will be remembered. Noticing the "bad" is not so much the problem; rather the problem is letting the bad obscure any good because doing so completely distorts the picture of how things really went. After your child has "dumped out the bad," encourage him to rewire a new string of bulbs, spotlight other facets of the experience, such as what went well, and how he would want to improve next time.

Trouble Number Two: Perfectionism: Guaranteed Unhappiness Every Day

A lightbulb moment came to Georgia when she was thoroughly enjoying the Christmas tradition of watching the Rockettes perform at Radio City Music Hall. In the middle of the show, she turned to her fourteen-year-old daughter, sitting on her right, and asked how she liked the show; looking very tense, her daughter replied, "I'm just waiting for someone to mess up." Dumbfounded, Georgia posed the same question to her husband, on her left, who also looked tense: "I just know some-one is going to mess up." To Georgia, the performance was spectacular entertainment; mistakes were the furthest thing from her mind. For the perfectionists whom she was sandwiched between, the specter of a mis-take loomed so large that they—through a process of identification—were feeling the strain of a possible false move. The Rockettes have been trained to hide their mistakes, but for Georgia's husband and daughter, there's no hiding.

Perfectionism—the rock-and-a-hard-place mind-set of having impos-sibly high standards (I have to be perfect at everything I do) and excessive self-criticism (If I don't do everything right, I'm a total failure)—is on the rise. A recent study found that more recent generations of college students (and you can be sure, it didn't just start in college) reported significantly more perfectionism both in the expectations for themselves (up 10% between 1989 and 2016) and their sense of being judged by impossible standards of others (up 33% in that time period) as well as their judgment of others needing to be perfect (16%).[1]

We don't need the research to tell us what we see around us, the striv-ing for perfection evident in every flawless corner of our picture-perfect airbrushed lives. But still, given how unpredictable life is (sometimes in exciting and inviting ways), clinging to an everything-needs-to-be-just-right orientation is not sustainable and is going to lead to disappoint-ment and frustration every day, and over time, perfectionists can get really irritable! Their misery that those around them experience is just a fraction of the misery they feel inside.

A hallmark of perfectionistic thinking is that everything feels of equal and paramount importance. Perfectionists are always on the clock; when there's perfection to be had, anything else is wasting time. In short, be-ing a perfectionist is like working for a really bad boss who demands all of your time and is never happy. And this is why we say these kids are not their own worst enemy, their perfectionism is. Fortunately, they are actually the boss, and they can retrain the tyrant to focus on *excellence* (having integrity in what they do) as opposed to perfectionism.

What's a parent to do? Watching your five-year-old throw out paper after paper when he can't make his B's just so, or your middle schooler refuses to turn in an assignment because it's not good enough even though he's worked on it for ten hours when the teacher said it should take two, or seeing your teen anguish for hours over her appearance or which picture to post on social media and is profoundly dissatisfied with them all, parents universally just want their kids to relax. They want to take the pressure off. But this is like telling people on the edge of a cliff to just relax. They are not going to listen. You are not credible in that situation, not until you see it like your kids do. Not until you see just how far they feel they can fall.

Perfectionism isn't about actual consequences. This is why no amount of urging to relax will work. It's a mind-set of absolutes. There's only one bull's-eye, and if you don't hit it, you are nowhere. Teaching kids about the perfectionistic mind-set is how you depersonalize the process: Don't make it a criticism of them as a person, and join with your child in understanding that, like other anxieties, the fear feels very real, but that part of their brain is not giving them reliable information.

People with perfectionistic thinking are limited by the idea that there is one way things *should* be—meaning, that if you are not living life and acting in that "perfect" way, you are a slacker or making a bad choice. They won't give up easily. So, the first line of business is to support their desire to work hard and be successful, and while everything may seem "essential" to them, chances are they aren't happy. Help them name that and find what is meaningful, what's in it for them. What are the hard parts of the way things are now. Then, help them sort out which behaviors support their success, and which do not. This project is not a race, it's an important fundamental shift in their value system. You are not asking them to give up striving for excellence, but to take risks with the parts that ultimately are hindrances to their success.

Talking to many, many children and teens (and their parents!) about perfectionism over the years, I find it best to stick with my long-distance learning model: point to *other* people's examples first so the lessons feel more palatable. In the case of perfectionism, I talk about professional athletes and entrepreneurs who have to embrace the growth mind-set (see Chapter 4) because many have perfectionistic tendencies, but they had to overcome those or they would never have been successful—because success requires being able to improve and do better and better, and that requires learning and taking risks—which may be very much not perfect and messy in the process. And while we are at it—why do those athletes, musicians, entrepreneurs, you name it practice so much and work so hard? Must be because that's how they improve and get things done. I talk about how successful business people (somehow they have the most clout with many kids!) have to leave their perfectionism aside or they won't be good collaborators (because they'll be judging their coworkers), won't be happy or healthy (stress negatively impacts health), will cause friction in the office (because being constantly dissatisfied causes tension), will be risk-averse and less creative and innovative (can't take a chance unless you know it will work), will waste time on inessential details (because everything big and small has to be perfect), and will miss big picture opportunities (can't lift head up from desk with the project at hand).

Take Steve Jobs, who changed the world, not only of technology and computing, but by developing the iPhone, he changed the shape of how we live our lives. His relentless pursuit of perfection in the early years caused friction with employees, he fired talent who wouldn't follow his detailed instructions, and he delayed releases by being essentially a micromanager. Ultimately, these issues led to Steve's being fired from Apple. It was only when he made changes in his thinking and interactional style that he was able to come back and lead this unprecedented success of Apple computers.

Here are red flags to see if your child's or teen's struggles are more than just wanting to do well, and are actually a sign of perfectionism.

- Ruled by the idea that things "should" be a certain way or people "should" act a certain way, both themselves, and others

- Becomes highly anxious, upset, irritable, or angry about the possibility of making mistakes or doing less than what they envisioned for a task

- Because of inflexibility, easily frustrated and upset when doesn't understand or things aren't going as expected

- Sees life into all-or-none terms, no continuum; if it's not good it's terrible; people are mean, not sometimes unpleasant; if a strikeout in sports, they are a failure

- Won't delegate or does all work in a group project because others won't do to same standard

- Everything must be perfect: schoolwork, appearance, room, social interactions

- May review interactions to make sure has not made any "mistakes"
- Difficulty starting tasks, ongoing procrastination to avoid getting stuck
- Excessive thoroughness and time spent doing and redoing, rechecking, rewriting
- Refusal to try anything unless certain of the outcome
- Extreme fear of embarrassment or humiliation, disappointing others, or appearing unprepared in any way
- Fixates on what did wrong
- Insists that one must make one's best effort at all times, and judgmental of those who don't
- Inflexible thinking—there is one way that things *should* be done that is the right way

For some kids, they experience perfectionism as an unwanted and intrusive, internalized Mr. Perfect who is relentlessly unsatisfied. They would love to dump their perfectionism and make their own standards. Although the process will take intention and effort, they're already on board. Bossing back Mr. Perfect, debating him, saying thanks but no thanks, and starting the brave task of establishing their own standards (even though it will feel very wrong at first) are the tacks to take.

For kids whose perfectionism is more entrenched—they aren't totally unhappy with it, can't debate it, can't see anything wrong with it except that everyone is bugging them because they are taking too long—the goal is to help establish flexibility and a sense of scale and proportion.

Change the Language. Instead of saying "you are being a perfectionist, say, "Mr. Perfect is bossing you around," or for older kids, "those perfectionistic thoughts are really trying to control at you right now."

Change the Narrative. Create the same distance and choice as with all other types of negative distorted thinking. It's not you, it's your inner Mr. Perfect, and you can give him the boot. What else can happen with frustration besides insisting that it not be so? We can relabel what is happening, change the narrative, catch that moment of frustration, say yes to it—normalize it, help kids and teens to see that this is part of a process of growth. This is what humans may want—no frustration, no ambiguity, no error, but this is not what human beings can do, and that's okay.

Discuss Beliefs About Success and Failure. In a calm moment, zoom out and talk with your child, whether eight or eighteen, about what success means, how it happens. Explore the beliefs in the relationship between success and failure (see Chapter 4 for more ideas). Likely your child thinks they are mutually exclusive instead of inextricably linked.

Look for the Partial Successes. Have your children look for the excellence or even good enough progress amidst what feels like the "unfinishedness" or imperfections.

Talk About Sustainable Standards. Help them find their own reasons why there are costs to this mind-set. Discuss how perfectionism is interfering with the quality of their life.

Switch out "Should" for "Preferences." Kids may say, "I *should* do this presentation perfectly; I *should* get an A on this test; I *should* have the perfect outfit every day." This creates a false sense of urgency; help them hear that, gently, by reflecting back, "Is that a real *should* or something you would prefer?" Substitute the word "prefer" early and often.

Do Small Experiments. Mess up on purpose! The goal is to help kids see how to get the *positives* without so much unnecessary effort. Ask them to think about how they can have the good (reaching for excellence) without the costs—exhaustion, fear, missed time, never feeling happy, etc. What small step are they willing to consider? For kids—can they leave a Lego construction unfinished, or one part "wrong" (on purpose!)? For teens—can they leave one book at home that they usually bring but never need, not recopy notes, and check math once instead of twice?

Set Time Limits and Expectations. For younger children: use careful "turtle speed" for very important projects, racer "rabbit speed" for quick ones, and "pony speed" for everything in between. For older children, because perfectionism is about "never enough," have them set time estimates for how long they'll work on something—whether it's styling their hair or studying for a test. They can set a timer on their phone; even if they go over the time, it will likely be shorter because they have that external reminder of the passage of time that gets completely lost when perfectionism-brain is in charge. Have them establish benchmarks or expiration dates for the importance of their work: Does this matter for this week, this month, forever? Help your child define his own scale; have him write it down or draw it, and when he is getting stuck, ask, "How big or important do you want this to be? Is this how you wanted it to go?" Ask him, "How much time do you want to devote to this?

Keep a Check on Your Own Expectations for Your Children. While we all take pride in our children's successes, this can't be the only game in town for us or our kids. It is important to make sure that your children don't feel that *your* happiness and approval are contingent on their achievements. This leaves your youngster balancing on the head of a pin. What if they don't get into the "best" college? What if they don't make varsity? What if they get a C? Seeing these as deal-breakers for their self-esteem and yours is unhealthy. They don't control their grades or college acceptances. They only control their efforts. Take your expectations out of the equation; "child-contingent self-esteem" is a term psychologists have coined to describe parents who, whether secretly or overtly, gain their self-esteem through their children's accomplishments. Which, you might say, well that's too bad for the parent, but the fact is, it's too bad for all. If parents' self-esteem is hinged on their children's achievement, they are going to not only exert the amorphous "pressure" in subtle and not so subtle ways, they are also going to be more controlling in their interventions, which as we've seen is a parenting style associated with anxiety in children.

Trouble Number Three: Competition: Children Losing Badly

Anatomy of a Wounded Loser: All or None

"I rolled up the window faster than you—you lose"; "I got upstairs first—you lose." Even children who lack resourcefulness in many areas of their life have an uncanny knack of being able to turn any ordinary moment into a competition—when they're winning, that is. When they're losing, children with a negative mind-set are not sore losers; they are mortally wounded losers. It can be embarrassing for parents to whisper apologies for their child's public meltdown or explosion in the face of failure; at the same time, these parents are baffled and wondering to themselves whether their children are just not *willing* to lose, or their reaction is somehow out of their control. Should the parents punish the child or be understanding? Children in the loser-lose-all mind-set are approaching competition with the idea "If I lose, I'm a loser; if I miss the shot, I suck." What these formulations have in common is that there are zero degrees of separation between the *performance* of that person at that given time and the *worth* of that person, past, present, and future. Everything rests on that one moment. The magnitude of that loss for children overtakes their whole being, there is no point to their lives as they see it; as when a tidal wave hits a shoreline, there's nothing left but debris.

> I've missed more than 9,000 shots in my career, I've lost almost 300 games. Twenty-six times I've been trusted to take the game-winning shot and missed. I've failed over and over and over in my life. And that's why I succeed!
>
> **—MICHAEL JORDAN**

When we lose, we are in good company. Professional athletes provide the clearest examples, as there are so many examples of the extremes of winning and losing (all in one person, often even in the course of one game): Wilt Chamberlain is *still* one of the greatest basketball players of all time—but could not master the free throw. His record was 51 percent; the average pro player's is about 75 percent. Still, Wilt Chamberlain is the only player ever to score a phenomenal 100 points in a game and is in basketball's Hall of Fame. In baseball, Ryan Howard, first baseman of the Philadelphia Phillies, won the National League Most Valuable

Player Award in 2006. In 2006 and 2007, he hit more home runs (105) and had more runs batted in (285 RBIs) than any other player in major league baseball, but he also had 199 strikeouts in 2007—the all-time strikeout mark for a hitter in a season! Serena Williams, the most decorated women's tennis player in history, and the oldest player in history to be number one, won thirty-five Grand Slam titles and four Olympic gold medals, came back from a near-death experience after giving birth to her daughter, and went on to be a finalist in Wimbledon 2018. Although ultimately losing the title, it was a win, for her perseverance, grace, and sheer power.

And grown-ups aren't the only ones who know about perseverance and handling loss. Superstar Mo'ne Davis, from my hometown of Philadelphia, who famously said, "Throwing 70 mph—THAT'S throwing like a girl" in 2014, was the first girl in Little League World Series history to pitch a winning game. But Mo'ne knows about bouncing back from failure. After her team lost a key game in Cooperstown, New York, going against the number one team, all because of a few bad calls, a couple of weeks later, she and her team went on to win the Little League Championship. In Mo'ne's words, "you have to lose to win." There are many more examples of winning and losing all rolled up in one in our heroes in many other arenas in life. See the resource guide at the end of the book for more ideas.

Children can be "obsessed" with winning, not necessarily because they want others to lose or are looking forward to the sweet taste of victory. Rather, the obsession to win is an overprotection from the feelings of disappointment they are anticipating as being unbearable if they lose. For some children, there is a thin line between winning and losing, and there can never be enough protection. The strategy of expecting the worst so as not to be caught off guard *if* it happens often backfires, either because children are so convinced they will lose that they make this conviction come true by not even trying, or because they wear themselves out grieving about the loss in advance. To top it all off, when they find that they didn't fail at all, they're too exhausted to appreciate the success: It has been ruined by the obsession with winning.

How to Make Your Child a Smarter Loser:
Talking Your Child Through Losing

- Be empathic; share the experience with your child: *Everybody loses sometimes. Everybody. But that doesn't mean it feels good; it feels bad. It's okay to be sad. I feel sad when I lose, too. It feels really hard at first, but it doesn't last, and then you get to try again. Everybody feels this way when it happens; that's normal. We don't lose all the time, but when we do, it feels big and forever, but it passes and then you can figure out what you want to do next.*

- Expectations and consequences: Rather than telling your child that this doesn't matter, ask him, *What was the picture you had in your mind? Tell me what you were thinking, what this means to you, what do you think is going to happen, or not happen now?* If your child says that this loss means that he isn't the best, you can explore with him whether this one loss means that he isn't the best, and also whether he really needs to be the best to enjoy himself.

- Find the partial wins and the partial losses: If you want your child to have a balanced view of his performance, model that view, and ask him to find what went well, as well as what went wrong.

- Intrinsic value: There's more to playing than winning. Once you have discussed the basic plan for resetting expectations for winning and losing, and for managing losses, refocus on the purpose. What else can he derive out of the experience? Is he improving his game, is he enjoying himself, was it a stretch to try something new, and what is it that he'd like to accomplish by the end of the season?

- What if you were the only winner? Broaden the perspective and do a table turner with your child: *Imagine if every time you played with your friend Charlie, he had to win. He would choose only games where he would win; he would leave the game if he wasn't winning and get angry. What would that be like for you? What would you want to say to Charlie?* See whether there is something that your child can write down to remember for the next competitive situation that comes along.

- Refocus on the learning curve: Sometimes what you learn from losses is what you want to do differently next time. If we look at Olympic athletes, almost as amazing as their feats of athleticism—the triple loops on the ice, the slaloms—is the levelheaded way they manage their successes as well as their disappointments. Whether they've won or lost, they talk strategy: "Well, I just focused on the board," or "I need to work on my footwork." The fact that these most skilled and gifted human beings on the planet humbly bring the subject back to strengthening their skills must mean that this is a good way to go.

- Encourage good sportsmanship: If your child has made a scene in the past when losing, you can see whether he is ready to apologize and explain, "That loss really got to me that day. I'm sorry I never said, 'Good game.'" Going forward, your child can choose his one-liners for being a good sport (giving specific compliments to fellow players, congratulating the winners) and practice them with you so that he feels he can say them sincerely. To get to the heart of the project, ask your child what compliments have meant most to him when he has won something, and see if he can find a way to honestly share that gift with someone else. You can help him anticipate how he'll feel when he says it; while he may think that he is giving something away by giving a compliment, you can help him remember from his own experiences how receiving a smile and knowing that he was the trigger for that other person's happiness can be very rewarding in and of itself.

- Find opportunities to win some, lose some: Sometimes parents think the solution for teaching kids to cope with losing is to let them do it all the time. But if it isn't a "fair fight" and children know that they are going to lose every time, they will likely give up, and that would actually be an adaptive response in that circumstance. If you were arm wrestling with your young child and you played your best, you would win every time: Where's the fun? There is no set formula for number of wins to losses that your child should experience (if you are playing games with him), but watch his face. As in any growth process, it's better to look for steady progress than to overwhelm your child.

Obstacles to Dealing with Losing Gracefully

Pregame Huddle: Expecting to Win: A Losing Strategy

Whether they are gearing up for Monopoly or a wrestling match, when children go into a game focused on winning, it not only creates added stress but *distracts* them from doing their best. See how Olympic soccer gold medalist Brandi Chastain focuses—getting into the moment before the game: "When I put my uniform on over my head, my game face goes on. It's letting nothing on the periphery penetrate my focus."

Talk to your child about her "game face"—what she wants to focus on and how she can turn off her competitive head and say, "Not now!" to her distracting thoughts about needing to win. Your child can't predict the outcome of the game, but the one thing that she and she alone *can* control is her effort. Ask your child to identify the specific strengths and strategies she wants to bring to the game. This way, with her own personal agenda set beforehand, regardless of the outcome your child can see how much she improved and met her own personal goals.

The Postgame Recap: Not Only Criticism Need Apply

If at the end of knocking himself out on the field for two hours, the focus in his head and broadcast in stereo from his coach and/or parents is everything he did wrong (even if that is presented constructively), your child is going to develop a very negative relationship to losing, and to playing altogether. It's a double whammy: You not only *don't win,* but as your consolation prize, you get to hear everything you did wrong. Eleven-year-old Kent dreaded talking to his dad after a baseball game because the whole ride home would be a recitation of how to improve his game. Although Kent's dad was well meaning and very dedicated to his son's success, his timing was off. His son was feeling dejected hearing all he did wrong. Instead, point out the good moments to your child, and it may be even more effective and enjoyable to ask him to point them out first and then echo his pride with your own. After you've talked about what went well, *ask* your child whether there is something he'd want to do differently. The question will be more meaningful and he'll be less defensive if he's discovering it himself. If you have additional concerns, let him know *after* you've focused on the good.

In the following dialogue, where ten-year-old Sally lost her first tennis match, we see the self-discovery happening, with her dad's questions as a guide.

SALLY: They are so unfair, they are so awful. I should have won!

DAD: That is really hard when you really thought it was going to happen. Do you want to talk it through now so you can be ready for next time, or do you want to give it a rest?

SALLY: Next time? There's no next time. I'm done. It is so unfair.

DAD: You're really mad about not winning. I bet you don't even want to try—because you think it might happen exactly the same way again.

SALLY: Well, not exactly the same. I don't know what's going to happen.

DAD: You're exactly right—that's true. We don't know exactly what will happen. We can make a basic prediction, and well, what else can we do to make the outcome we want?

SALLY: What do you mean?

DAD: Well, we can't control how the other players will do. What is the part that only you can control?

SALLY: What do you mean?

DAD: Well, what do you think athletes do to prepare for a game or competition? Do they hope for the best, or is it more technical than that?

SALLY: They practice. They work on what they need to improve, that kind of stuff.

DAD: Okay. How would that strategy look on you? Are there things that went well that you want to just practice a little, and then are there other things that you want to build up your skills with?

SALLY: Yes.

DAD: You know, I wonder if there is another part of this that could help. Athletes say if they are putting a lot of pressure on themselves about winning, that gets distracting and stressful. When I pressure myself about doing a presentation, I get nervous, so I just focus on *what* I'm doing instead of *how* I'm doing, and my focus and performance are much better. What do you want to say to yourself next week?

SALLY: Focus on my follow-through. Focus on—focusing!

DAD: Hey, that sounds really good. I'm really proud of how you worked through this. I know you're disappointed in how things went today, but being able to manage the disappointments is what is going to keep you in the game—not the number of trophies you win.

SALLY: Yeah, I feel better now. It doesn't feel terrible anymore. I did do a good job with my serves; they were always strong. I just need to work on the power of my returns—my backhand especially. I knew it, I just didn't practice it enough.

DAD: Well, hey, that's really neat that you went for it—and that it isn't a mystery what happened. Now you know what to do: Just keep at it.

Trouble Number Four:
Disappointment: Crushed by Expectations

"The worst day of the year is coming up." Would we ever have guessed that thirteen-year-old Michael was referring to Christmas, the day that so many children consider the best day of the year? "I'm never happy on Christmas, because I'm sure I'm not going to get what I want, and even when I do, I've been so upset about it already that I don't even feel good when it turns out the way I want it to." Understandably Michael's mother's reaction to this statement vacillated between empathic concern and flat-out frustration. If words like *ungrateful, selfish,* and *bratty* are popping up in your mind, that would be a very normal *first* reaction to Michael's seemingly self-inflicted predicament. But on consideration that it's not likely for a child to knowingly make himself miserable on Christmas, our *second* thought must be that there's got to be a no-fault explanation!

I have to watch what I say all the time. If I mention anything—any plan, purchase, idea, whatever—in an offhanded way and then I don't do it, Joey will totally fall apart and say, "But you promised." I think he really believes it, but I don't understand why.

—FATHER OF AN EIGHT-YEAR-OLD

Disappointments are to the soul what the thunderstorm is to the air.

—FRIEDRICH VON SCHILLER

Anatomy of Disappointment: When Life Rubs You the Wrong Way

What could create such intensity of feeling, whether anticipating disappointment like Michael, or in the aftermath when kids like Joey feel truly devastated? These children, by no fault of their own, get an idea, and it becomes set in stone. Their ideas, desires, and expectations make deep impressions; they are not dabblers about their plans—they are committed! It can be all the harder when it doesn't work out. Like the thunderstorm that Schiller described, with disappointment these children are juggling several elements of compounding difficulties: a surprise, a change, a transition, and a dissatisfying setback all rolled into one. Imagine that all of the molecules in your child's body were organized around one idea, and suddenly the idea vanished, and all the molecules were scattered, all charged up and nowhere to go. Until they regroup, there is chaos. Often, children get stuck in the "scattered" phase and get very unglued, demanding, and cranky; it's not a pretty sight. The goal is not to avoid that phase, rather, kids need to release it, find a safe way to contain it, work through it efficiently, and help them regain control because that self-control is the other thing that got lost in the shuffle.

Some children are so afraid of being disappointed that they create the very situation that they are afraid to face. Michael and kids like him need to understand that what is fueling those very uncomfortable feelings is the story they are telling themselves about the situation. It may be bad to start with, but their thinking is making it horrible. Yes, it is disappointing when you don't get the gift you wanted, but the caption on that picture—"I never get what I want! I'll never get what I want!"—only turns up the heat and makes you feel more upset. If Michael's mother used the brain train exercise from Chapter 2, they could both see that Michael's initial thoughts ("This is my only chance. I'm going to hate my gift. They probably won't get me what I want. I never get what I want.") are sending him down the negative track, creating feelings of anger, frustration, and upset; and the action, by Michael's own admission, is being mean and grumpy. They could then head down the accurate track: *How do you want to be thinking about Christmas if you were in charge in your brain? You can rewrite the program. What would it say? Do you really think that you'll be disappointed? Even if you are, is this your only chance in your life to get a present?*

With new expectations and thoughts in place, Michael's stress temperature would come down, and he could be more relaxed about the holiday and start enjoying some of its other aspects, rather than anticipating it like a test that he's sure he'll fail.

Goal: Containing the Spill and Moving On

For children with a tendency toward the negative, disappointing experiences don't just ruin that one event; they spill over and ruin all surrounding events. The game plan is to help children learn to be more flexible with their expectations so they can be better buffered from any eventuality.

To explain the basic concept of managing disappointment, parents—in a calm moment—can introduce the idea of *strong expectations* and how they can sometimes do more harm than good, by telling a "long-distance story"—about themselves, an invented character, or, as in the following script, man's best friend:

Dogs think that every outing is to the dog park. In fact, every time you go to get your coat or walk to the door, they may bark excitedly, thinking, "Ooh, walk time, walk time!" Because they are so excited about the dog park, they may get sooo disappointed when you're just going to put the trash out. We might laugh and think, "Hey, Fido, you can't go to the park all the time, and you don't need to go to the park all the time," but in a way, when we leave the house, we may think we need something good to happen all the time, too, and we kind of stick to an expectation and then get disappointed when it doesn't come true. Is the solution for Fido to forget about the dog park and think, "I'll never go to the dog park"? Will that be any better for him? Right, he'll just be guaranteeing that he'll be miserable by telling himself the "bad" message. Can you think of a different solution? What if he thinks, "I'd like the dog park, but I could also chew on this marrow bone and bark through the window at squirrels. Either way I'm covered." Well the good news is that though dogs may not be able to come up with those options so easily, human beings are incredibly well suited to the job. When we are disappointed, it feels as if we are stuck in a room of disappointment forever, but we need to know that the door is always there to step out and see what else is possible. Give yourself time to recover. The speediest plan isn't necessarily the best plan for you, but when you're ready, you can decide on your next move.

Key points to work on with your child:

- *How big is the problem? It feels like a disaster. On a scale of 1 to 10, how bad is it?*

- *What is the worst part of it for you?* You may be surprised to hear your child's response to this—"I have to get the new game today; if I bring it to school next week, no one will care; it will be old already"—and it will help you clear up distortions and brainstorm what else your child can do.

- *How long will the disappointment last? A day, a week? How upset do you want to be about this now, given that it is going to feel better soon?*

- *Is there a part of this you can control, change, or improve?*

- Put a time limit on the venting but blame Disappointment Guy, not your child: *How long do you want this disappointment to make you feel bad about these things?* or *How can we make sure that Disappointment Guy doesn't mess up anything else in your day?* If your child isn't naturally winding down but becoming more convinced of the injustice that has been done, it's time to cut it off: *Okay, it's time to move on now. I think the sooner we get going on Plan B, the sooner you'll start to feel better.*

- Help your child find alternative things to say to himself to counter the alarm messages going through his mind.

Things your child can say:

- *I wasn't expecting this. Change is hard for me, but it's okay.*
- *This is a big change—it feels uncomfortable.*
- *I need a minute to regroup. I know this feeling won't last.*
- *I'm going to take a deep breath and reassess the situation.*
- *This isn't what I wanted, but I can handle it.*
- *This feels bad, but that feeling is temporary. I'll feel better soon.*

Obstacles to Managing Disappointment: Getting Stuck on Just So

Some children are born with a "just-so" stance toward life: It isn't their fault and it isn't about being perfect or controlling, it's just about *not* being surprised. These are the children who ask lots of questions and need to be able to foresee exactly what is going to happen each day down to the minute, who is going to be there, what it's going to be like. For these children, when things change, nothing is left in the bank: Everything was tied up within the picture they had in their mind. To increase their autonomy, don't plan out every second; *ask them* to try to answer their own questions about the possible plans for the day. They will be less locked into the "one and only" answer. To get their flexibility neurons limber, ask *them* to brainstorm "glitches," places where the plan could go off track (e.g., the movie is sold out, the restaurant doesn't have tables, there is traffic, and we're too late for the game), and then ask them to brainstorm "fixes"—the array of options they can generate to solve the problem. For more ideas about developing flexibility in the face of disappointment, please see the end of Chapter 3 on big feelings.

Trouble Number Five: Jealousy: Self-Inflicted Misery Courtesy of Another Person (Other Person Incidental)

It's not surprising that jealousy is a frequent companion of children who pick out and emphasize the failures in their life. In contrast to the painfully skewed view they've constructed of their own situation, it is not hard for them to see others looking as if they've got it made. Children who feel jealous think that the problem and the solution reside with the other person: That person is *making* their life miserable; if they would just stop it, everything would be fine. The good news, as we well know, is that we actually hold the key to both the problem and the solution. We may not be able to have what others do—but the story we tell ourselves about how terrible or unfair that is, is completely open to our revision.

> Jealous people poison their own banquet and then eat it.
>
> **—UNKNOWN**
>
> To cure jealousy is to see it for what it is, a dissatisfaction with self.
>
> **—JOAN DIDION**

Anatomy of the Green Monster

The formula for jealousy is a two-part punch: First, there's the sadness and inadequacy for not having what you want, but then—the clincher—there's the anger and hostility you direct toward the person you're jealous of, as if that person expressly *caused* your distress. Not only is the child jealous of another child's accomplishments, but he perceives that lucky child as an *obstacle* (the obstacle is that person's advantage) to his achieving his goal. He then becomes focused on that child (rather than on the goal itself) because he thinks that without knocking down that child in one manner or another, he can't achieve his own goal.[2] This is where the opposite of negative thinking being *possible* thinking is so important. Fixated on the one pathway that he perceives as blocked, the child in a negative tailspin doesn't see that there are many other roads leading to Rome—Rome being either a new toy, a good grade, or a playdate with a friend. Let your child first briefly spill out the jealous feelings freely (you can curtail them with a kind, but firm, "Okay, now I think we need to move on" if the ranting is ramping up rather than resolving). You also need to help your child move on if his efforts to console himself turn into a negative rant about the other child or children. Aim away from people. Redirect your child to express his anger or frustration without it being at another's expense. The longer your child stays wrapped up in his anger at the other child, the longer it will take to solve the problem because the heart of the matter is how your child is feeling about himself.

The Goal: Refocusing Your Children on What They Need

As in Ms. Didion's quote, the quagmire of jealousy is that our feelings of inadequacy in ourselves get mixed up with our feelings of anger at or envy of other people. Just as when we approach a big tangle of yarn, it's hard to find the end to start with to set things right.

Talking Your Child Through Jealousy

Help your child separate what belongs to whom by dividing a piece of paper in half and having her write down: "What upsets me about the other person? What upsets me about me?" Sort through these thoughts by asking other questions:

- *Is it more that you want it, or you don't want him to have it?*
- *What matters most to you about this?*
- *What did you think would happen if you did get this [coveted item or recognition]?*
- *Do you think that is realistic?*
- *Is there still another way of getting there?*
- *Is that (item or recognition) a nice piece or an essential piece in your reaching your goal?*
- *Will it matter in the long run, or just in the short run? How short-term is it? How soon do you want to be over it?*

Because problems are meant to be solved, add a third column, "Steps I can take to change things." Once you have helped your child redefine his goal by using the suggested questions, then you can think through with him what is the best way to invest his time: How long does he want to stay angry? When and how does he want to get moving toward his goals?

Talking About Jealousy with Your Children

Because temperatures rise when jealous feelings are in the mix, it can be helpful to have a way of explaining the "why" to your child. Sometimes the more angry kids feel, the more true or justified they think the source of the anger is. This is not the case. This is how feelings work, this is not how life works. Our feelings can quickly intensify when we feel threatened or blocked from something that matters to us, but remember the quick but inaccurate amygdala we learned about in Chapter 3. Our reactions happen first, and our logical mind might not catch up with us until later. These scripts will help to normalize and defuse the intensity of jealous moments.

Script for Young Children

It's hard when you want something that someone else has, or want to be able to do something as well as someone else. Everyone feels that way sometimes. Did you know that? Sometimes I get mad that Dad can draw and I don't know how. But you know what's worse than that? It's when my Meany Brain makes me feel that if I can't do that one thing, I can't do anything! It is playing that everything/nothing trick on me: Drawing is everything, and if I can't do it, I've got nothing. So I have learned to boss back and teach Mr. Meany about this with the One Thing, Not Everything strategy: It's just one thing, and I still have everything else I know how to do. Here, I'll name a few things to show Mr. Meany how he's wrong. And you know what? I bet if I wanted to draw better, there are things I could do—can you help me think of some? Or sometimes it feels as if we have a Gimme Guy inside, and if someone has a toy we want, Gimme Guy says mean things like, "You don't have anything good; that's the only thing that's good; your toys are bad." Is Gimme Guy right? What can we tell Gimme Guy?

Script for Older Children

Jealousy is such an uncomfortable feeling. It almost feels as if you're not your-self when you feel jealous. You might not like things about yourself and think that what other people have, or who they are, is the best way to be, and you've got nothing. It's as if someone has seized all of your valuables (your strengths, all the things you like about yourself), and you don't have access to any of them; they are all on hold or suddenly not of value because in that moment it feels as if the one thing that you want, or the only thing that matters, is the very thing you don't, or can't have. It's not fair to compare yourself to others when you are feeling empty. Open up the safe. You have unlimited access to those assets. You may need to cool down first before you do this, but once you've filled up the safe again with what really matters about you, then you can ask yourself, "How important is this thing to me? Do I really want it? Will I want it in a few months? Are there things that I can do to make it happen in my own life? If I switched shoes with that person, how would I feel if they were angry at me? Would I think that was fair? How would I want them to feel—happy for me, or even just neutral? Is there a way to express that in this situation?"

Obstacles to Managing Jealousy: Eliminating the Conditions That Foster Jealousy in Your Home

We know we don't like it when our kids speak the jealous language, but it may be that our interactions are making conditions ripe for our children to get lost in those feelings. The following checklist is a starting point to do a "green" cleaning, ridding your home of comparisons, blaming others for your shortcomings, and other things we all do (but would do well to do less of).

- Be aware of your own double standards. Are you letting jealousy of someone else block the entrance to a goal that matters to you? Keep an ear out for that. You can be sure that your child is listening in.

- Be careful not to compare your child to others (even in a positive way). Comparison sets up the tracks for the jealousy train. Rather, appreciate your child's strengths in her own right, and discuss weaknesses relative to her own situation.

- Model generosity: give compliments, demonstrate good sportsmanship, and admire others aloud, to show your children that these actions don't diminish your portfolio; they only add to it.

- Share the stage: In your household, make sure that everyone has moments in the spotlight.

PART THREE: WHEN LOSS HAPPENS FOR REAL

In contrast to the day-to-day frustrations of life, losses such as divorce, illness, and even death, while universally challenging, can present to negative-minded children added dimensions and layers of meaning that ultimately interfere with their resolution of these already difficult events. It may seem out of place to consider these major events in the same breath as losses of a much smaller magnitude, and yet the skills for processing both are the same, as are the risks in misinterpreting them. In the end, we need to honor all of our children's experiences—big and small—and always help them reach for freedom. In this section we look at two examples of coping with real losses: death and divorce.

Coping with Death: Nothing Will Ever Be the Same

Troy, a very bright, soulful eight-year-old, was struggling with the loss of his beloved grandmother a year before. For Troy, complicating the normal reaction of grief were his ideas and expectations about the grief. Whenever he got upset, he would start to think, "This is never going to stop; I'm always going to feel this way; I'm never going to feel better again," and then he would get frustrated because he couldn't enjoy anything and was feeling so sad; he was grieving not only his grandmother, but the loss of his life as he had known it. Rather than consoling him in his hour of need, his thoughts were compounding the scope of the problem exponentially. We talked together about how grief comes in waves, and even though when the wave hits it *feels* as if it won't ever stop, it does pass, and you kind of keep going until the next wave hits. Instead of thinking ahead and borrowing grief that hadn't even happened yet ("Tomorrow is probably going to be ruined because I'll probably be too sad to have fun with anything"), we worked on the idea that Troy didn't have to look for his sadness: When it came, he would manage that wave, and when it passed, he would go back to what he was doing. I explained to Troy that this is the way grief works for everyone: It comes, and it goes, and while we never forget the person we've lost, little by little we resume our activities because that is what our loved ones would want us to do. Troy hadn't thought about how his grandmother would want him to be happy; that idea was a relief to him. Troy wrote down a few thoughts on a card to keep with him:

New Track:
Grieving is part of life. It is normal and it comes and it goes. It changes some things but not everything changes. I have to have faith that it won't always feel this way. My grandmother would want me to enjoy myself. I loved spending time with my grandmother, but I can also share my gifts with others. I will be okay in time. Be patient.

Thinking these thoughts helped lift the load off Troy's heavy heart, and he was able to move through the grieving process—working on a memory book of his time with his grandmother, writing messages to send up in a balloon to her, and finding other people to play games with that he had enjoyed with her. Troy had trouble accepting her death, and he wanted to insist that things be the way he wanted them to be. This was one situation he couldn't change: His grandmother had died, but he could decide whether he was going to cling to how he wanted things to be or tell himself that he didn't need everything to be the way he wanted to be happy. Over time, Troy's mood brightened and he felt more empowered that he could be back in charge of his life again, rather than having it be on hold every day.

Coping with Divorce

For ten-year-old Constance, her parents' divorce was devastating. Divorce is devastating for any child initially, but Constance's distress grew over time because she felt that the divorce was her fault somehow, or that it had been her responsibility to prevent it. "I'm the fixer in the family," she explained. "I always know what to do to make things better. I write notes to people, I do nice things, I can break up fights, but I failed at this, and now look what happened." Constance didn't even want to tell her parents how she was feeling because, true to form, she didn't want them to feel any worse knowing that she was feeling so bad.

Constance and I took the brain train ride. Her thoughts—"This is my fault; I'm a failure; I can't do anything right"—were leading to feelings of sadness, and as a result, she didn't want to be with her friends, and even when she spent time with her mom or dad, she kept thinking about how sad she was and felt doubly bad that she couldn't even have fun when she was supposed to. We talked about what a caring, loving person Constance is; about how sometimes people like that—because they are so good at caring and figuring things out—start to feel as if it's their job to take care of everything; about how that's not true; about how it was her job to do things that she enjoyed; and about how the blaming thoughts in her head were keeping her from doing that. Going down the smart track of the brain train, she came up with some new thoughts: "Divorce is hard, but it's nobody's fault. It's my job to take care of myself. My parents are there for me. I'm allowed to have fun. Things are going to be different, but different doesn't mean bad." When she was thinking those thoughts, she felt more peaceful and comfortable, and even though she was still sad sometimes, she knew that it was okay to feel that way. But behaviorally this new thinking freed her up to get back to seeing her friends because now she knew that she was allowed to, that it didn't mean that she wasn't upset about the divorce, and because she now understood that it was not her job to be upset about it all the time.

CONCLUSION

In this chapter we've explored strategies for managing adversities in life, those that we may think our way into, and those, such as death and divorce, that are not under our control. No matter what the circumstance or event, we *always* have choices about how we talk to ourselves about these events. Our thinking can turn an already bad moment into something much worse, or we can use our thinking in the face of adversity to rally, regroup, and start again, in Henry Ford's words, "more intelligently." We can try to gloss over these moments with our kids, gritting our teeth till they're over, biting our tongue, or we can step up—as we want our kids to—and face these difficult often messy feelings and see that they come from narratives that need some good revising; the first draft of our reactions to difficulties is never accurate. It's not our fault. It's our wiring and we can learn to connect the wires differently going from failure, disappointment, and grief to growth. Our children can learn from us that what starts out feeling so bad, or impossible, or wrong, or messy is manageable, survivable, and potentially holds for us invaluable lessons to learn. Managing adversity is one of the great secrets to success. Don't keep it from your child; pass it on.

Family Activity

We briefly visited the famous failure examples in Chapter 4. Have your child choose a hero whose "failures" can inspire her to persevere in life when things don't go well. You can choose one, too. Do a little Internet searching together; there are so many inspiring stories to choose from, you could make this a monthly family ritual. Have everyone share their favorite stories, and when your child is struggling with a disappointment or failure, ask her what she thinks her hero would tell her. For example, one child who chose Michael Jordan as her hero—not only because of his amazing career, but because of his understanding that losing is inherent in winning—would cope with stress and disappointment by saying, "This is one situation to run by Michael," and in doing so, she essentially gave herself the will to not give up.

9

NAVIGATING SOCIAL MEDIA: TAKING CHARGE OF A LIFE LIVED ON-SCREEN AND OFF

In *Eighth Grade*, a film about teenagers and social media, the protagonist Kayla Day has her own YouTube channel, gives advice about friendship, fashion, and school and exudes nothing but confidence. But once the cameras are gone, she's a scared young woman who doubts everything: her appearance, every word she manages to utter, even the possibility that she will ever make friends, given how weird and different she feels from how she perceives everyone else. She's hiding behind her on-screen persona. But who is she hiding from the most? Herself. By the end of the film, through trials and tribulations and embarrassing moments at pool parties and close encounters with boys, she begins to realize that she doesn't need to conform to some idea of how she *should* be, and she starts to be herself, embracing in full teen mantra: "You can't be brave unless you're scared." She makes a time capsule to be opened on her high school graduation, which captures the sense she has of the future promise of growing into her authentic self: "Stay cool," she says, "I can't wait to be you."

•

We need look no further than our own inner dialogue when we check social media (did they not like that picture? Am I not as close a friend as she is? He went to the shore with that family and not us?) to appreciate the powerful relationship between this monolithic cultural experience and arbiter of approval and rejection, and the kindling of daily self-doubt. We saw in the Introduction how psychologists have identified that the increase in depression or decrease in sense of well-being is correlated with the rise in popularity of smartphones as a staple in kid's lives, and correlates with time on social media,[1] especially for girls;[2] the constant parent-child conflict trying to get kids off devices; the tragic consequences of cyberbullying. Even though we can't know exactly what this is like firsthand, we can help guide our kids through this, not by "caving" to our kids' demands, nor unilaterally refusing to listen to them, but by being willing to step into what feels like the uncharted waters between those extremes.

MAKING THE CONNECTIONS, WITHIN AND BETWEEN

What are we trying to help with? Kids connecting with themselves—and most important—kids connecting with each other. Child psychology expert Dr. Michele Borba, in her book *Unselfie: Why Empathic Kids Succeed in Our All-About-Me World*, connects the dots between the excessive self-focus of the look-at-me selfie-generation and their diminishing empathy skills.[3] Empathy may seem like a luxury, but a lack of empathy will actually impede kids' ability to work together, innovate, and acquire the flexibility and problem-solving skills they need to be successful in school, work, and life generally. Negative thinking and anxiety burden kids with a constant pull toward self-focused attention, analysis, and critiques, which preclude attention and focus on anyone else. There is a pressing need to right the ship, and parents can help equip their children with these four important lessons:

1. *Don't believe everything you see:* We teach kids that commercials are "fake" at a young age; similarly, they can learn that on social media everyone is doing the best commercial for themselves—it's not accurate, it's not comprehensive, it's highly curated and choreographed to create a specific and alluring narrative and get likes. In fact, if social media posts do not garner positive attention (at the rate of one like per minute), some kids will delete them.

2. *Everything in moderation:* We don't eat candy all day long even though we like it (but kids might have it for breakfast if we didn't set down some rules). Research on teens and social media support a "dosage effect": Some online engagement can have a neutral or even positive impact, but after a certain level, the dramatic dip in well-being is clear. Have the discussion with your kids to find healthier alternatives to social media, and help them learn to pay attention to their reactions and know when they've had enough.

3. *Trust yourself!* Throughout our kids' social-emotional development, we are working on the project of learning how to trust, whom to trust, how to trust your gut, and how to be trustworthy. Social media is not a substitute for real life. Support your child's process in making their own decisions and interpretations about what qualities are important to them, who and what they respect and trust in a friend, rather than accepting as a done deal the importance and popularity algorithms that social media platforms provide. It works both ways, so talk frequently with your youngsters about the kindness and appropriateness of their online behavior—just because everyone is doing something to be funny that's actually *mean* doesn't mean it's right.

4. *Don't go it alone—ask for help when you need it:* Part of what compromises kids on social media is getting into situations they don't know how to handle and might be challenging for anyone! They want to be independent and may make snap decisions that they later regret; they didn't stop to think—*Stop and think!* Kids don't understand (unless we teach them!) that true independence and maturity means asking for help when you need it with things, large or small. Your goal—through open communication with your child—is to help them to become good decision makers, and to model what that looks like for yourself. Whether it's a friend posting something sexually inappropriate (or asking your teen to), a classmate talking about suicide, a stranger asking for their address, it's important that kids know that when they feel unsure or confused about something, don't act, *ask*. Everything can wait. Feeling unsure about what to do may lead to more impulsive decisions, but being unsure is exactly the time *not to rush*. You might open up a discussion by showing your seams first. You can acknowledge that while you know it's also very different for

you in some ways, in other ways, even as an "old person," you may have trouble asking for help because you don't want to seem like you can't handle something, or that you're not cool for not understanding, or that you're bothering someone. You can give an example of when you tried to do something on your own but it would have been so much better if you'd asked someone for guidance. As parents, we know that this apparent "strength" can be a weakness; we need one another. End of story. Whether they are having trouble with the content of social media, or are feeling stuck, irritable, afraid, and addicted to the process in a social media context, kids should ask for help.

We are living in a time when technology and social media are like the air we breathe. Kids have grown up not knowing any other reality than the one they see on-screen, and they may be unaware that they have choices and agency in what they do with it—how much to be on social media, if at all. This is our starting point: Making life online a conscious process for our kids. Just like we discuss "IRL"—in real life—interactions that occur at school, we must do the same for the interactions in what may be thought of as the virtual cafeteria and hallways online. Is their social media helping them to feel connected or isolated? What parts do they enjoy? What parts are hard for them? How do they keep tabs on their experience? What signals can they use to determine what they need, how will they decide? Although our discussion here is primarily in reference to social media sites, such as Instagram or Snapchat, similar guidelines apply for video gaming and YouTube watching.

We must be willing as parents to "go there" with our kids; step into this territory that our kids may know more about than we do, and be two places at once: the aerial view of normalizing and understanding the instability of the teenage years, and the nitty gritty of being in touch enough (while granting reasonable and respectful autonomy) with what our teens are up to so we can help them translate and make sense of the experiences they are having online and in general. We can't opt out and throw up our hands; at the same time, we can't blame it all on social media. Kids made social comparisons long before the iPhone arrived. Daydreaming about how this person has more friends, better clothes, better teeth, better hair, whatever it was, we might come up short. Nor can we pretend we have all the answers. With our authoritative parenting hat on, we go in to help our kids learn how to equip themselves—that inside job of happiness and healthiness—to lead their lives in a way that is meaningful and fulfilling.

PARENTAL STANCE: DON'T CAVE, BUT DON'T DIG IN

We may take quick action out of our own fears and desire to protect our children from the lack of control that we perceive follows them on social media, but phones should not be whisked out of kids hands lightly. Teens are ready to be disappointed by our lack of understanding—the daughter's refrain in Freaky Friday, "You're ruining my life!" when her mom shuts off the breaker to her daughter's band practice in the garage or takes the door off its hinges. Parents have to find a way into their teen's life and the social media conversation is no different. Simple punishment—taking your teen's phone away—is not the way. They won't learn better habits for recognizing problems and regulating their use. It's about the conversation. Helping your teen to know the signs when they have had too much (irritability, sadness, hunger, depression, self-criticism), creating phone free zones (you must follow this, too!), and turning phones in an hour before bedtime as late-night phone use is especially associated with depression (and sleep-deprivation) in teens—they can use alarm clocks to wake up! Common Sense Media, a digital advice group, found recently that half of teens feel "addicted" to their phones, and 69 percent of parents agreed with that assessment. The addiction leads to daily tug-of-war, or tug-of-phone, and lots of conflict. However—parents do have influence—have the conversation, set reasonable limits and consequences when lines are crossed. Yes, sometimes that will mean kids' turning in their phones—but better that they get credit for handing them over than your whisking them out of their hands.

TO SPY OR NOT TO SPY, TO TAKE AWAY, TO NOT TAKE AWAY: THESE ARE NOT REALLY THE QUESTIONS

Parents wonder whether it's okay to use parental controls to monitor their kids' phone use and social media activity, or whether they should instead take their children's phones and spot check for any concerns. A phone is a privilege and likely parents foot the bill, but you also pay the rent or mortgage and it doesn't mean you should barge in on a closed door, especially when you've taught your kids that they should always knock. While in a sense, parents have the right to spy on their kids' phones (and yes, take away a phone), consider this: The phone can feel like a teens' lifeline; it's how they connect, socialize, and grow. If you take away that lifeline there will be backlash. Which may be worth it at times, but not when things are going well. Teens are working on the developmental tasks of autonomy and individuation. If your teen is doing her job of being honest, reliable, and respectful—the things she needs to do to earn your trust—it makes sense to show her that trust. If things change and you suspect that your teen is struggling or is in any sense in danger—and has not been able to tell you when you've first asked her what is up—then it is your job as a parent to protect your child, often from herself, and let her know that you have concerns and you want her to show you her phone. Your goal in this intervention is not to strip her of her rights, but to say that yes, you'll go to that uncomfortable place of questioning and searching—if she is not seemingly willing, or emotionally able, to tell you what's going on. Broaching this conversation with, "I really wish that you would tell me what's going on because I want to help, but if you can't, I'll need to step in myself."

A Word About Video Game Playing . . .

In this chapter, we are focusing on the challenges of not losing your teens to social media. Video games, while generally freer from the risk of embarrassment and blatant social comparison, can lure kids into a trance, making them forgo food, water, and the bathroom. We don't need research to tell us that kids spend too long in front of a screen, but how long do experts recommend that kids *should* be playing on game systems? Shockingly, one study published in the *Annals of Neurology*[4] concluded that just *one* hour of video games per week was associated with better motor planning and school achievement, but beyond that there was no benefit, and playing nine hours a week or more was associated with peer conflicts, conduct difficulties, and reduced social skills.

Establishing Tech-Free Zones

To make sure that your kids are cultivating life beyond the phone or video game talk to them about it. It may take some exploration and some . . . boredom, but eventually if you set the limit, they will figure it out. If you set the limits without any input from them, they may be inclined to sneak around and hack into your system, so better to discuss this together. If your child prefers to play video games all weekend or sit on Snapchat, talk about reasonable time limits and introducing other activities. Try to make this a collaboration. Some families put phones in a basket or shared charging dock during meals and before bedtime (30 to 60 minutes before). You can assign different family members on "basket duty" to collect and monitor the process. Ask your child to line up another activity to be ready for after tech time to ease the pain of withdrawal. There are also software programs or apps that parents can use to shut off the Internet on individual devices—parents can challenge their family to *not* need this by cooperating with time limits, but if it is needed, it's good it's there.

What's It Like to Be a Teen These Days?

Let's do a thought experiment. Imagine if one day your child came home from school and told you the teacher said, "Raise your hand if you like Susie or Johnny. Let's have a show of hands. Do you like their clothes? The way they look?" If such a vote ever took place, parents would be storming the principal's office. How arbitrary, how harmful. This is similar to how social media feels—with all the likes, views, and comments, people are, perhaps unknowingly, creating a hierarchy of what is likeable and successful—and it's not just in one class period—it's 24/7/365. Is social media to blame for the painful social comparisons and disappointments teens feel? Yes and no. The social comparison, fears of not measuring up, fears of being different, isolated—weird, unpopular are venerable guideposts on the terrain of normal adolescent development. We all may remember similar concerns from our day. But unlike our day—our status was not broadcast through real-time updates memorialized on the continuously updated iPhone stage for all our peers to see. This constant barrage of perceived inferiority has been correlated with increased rates of anxiety, sleeplessness, depression, and even suicidal thoughts in research studies.[5] At the same time that social media is tailor-made for addictive behavior (the dopamine rush with the promise of new information has been widely documented for all ages), we—and more important, our teens—are not helpless in the face of it. There can be benefits to social media use—kids connecting around awareness of causes in the news, sharing moments of beauty, but as with anything, we aren't defenseless, we need to go in realizing the risks and effects.

TOOLS AND STRATEGIES FOR SURVIVING AND THRIVING IN A SOCIAL MEDIA WORLD

Safety First! Before any detailed processing of the emotional risks of social media, every parent needs to make sure that their child or teen knows how to physically protect themselves online. Start with the basics: Although it may seem obvious, state the obvious. Emphasize that kids need to know who they are talking to, what constitutes a safe person, what constitutes a stranger, and in general to know not to give out any identifying personal information, address, birthdate, vacation plans, and so on, to never agree to meet someone in person who they met online without consulting their parent, and always—when they're not sure what to do, don't hit Send, ask an adult. There is no rush; nothing has to happen quickly online even though it may feel this way. This pressure is no different than the peer pressure that they might feel in person; teach kids that other people can wait for you to make a decision that's good for you.

Normalize the "Abnormal" Feeling. Help teens know that they're in good company when they have that "less than" their peers feeling. Before asking them to challenge that thinking, zoom out and ask them to imagine how many people they guess are feeling "less than" right now. Ask them how reliable they think these posts are in conveying the real picture of those people's lives. Remind them that these platforms showcase people's best moments, or best-looking moments anyway; all posts are highly edited for a certain effect. Nobody posts that they feel lonely, ugly, scared, or left out, even though everyone feels that way sometimes, but if they do post something like that, it may be a sign of distress, or even a cry for help.

Remember: Comparing Leads to Despairing. Separate Self-Worth from Selfie Likes. Highlight with your kids that when we determine our self-worth by seeing how we stack up against someone else, no matter who we are, this is not going to end well. Self-worth comes from within, so kids need to see that it's not personal when this leaves them feeling wanting—it's a flaw in their methodology and we all do it sometimes. Kids are comparing a flat ticker tape of everyone's best moments at a party, or concert, against which their moment of being at home in their pj's can't compete. But that's just it. No one can compete with that. Even those momentary celebrities at the concert will be at home later looking at someone else's great moments and they'll come up short. They will feel left out, imperfect, and isolated. When your teen is misinterpreting the positive airbrushed version of someone's feed, ask them: What are the parts they are leaving out? Who are the people they feel jealous of? And once your teens have worked through this a few times, see whether they can take shortcuts when they start comparing, catch themselves sooner, wish that person well who they are envious of, and remember: that person isn't getting in the way of their social success. Instead of focusing on others, ask your teens what things they can do right now to feel more connected.

Get Distance and Perspective: Fact-Check Your Thoughts and Fears. "Am I replaceable? Does he like her more than me? Do I have any friends? Do people think I'm lame?" A fury of fears and worries can be unleashed when teens go on social media. Yes, they feel those feelings authentically and painfully, but you can teach them to not trust their fears, but instead to "fact-check" them. Take each one and have them put the fears to the test. Is this how they would feel on a day when things were going well with friends? When they're feeling better about themselves? Then they know these instant and seemingly permanent conclusions about their lives and social standing are really temporary reflections of what they are seeing on their news feeds. Help them do appropriate attribution: if they are feeling like a loser and humiliated—help them determine whether this is really about them or has their explanation mistakenly attributed something to them that really is not personal. Help your teens find their ways of running their reactions past their Internal Board of Directors (see the Possibility Panel, page 142), their future self, themselves on a better day, and so on. so they can rethink the meaning of these moments. Teach them to label emotional reasoning: no matter how bad we feel about something, no matter how convinced we are that we are losers because we weren't invited to a party—it doesn't make it true. Self-worth comes from the inside, not from the number of likes and invitations.

Make a Mantra. Ask your teen whether she wants to create a mantra, write it down, set it to music if she likes: *This feels bad, right now, but it will pass. I don't have to be doing this. This is not about me, this is fake, this is someone's fifteen minutes of fame, it will not matter to me in a month (or maybe even tomorrow)! My life is bigger than this platform, my real life is real, this is not.* Encourage your child to center herself with a mantra before she opens up a text or clicks on her Instagram account.

Take a Break! Get a Life! As much as kids feel that they need to be on their phone, and feel anxious when they are not, many see there is a problem. A recent poll found that teens themselves reported that they spent more time on their phone than they wanted to. When kids are at camp or in Wi-Fi–free vacations after a couple hours of withdrawal, they don't look back. "I'm so happy to be free of the drama." "I am just living my life instead of thinking of what my standing is or how people are judging if my life is good enough." We can help kids to try these breaks or moderation even when they are five bars full and to cultivate life outside the phone—talk to your teens about getting lost (in a good way!) in meaningful activities—ones that to them define a good life.

Put Yourself in the Driver's Seat: Make a Schedule. You are not criticizing your teen when you say he can spend hours and hours online and have no sense of the passage of time—because, be honest: That happens to parents regularly. These days, there are apps that show us how many hours per week we've spent on-screen. But you are letting them know they need to act on the information in some way. Some kids decide to take apps off their phone to make it harder to check social media and easier to resist. Ask your teen to do his own experiment—what's a good time period to be on social media? Does it differ on weekdays or weekends? Is he willing to experiment with making "appointments" to check in a few times a day so he can be aware and know what he's doing, rather than expose himself to the constant onslaught of information? Talk to your teen about what else he might want to do with his time.

Self-Regulation: Breaking Through the Trance and Noticing When Something Doesn't Sit Right. It's not just a sense of time that can elude us on social media. We may not notice how we are slowly sliding into a slump and losing perspective. To help your teen start to notice the reactions that matter most, ask her: If social media came with a warning label, what would it say? Then, ask how she wants to keep track of her reactions and triggers to make sure she is checking in with herself. Just as with food choices, your teen needs to learn when it is enough and how they are "digesting" the information in front of them. Ask your teen when the difficult times are—if it's nighttime, you may need to get at other difficulties at night—maybe she needs help to establish relaxing activities to help prime her for sleep.

How to Handle the Disappointment: Get Specific. When your teens see a gathering that they weren't invited to splashed across their screen, it hurts. Don't deny it or diminish it. Accepting the hurt first will help your teen not feel judged or silly on top of feeling bad already. Then help them process the feeling—name it ("I feel excluded, like a loser") watch how those feelings turn into facts. Help them fact-check, look at context. Should a friend draw the same conclusions? We won't be included in everything, and that's okay. Name the catastrophizing or the chain of thinking that underlies the meaning of that rejection to your child. Help isolate the event and see whether there are proactive steps they want to take to improve their social connections. Before this event, how were they feeling? What does this really change? Decide what it means—help them see they don't need to reshape the idea of themselves because they weren't invited to a party.

Make a Feel-Better Kit for Quick Inner Boost. It's crucial that our teens learn how to self-monitor when things are going south in their mood on social media and in general. Ask them (in a calm moment) what they'd like their go-to to be that makes them smile, or gives them a lift or a sense of purpose. Tell them what you like to watch (they'll get a kick out of what you like to do . . .). Ask them to name something they enjoy doing: YouTube videos of kittens or puppies (or actually playing with their real-life kittens or puppies!); watching their favorite comedian. What about learning ten more vocabulary words in Spanish? Suggest that they set up a pick-me-up playlist on their phone. It is hard to generate these ideas in the moment when you need them most, so suggest to your teens that just as you wouldn't want to have to search for a fire extinguisher in an emergency, they should identify their getaway plan and have it within reach for the moments when they need it most.

Getting off the FOMO Loop. When teens feel left out, they may try to fix that FOMO—fear of missing out—feeling by going to the very source of likely more missing out—social media. How can they fix that empty feeling? Address it directly. There are distraction techniques that they can use to have a change of pace (play with their dog, etc.), but that's missing the opportunity to shrink down the meaning of this particular event from the huge, absolute "this means I'm a loser and have no friends" interpretation that is weighing them down. Sometimes, teens do intentionally leave someone out, but more often than not, teen plans happen spontaneously, and kids don't look beyond the immediate to consider the feelings of others and how they may feel left out. They're so busy protecting their own "fragile" social status. Has your child made a plan and not included everyone? It happens. To go even bolder, ask your teen what if she skipped checking social media on a weekday—on purpose—to dose herself with "missing out" to see that it's not so bad.

Make Time to Connect IRL (in Real Life). According to a recent UCLA survey of freshman,[6] the number of students reporting at least sixteen hours per week of socializing with friends decreased by 50 percent in between 1987 and 2014. Research by Dr. Jean Twenge[7] found similarly that this generation—iGen—having grown up on the Internet, spends less time socializing in person than any previous generation. But kids are craving real contact, so tell your kids to initiate it—reach out, make a plan: "Your friends will thank you, and you'll thank you, too!"

Do a Social Media Switcheroo. Advise your teen to find a replacement habit when he's tempted to go online: write haikus, practice a skill in sports or his musical instrument, learn a new skill, such as a new language, enroll in a free online coding program, play with the dog, go for a run, organize their room or backup, or even . . . hang out with his family.

CYBERBULLYING IS A CRIME: IT'S NOT CHILD'S PLAY

Today kids have, at the touch of a Send button, the power to spread rumors, pictures, secrets, destroying trust and tragically, destroying lives. Each heart-wrenching story of children and teens bullied on social media making that desperate decision to take their own life confirms that bullying is not "kids will be kids"; it poses an extremely serious, potentially life-threatening risk. Schools are taking a strong stand against bullying even if it occurs "outside of school," and against cyberbullying as well because of the serious risk it poses to children and teens. It is dangerous and it is illegal. It is best to have the conversation with your child proactively. Kids need to know that for everyone's safety, bullying of any kind is unacceptable, schools and law enforcement take it seriously and are there to help, and, it is part of kids' job to let adults know if they are aware of any bullying online or otherwise. It is then the adults' job to take it from there. According to the Cyberbullying Research Center, parents should keep open lines of communication with their children about these issues, collect evidence by taking screenshots of pictures, messages, postings, and so on, which can serve as evidence, and report dangerous behavior through the platform's harassment and abuse reporting links. While these platforms have the right to assess and decide in each case whether the actions constitute abuse, and have increasingly been criticized for their leniency and lack of action, they can suspend users' accounts and cooperate with law enforcement. Rather than approaching the parent of the perpetrator directly, parents should contact the school or the police. In addition, parents can seek counseling for children or teens when the need for therapeutic support is indicated.

In addition to the general safety guidelines on page 234, parents should have a conversation with their children about online behavior. Make sure they understand what bullying means—get a working definition together; for example, calling someone a mean name, or saying "I hate you" on a social media platform is bullying, but so is sharing an embarrassing picture or anecdote without its subject's permission. Teach your child to take a screenshot of anything that feels harmful or uncomfortable (whether the subject is themselves or someone else) and show you. Have your child practice a one-liner for instances when they witness cyberbullying: "That's not cool. Friends don't do that. That's cyberbullying. That's wrong. I'm not going to participate in that."

It is horrifying to parents when they found out it is their own child doing the bullying. It's important to take this action as seriously as you would hope other parents would. Remember the point of discipline is to *learn* not to frighten, so the goal is to make sure your child learns what they did wrong and to not do it again. Likely, your child knows what mistake they made, so give them the opportunity to own it: Have your child explain to you what happened. Ask *them* to explain to you why you are upset about it. You can fill in the blanks with any information. Make sure they understand not only the possible legal consequences for them, but the emotional consequences of the person they bullied. Ask your child how they are going to repair the break in trust with you, with the other person, writing an apology and/or an essay on why cyberbullying is dangerous and what they're going to do now to be a steward of safety in their community. Suspension of technology privileges for weeks or longer following an incident, sends a powerful message that there are consequences for misusing technology, breaking family rules, or laws. Although your child may not like or agree with those consequences, ultimately you are doing your part to protect your child and others. If kids don't grasp the seriousness of these incidents, there can be grave results, so as parents we need to make sure we are doing our part in preventing suffering, and making a safer world for our kids, online and off.

CONCLUSION

Like it or not, helping your child define his or her relationship with tech and social media is a de facto part of your parenting job description. Yes, it is their "world," so you must tread lightly, but tread you must! As one parent described, social media is a powerful tool, like learning to drive a car, so parents must be involved to some extent because kids' safety could be at risk. You can be greatly influential as a good sounding board for your child making decisions that are in their best interest and support their well-being. Yes, your child will say that no one else's parents care, and yes, they'll say that everyone else's parents let their kids do whatever they want. You can be generous and empathize with how that must sound so good to your child, but make it clear (with levity) that they're stuck with you, and it's just not going to be like that at your house. Remember that you don't have to have all the answers to the social media situations that come up; you can "consult" with your child—ask for their opinions, while being clear that in the end you've got to do your job of being the decision maker. Be a good listener and be a good role model with healthy habits for your own social media use—when you try to do so, you'll see just how hard (but necessary) it is! The new reality of life with social media can feel terrifying, and it can also be uplifting. Either way, it is pretty clear that social media, for better or worse, is here to stay, so let's make it for better, together.

10

THE PARENT'S ROLE

*Teaching Without Getting Tangled Up:
How Not to Turn One Negative Person into Two*

> The hardest part of raising a child is teaching them to ride
> bicycles. A shaky child on a bicycle for the first time needs
> both support and freedom. The realization that this is what
> the child will always need can hit hard.
>
> —Sloan Wilson

All parents want their children to thrive. We know that some unhappiness, some knots, some tumbles, some frustration and wrong answers accompany the process; the question is: do our kids know this? The answer:
only if we teach them. Back in the day, struggle was normal. It didn't seem
to need to be taught. The more we teach our kids to expect and embrace
things that are hard, to see the struggles as normal, temporary, and universally expected steps in the process of growth, the less they will have the
added hurdle of thinking something is wrong whenever it's not instantly
right. How do we teach this? As we've seen, it's not by changing the situation, racing ahead and preventing problems, or doing scoop-and-rescue
missions when that shoe won't tie itself or the calculus problem is insolv-
able (not that most of us could be of help in that scenario!); it's by changing our reaction when our kids are struggling, so they can change their

reaction, too. This is how they will learn to persevere, to figure out what they need to and continue on the grand path of their life.

GROUNDING THE PLANES

The other day, I sat with a teenage patient and we heard what he immediately identified as a medical helicopter. "How can you tell?" I asked. It's the rhythm, he said. It's an emergency.

As parents we are wired to look for and prevent emergencies, but we still need to convey to our kids that most of what feels like an emergency isn't one, and share with them how we juggle the emotional and physical challenges of life, so they can increasingly internalize how to be successful jugglers themselves. Take Charles, for example. He is seventeen and has not once ordered his own food at a restaurant, never talked to a teacher about a grade, never did an oral presentation, and certainly never raised his hand in class, never bought his own supplies for school projects, and truly didn't do too many of his projects himself. Charles is suffering from depression and social anxiety. I asked Charles whether his parents were supportive of him with his anxiety when he was younger. "Absolutely," he answered, and without missing a beat, he continued: "They did everything for me. I never had to give a presentation, ask for anything." How did that work for him? I asked. He replied: "I don't know how to do anything myself, and don't really believe I can learn." This may sound hyperbolic, and perhaps most parents don't rely on swoop-and-rescue to that extreme, but there are many similar situations where parents, thinking that they want to make things better, work around the discomfort that their children are feeling, and kids are left not knowing how to regulate their own feelings, to know what's normal, what's not, how to ride out uncertainty or discomfort, and in the end, don't trust themselves to try.

Holding steady with our patient stance conveys to our kids that even though things are hard, this is expected, manageable, not wrong. Parents are bestowed with their emergency voice for a reason, but just as we say to our kids, we should only use it in an actual emergency. Not with the B–, not when your teen loses the book for his book report. Yes, we can say the words to convey that uncertainty and challenges are safe, but sometimes it comes down to the look on our face.

We've all had that experience of our child's falling and looking up at us and, depending on our reaction, they either burst into tears or brush it off. Our reactions are so powerful in shaping to our kid's understanding of the world and it doesn't stop at toddlerhood. One way to remember this is to consider the classic psychological study conducted by Eleanor J. Gibson and R. D. Walk[1] in the 1960s that had babies placed on a solid counter across from their mothers. The hitch: half of the counter was checkerboard, the other half was clear Plexiglas, creating the appearance of "the end of the table" that might well be the end of the world to a crawling baby. To get to Mom, babies had to crawl across the table. Babies who saw their mother smiling at them crossed the great divide. If Mom had an angry face, they stopped and didn't dare cross over. Of course, these days, the experiment would be done with *parents*, not moms, but the tagline is important—kids are watching us to provide them with an interpretation, an emotional barometer of the manageability, risk, or safety of a moment. We can take time to consider: Are we, by our reactions, saying, "It's okay to venture out across the unknown of that moment," or are we saying, "Don't attempt it"? Because ultimately, we want our kids to internalize the idea that typically, it's not the situation that we need to change; rather, we need to change our reaction to it. Which brings us to the discussion of the popular criticism/accusation of well-intentioned parents: helicoptering.

SHARING THE JOB

Let's consider that helicopter parents are as well intentioned as the rest of us, or, even better, that we all can hover at times, and maybe that's not a bad thing. The issue is this: Helicopter parents may hold the belief that wanting the best for their kids means giving it to them on a silver platter—no effort required on the child's part. This leads to kids who are passive, confused, and yes . . . even entitled. All parents do want the best for their kids, but grounded parents know that the "best" means equipping their kids with the tools they need to hold up on their own in life.

I think of it as "job-sharing" and it isn't always easy! Babies, learning to crawl, reach for a toy that is just beyond their grasp. Do we push the toy closer or do we encourage the stretch? This is the blueprint for everything that comes after. Do we keep zipping our kids' coats, or leave a little extra time so they can learn themselves? Do we write our teens' college applications, or offer to be a reader? When we take over, we aren't being supportive; we are doing *for* our kids and communicating both that they can't do for themselves, and that they shouldn't.

The optimal alternative for your child's resilience is to include your child in the process of solving problems rather than magically swooping and rescuing them when things go wrong. Showing children the "the messy seams" of how things work in life is crucial. Who is going to show them, if we don't? They certainly won't see the backstory or trial and error effort online. Modeling and walking kids through the often messy process of disappointment, failure, and losing, and showing them that these experiences are temporary, are invaluable. Even more important is showing kids that great knowledge can come out of these adversities.

A good way to reinforce problem-solving skills is to enlist kids' help with someone else's problem—like your own! The next time you forget something, have a problem at work, or lose at something that matters to you, don't hide those experiences away. Once you have processed your initial raw emotion, share the story with your kids and solicit their input to see the problem in a more realistic light, and to brainstorm how to resolve it. They will be amazed that things like this happen to adults and that adults can freak out (temporarily), too! They think that only they have problems. Sometimes kids learn the belief that failures (a.k.a. glitches, missteps, disappointments) are insurmountable from the way their parents handle those situations themselves. So, parents need to check out their own beliefs about success and failure first. If parents are deathly afraid of things going wrong and believe that problems are irrevocable, this will have at least two outcomes: first, parents will hover to protect their kids, and two, kids will be so afraid of failing that they won't try. The alternative is for parents and kids both to work on shrinking their disproportionate, catastrophic beliefs about adverse events and then figuring out what is the actual problem at hand and what can be done to solve it.

It takes two to make things go as best as they can, but things going "best" doesn't mean that your child ends up more "positive" (not in the immediate anyway). Although it may be counterintuitive at times, your

North Star in these tough interactions isn't to be positive, or even to fix the problem, it's to try to make a connection with your child and help them think more *accurately*, not more positively, about what just happened. Think about when you are upset and you make a global statement: "Everything in my life is a mess; I can't do anything right; and on top of that, I overcooked the pasta!" Close your eyes and imagine the response you'd like, and that you wouldn't like. If right away someone rushed in and started to debate whether everything was *really* a mess, or if that were an exaggeration—well, you know, no one would feel better. If instead, you heard "You are having a tough day," you might just get that "nodding head" we saw in Chapter 3, and even that supreme exhale that comes with being understood. Using this approach, your child will be in a better place to fact-check, shrink the problem down to something specific and likely temporary, and wrestle themselves free from the tyranny of the "no," "can't," "never" rant in their head.

THE FINE ART OF WALKING ON EGGSHELLS

As a compassionate human being, you can't help but get pulled into your children's unhappy moments. But also as a person who has compassion for yourself, you can't help but get stressed out when the very help you are trying to give is reciprocated with anger, accusation, or meltdown. While scrambling to find the Off button, you feel as though you are walking headlong into the spray of a wayward or seemingly possessed sprinkler; in trying to approach to turn it off, you get soaked, too. Let's face it, our own internal negative nozzle is wayward, too. It turns on us. Especially when these moments are a regular occurrence for you, the meltdowns of your young child, or just the downs of your teen, it can be challenging to approach these situations with the grace, equanimity, and even just concern that you might once have had. Anticipating the failure of your efforts to "cheer up" or even get through to your children through the din of their own upset, you may be discouraged before you start, resulting in dueling pessimism that I call negativity in stereo. Your buttons are pushed. Your desire for it to be different pushes your child's buttons. It doesn't have to be this way. In moments like these, it's a good time to spot out of the corner of your eye that "table for two" that we discussed in the Introduction. Lean back in your chair, exhale, and remember—your child doesn't want to be feeling the way she does; her wiring grabbed her before she could stop and think it through. Your wiring may have grabbed you, too, when your mind was racing with such thoughts as, "Will she be like this forever? Will she ever be able to have a 'normal' life? What if she gets upset like this with her friends?" Do your part to snap back to the present. Get specific, keep the problem small and temporary: What's happening right now. Helping your child wrestle free from negative thinking means first separating the "negative" from the will of your child. Seeing them as saddled with a burdensome reaction rather than intentionally trying to burden *you* will help you to enter the situation as their ally rather than one more bad guy.

THE PREDICAMENT: TO EASE UP OR NOT TO EASE UP

"You're not helping me!" your eight-year-old screams at you in tears, throwing her papers on the ground. The sweat is running down your face after an hour of working on memorizing multiplication tables (which you mastered about thirty years ago yourself, but no matter), and the tension is rising in your chest. You compose yourself, grit your teeth, maybe even manage a smile, and say, "You can do it; you're doing great." But the fact is that she *isn't* doing great, and apparently she *can't* do it, at least not the way it's going right now. What is your role? Should you keep encouraging and insist that she is smart and do it, or let the steam come out of your ears and pour out your frustration? Maybe try tough love and just *make* her comply? Walking away might work, but she may follow you. And then there's still the unfinished and perhaps doomed math assignment, which might be okay, if you weren't so sure that the assignment is entirely doable—if only your kid was in her right mind.

What do we do? Most of us start out with an instinctual and homey version of Isaac Newton's third law of physics: for every action, there is an equal and opposite reaction. When our children are miserable, we come at them with an equal and opposite response: We are positive, encouraging, and reassuring—that is, until our attempts to make it better seem to make it worse. At that moment, some other law of physics, based on the transfer of toxic emotions from kid to parent, kicks in and eventually leads to combustion. One miserable person has morphed into two miserable people.

These types of interactions, when they occur daily, take their toll on everyone. Parents are confused about whether they should just ease up on their children, running ahead to remove obstacles wherever they appear, or just stand firm and let their kids tough it out. Actually, the key is not for us to ease up on our children; our role is to show them how to ease up on *themselves*. Imagine if the next time our children fall into a thinking trap, they could say, "I don't want to feel this way, but my mind keeps tricking me into thinking this is a *forever* thing, and that is making me feel worse than the problem itself." If we resist the temptation to just make it all better, we can help our children identify how the thoughts of blame, disappointment, and sadness are getting stuck in a net—like the brain net illustration in Chapter 5. The longer these thoughts stay stuck, the more they *feel* believable, but that feeling doesn't make them any more true. Encouraging children to shrink the problem back to its original form will naturally lead to their feeling better. When children are stuck in a negative spin, they are reacting to a picture they have in mind and the story they are telling themselves about it: "This is impossible." If we just cheer them up without helping them see a different and more realistic picture, with a more accurate caption, we are not teaching them how to ride a bike; we are saying, "Don't worry. I can always hold onto the back for you." When we rush to the rescue, we are also echoing their feeling that what is a struggle is *unbearable*. What we need to clearly convey is that there is a *different* (don't say "better" unless you want an explosion) way out: "Look at the picture from this angle: It is *uncomfortable* but not *unbearable*; it is *temporary*; it is *manageable*."

In this context, the idea of letting go and letting children solve problems on their own may strike you as cold and unfeeling, but anyone who has experienced the indescribable magic of letting go of the back of the bike as his child rides off knows that *this* is the exquisite gift and privilege of parenting. In the words of sociologist Sara Lawrence-Lightfoot, "I love seeing the backs of my children as they move out into the world."[2] This saying of her mother's reminds us that the ultimate role of every parent, however bittersweet, is to teach our children the skills they need to leave us. And curled up in every interaction is the back and forth between the support and the freedom that will deliver our children to where they need to be.

While striking this balance is a lively undertaking for any parent, the child who is often unhappy and saddled with the frequent anguish of hurt, disappointment, or frustration poses greater challenges. Is it cruel—if even possible—to teach kids about managing distress when they are writhing on the floor because their reading homework is too hard, their friend had to go home, or the store had only the blue Matchbox car, not the red one? How can we not just take away our children's pain when it is wrapped up in such suffering? First, it wouldn't work. We can't just take it away, and if we could, whenever our children met with adversity, they'd be looking around for us to shoo it away. We can do better by being clear that distress is manageable, that there may be lessons to be learned through it, and that our children can withstand the lessons. We can give our children the opportunity to learn that they can eliminate their suffering themselves. And deep down, we know that *especially* since these lessons are harder to learn for children with a negative bent, one thing is clear: If we are going to see them off into the world one day, they need to be *more* skillful at these lessons than their peers who can go with the flow.

PART ONE: PARENTAL REACTIONS TO NEGATIVITY AND THEIR CONSEQUENCES: JUMPING IN, FLIPPING OUT, HOLDING STEADY

> I am too embarrassed to tell my friends how defeated I feel by Rachel's moods. She seems so great around my friends, but as soon as we walk in the door at home, I get slammed with everything that's wrong and how it's somebody's fault— usually mine. I find myself saying the most awful things back to her. It's totally unsupportive, but it's as if we're both pulled by this undertow, and our interactions become this awful dark mess.
>
> —mother of a fifteen-year-old

> I've got to get this kid happy. I feel like a trapped animal. He doesn't want to try anything, and when I bring up ideas, I'm the bad guy.
>
> —mother of a seven-year-old

Talk to my son when he's in a negative spiral? I don't want
to go in there. How will we ever get out?

—father of a thirteen-year-old

If only children's moods and negativity were self-contained like the cloud of dust and dirt that follows Charlie Brown's delightful but hygiene-impaired buddy Pigpen. Although he was always dirty, the dirt wasn't contagious; he kept it to himself. But when a child is in a dark mood, in an effort to get the dirt off him, he wipes it on you, and you may then pass it on to your spouse or your other children, and on and on. So, it ends up more like—to stay with the children's story references—the pink goo residue in *The Cat in the Hat* that is just transferred to more and more places (from the tub to the cake, to the rug, to the shoes)—but not eliminated.

The way not to *share* the negativity is to separate your child from the negative moment: Wrestle him free from Mr. Meany or the pessimist view in his mind, and he in turn will see that this interpretation isn't a given; it's not a banner he has to carry. It's a temporary circumstance; he has stumbled onto one path, and he can choose another. Your child may be negative by nature or by circumstance or may just be caught in a no-fault moment when the brain's circuits are lighting up a pathway connecting the dots in a pattern of impossibility. He doesn't *want* to feel this way; he is just following the path. Negative thinking is a "wiring issue." Your child is wired to respond in certain characteristic ways, and those ways, because they may be different from your neural pathways, may be frustrating to you. But here we will learn, in the words of my daughter Meredith, how "not to get tangled up in someone else's wires." Not rushing in is part of the solution, but what will help you to stay grounded is a belief in your child's ability to handle the unpleasantness, which means less work for you than trying to deny or ward off the unpleasantness.

This may prove especially challenging with teens whom, while we expect a bit of adolescent disgruntled-ness, we may also expect a little more respect, responsibility, self-control than we would with a five- or ten-year-old. We get fooled by the outward appearance that they are young adults and forget that inside they are in the midst of a growth crisis, identity crisis, pressures from friends, from social media, from school, they are tapped out. As parents, we will have to work extra hard to get into that Zen place in our chair of having compassion for our teens (while setting firm limits so lines are not crossed), but it may be best when you're sitting back in your chair to remember that adolescence has been called a "second toddlerhood" by many—and with no judgment. Both stages are characterized by steep acceleration in physical and socio-emotional growth. Think of how a toddler is bounding out into the world apart from you, a newcomer. Growth spurts, hormones aside, teens are having to find their own way bounding along with making choices—that are separate from you—the food, clothing, hair, their friends, their taste in music, their values, beliefs, imagine that they are all cylinders firing for things that you've already settled—this requires a lot of self-focused attention on a teen's part that can be maddening, but it's all par for the course. This is why the smallest thing can set them off, so tread lightly. To join with them without reinforcing the depression say, "I know you are overloaded," or "I know you have a lot on your mind," or "I know everything looks bleak to you right now," and "Remember, I'm on your side," or "I want to help, or "I feel that way sometimes." Whereas younger kids are just swept up by their feelings so they may not have the additional fear *this isn't normal, I'm not normal,* for teens, this question is the turnstile that they have to pass through all day long. If you have compassion for that predicament, it will be easier to not take things personally, not get tangled up, and help your teen untangle herself from her distorted and distressing perceptions.

Just as we don't want our children to walk the path of negative distortion, we ourselves need to pause, center, and accurately interpret our children's protests so we can respond to the *moment* rather than supersizing our reaction as if this were a permanent problem. We need to anchor ourselves in the understanding that how our child is reacting right now is temporary; even if it is a characteristic response, it is changeable, and we are helping our child to change. If, instead, we fall into seeing our child's worldview as permanent ("He is so inflexible! He'll never change!"), there's a double standard. We are accepting the tyranny of the negative as the final word and have lost a crucial leg from our table of interactional optimism. But equally important, we may be seeing as set in stone a behavior that, for our child, was more like striking a pose. Your child's upset or discouragement doesn't necessarily mean they can't or won't do something; it's just a negative blast. Like the parents I see who respond to their child's vomit phobia by running for a bucket every time she is afraid she might throw up, when parents take this first reaction to frustration more seriously than the child does, the negativity gets an extra dose of legitimacy and is on the way to becoming entrenched.

We see in Chart 10-1 that if we pause, rather than immediately try to make our children *feel* better, we can help them see how they can *do* better by actually solving a problem. Ultimately, that will feel better. If we short-circuit and just make solving the feelings our destination, we are focusing on quick arrival of temporary relief, rather than a deliberate path to lasting happiness. As we saw in the brain train illustration in Chapter 2, the feelings are a result of our perceptions of a situation. So while we can empathize with our children's feelings, we also need to discover the interpretations, explanations, or commentary that our children have attached to a situation that generated those reactions so they can detach from them. At first, when we reorient ourselves to these second reactions, they may seem foreign or even unfeeling, but they give our children the credit they are due: our belief that they can overcome their problems.

CHART 10-1

When Your Child Says	Your First Thought Might Be	Your Second Thought Needs to Be
I hate her; she's a terrible friend and I'm done with her.	Yikes, (a) I need to convince him that she's not terrible, or (b) that friend is terrible; I never liked her!	What happened that made him feel so strongly? What was the straw that broke the camel's back?
This won't work; you can't help me; no one can.	I need to convince him that it did work and that things can help him.	What does he think didn't work about it? What does he think the problem is? What does he think would work better?
I can't do this; this is too hard!	I need to convince him that he can do it; it's not too hard!	What part of this can he do? Is he ready to do it now? Let him show me where he's getting stuck.

Take a moment to recall a time when your child was melting down over her version of the multiplication table example from the beginning of the chapter. What were you thinking? Read through each section and check off which thoughts apply. You will see that the solution in each scenario is not to come up with the words to magically take it all away, but to help your child change her understanding of the situation, to see options and passageways out of the maze, where before she only saw dead ends and blind alleys. Support your child in finding these answers rather than stealing her fire and doing it for her.

Overly Compassionate: Superparent to the Rescue

What we may think to ourselves:

- I am afraid for him. This isn't good for him.
- I want him to be happy. Let's drop this. It's making him too frustrated.
- What did I do wrong that he isn't happy?
- He has so much to deal with. I'll just fix this one thing for him.
- I know it's not good for either of us, but I'm so tired that I'll just do whatever he wants. It will end faster.

What we may say aloud:

- You don't have to worry; I'll take care of it.
- This isn't important; everything's totally fine.
- You are the best. They must be wrong.
- I'll call the teacher; I'll take care of this.

The Problem. Kids may be frightened by our zeal in needing to eliminate their distress immediately and may understand that their negative feelings are unnatural, wrong, or dangerous and are to be avoided instead of being worked through. Switch your orientation from thinking that something is *wrong* with your child for being upset to looking at her upset as a challenge that can be overcome. Sometimes, too much compassion makes the situation seem much worse than it is, even to your child.

Don't play a zero-sum game. When your child dumps the problem, pause, and in your mind draw a boundary between you; look slightly away if looking directly at your child puts you too much in the line of fire, and practice *listening* without *fixing*. Picture your child's strengths—her toughness, her ingenuity—and incorporate that reality into the other reality you are seeing in front of you. Both are true. Ask your child questions empathically, bringing the ball kindly back into her court: "That sounds tough. What do you think your options are? What are you thinking that you want to do about that?" Not only will you be sending your child the message that you believe she has the capacity to solve these issues, but you will be protecting yourself from burnout and teaching your child that although you will always be there to support her, you won't carry her because she can carry herself.

The Solution. Use your compassion to first support your child's feelings: "I bet it does feel as if everyone is further along in the project," or "I understand why you feel that you can't do anything right *right now*." But then switch focus to distinguish between the facts and the feelings, as we saw in Chapter 2. Relabel the problem as a negative-brain distortion, and help identify the source of the exaggeration. In the case of younger children, is someone else—Give Up Guy—making it seem really bad? You may say to an older child, "It makes sense that it would look that way when the negative part of your brain is telling the story. I wonder what it would look like from another perspective—If you went with the facts, not the feelings. Are you willing to take a look from the other, more neutral side?" In the following anecdote, we see how being a superparent can backfire. What if your child *didn't* really want your help in the first place, but just wanted you to listen?

I was sitting with a parent and his ten-year-old son. An extremely dedicated father, Mitch wanted desperately for his kids to succeed, to learn the "tricks" to make life easier, and he took opportunities to show them whenever he could. On this particular evening, however, his son Jesse had spent thirty minutes working on a birthday present for his brother and, not very confident in his artistic skills, said to his dad, "It's not very good." Although we later learned while sifting through the aftermath that Jesse was simply fishing for a compliment, Mitch thought, *I need to help him so he can be happy with his project.* Mitch had Jesse rebuild the project, but then Jesse was *really* unhappy with how it looked and blew up at his dad. At this point, his father, who had just spent thirty minutes of his own time on a gift that wasn't even from him, became resentful, slammed the project down, and said angrily, "Forget it. You're on your own now." What went wrong? In all his zeal to make it all better, Mitch never *asked* Jesse whether he needed help, and Jesse, in all his insecurity, never thought to say no. If Mitch had used his superparent powers to be a spotter for Jesse, touring him through his own frustration, Jesse would have figured it out for himself, and Mitch could have felt proud that his son was learning to succeed on his own merits.

Angry/Frustrated:
Inadvertent Disapproval of Our Children's Feelings

When we feel frustrated—and how could we not at times?—our children will read that frustration, rightly or wrongly, as disapproval of their feelings, and from their perspective that means that they are either "dumb" or "wrong" to be feeling the way they do.

What we may think when we react with anger:

- I'm doing all the work. Why should I?
- I've got my own problems!
- He'll never learn if I keep cleaning up for him!
- He is out of control. It is his responsibility to stop.
- If I help him with this, I'm babying him.

What we may say:

- This is ridiculous!
- You're really not seeing this right. It's not a big deal.
- I can't deal with this drama. You have to stop!

The Problem. If your child feels as if he is in trouble or doing something wrong in addition to already feeling bad about it, getting angry at him turns one problem into two. Also, parents don't like to be the bad guy. It doesn't do much good, and it doesn't feel good.

The Solution. Remember that if you are getting angry at your child who is angry or upset, you have officially become tangled in the negativity knot yourself. How can you get her and yourself out without being mean, for instance, by saying, "You are being so negative!" When your child is free-falling, your instinct is just to get rid of the problem and push back. Instead of fueling the fire by adding your own heat, approach the situation as if your child's mind has wandered off the main road and is lost deep in the forest, and say, "We're not in a good place here. Let's figure out how to get back to a better place. Let's take a break for a few minutes. I need to clear my head, and then we can look at things with a fresh set of eyes." This is especially difficult to do when older children and teens push your buttons by cursing or insulting you. It's human nature to get caught up in the (very offensive!) words being hurled, even though you may know this isn't the best of how your teen feels: They are struggling. Rather than side-tracking the whole interaction by making it about the language, you can instead preface your response by first saying: "Look, I know you know that those words hurt," or "I know you know that we don't curse" and getting the business of correcting them out of the way without stoking the fires. Then get to the real matter at hand: "I want to understand what you're thinking that's upsetting you. I want to help. Do you feel ready to talk about it?"

Too Happy: The Out-of-Sync Parent

Seeing your child unhappy may be so confusing that you desperately want to push the "undo" button.

What you might think:

- Why is he so unhappy? That is not natural.
- Negativity is not good for him.
- This is a bad state of mind.
- I want to have a good day.
- There's so much to be happy about.

What you might say:

- You just need to have a good attitude.
- Let's go have fun. I want to be in a good mood today.
- There's so much to be happy about; let's not get bogged down in this.

The Problem. None of us want to be like the father in the film *Little Miss Sunshine*, whose oppressive and out-of-touch positive attitude drove his sullen teenager to a vow of silence. Even though that father had some wisdom to share, unfortunately he was not talking with his child; he was lecturing at him. In less exaggerated forms, asking our children to be *happy* (not even just neutral) when they are feeling bad feels (and sometimes accurately so) as if our aim is for *us*, not *them*, to feel better.

The Solution. If you are the kind of person who is blessed with a pleasant temperament and truly can't relate to or understand how your child seems to react to every problem coming down the pike, take heart, and then take a step back. You just need to find some common ground first. Rather than thinking that the goal is for your children to feel happy (i.e., making them say yes to life when their switch is set to no), you can say yes to where they are. Switch to their perspective and empathize with their point of view. Free yourself from the idea that your child needs cheering up. It will do you both a world of good. You will then be able to listen to your child's experience, and he won't feel bad for being unhappy and can invest his energy in helping himself rather than in opposing you.

As we saw in Chapter 3, part of your role is to get comfortable with feelings so that you can welcome them in any way, shape, or size. Remember what you aren't comfortable with and work on it. Rather than trying to rush your child, change him, or shame him, you can soften and accept what he is feeling and, by doing so, allow the change.

At the same time, when you are in the role of coach, don't feel pressure to jump on every experience as a learning experience. You can ask, but don't assume that your child is ready to hear what you are saying. Kids don't need to learn every second. If your message is consistent, they will come to expect your reaction to be accepting and supportive but strategic (even if the strategy is just leading them back to find the strategy for themselves).

PART TWO: STRATEGIES FOR REDUCING
THE CYCLE OF NEGATIVE SPIN

Listening: The Way into Your Child's World

We saw in the master plan that starting with empathy—reflecting our children's feelings—rather than immediately trying to convince them that they need to think or feel differently, establishes a good working relationship. Listening carefully and validating your child's words are a necessary (but not sufficient) first step to getting anywhere else. Many a child has said, "You never listen to me!" When we don't accept what our children are feeling (not that we endorse it, encourage it, or agree with it), we are like unhelpful tollbooth operators who say, "Only bills. We don't accept coins." We are telling our children that what they are presenting is not acceptable. Your child is then stuck at that toll booth. When we accept whatever our children are saying about their initial feelings, they then have entrée to the highway, and where they are *going* then becomes the emphasis of the interaction rather than getting bogged down with the words. If you want your child to feel heard, think EZ-Pass.

Wait, Wait, Don't Tell Me:
Ask Questions Rather Than Giving Answers

Many frustrated parents have come to the sad realization that what turns an otherwise perfectly acceptable suggestion into a doomed one is that the suggestion comes from them. Let your children be your prompter. Rather than being a broken record about the rules, let your children do the honors. Instead of explaining something for the umpteenth time, ask your children, "What do you think I'm going to say here?" Even though this may not be what your children want to hear, you know they know the answer, and they get some credit for guessing right.

Parents repeatedly say, "Brush your teeth, wash your face, get into your pj's," and feel as though they are talking to a wall. The same strategy that works for toothbrushing also works with negative thinking. Rather than reminding them to brush, say, "It's bedtime; what do you need to do?" When they are stuck in a negative spin, rather than telling them to stop being hard on themselves, say, "Things are getting really harsh in there; what do you need to do?" An interaction that usually ends in mutual frustration is transformed simply by a question, and gives children a sense of ownership and sets an expectation that they will eventually be able to handle these problems themselves. A side benefit is that you don't have to keep hearing the sound of your own tired voice.

Don't Ask the "Why" Questions

Parents are often baffled when their children get themselves in a lather so quickly over what may appear to be nothing. The parents are often tempted to ask, "Why are you getting so upset about this?" Unfortunately asking why in that context is like adding insult to injury. When a child is saddled with a borrowed vision of doom and gloom about herself, her future, and the entire world, asking her to justify why she feels this way is just adding more weight. We don't want our kids to feel like they have to defend their negative feelings, we want to help free them. Remember that our explanations for *why* things happen determine *how* we feel about them: If I think the game was rained out because I always have bad luck, rather than because a warm front met a cold front, I am going to feel very hopeless not only about this game but about all the games or moments of life to come. Bad luck is certain to strike again, so my distress is going to be enormous because it is distress on credit against all future possibilities. Let's reset the target of our questions from the feelings to the construction of the story. Don't waste time arguing with your child about why she can't forgive herself for getting 81 percent on her math test and doesn't feel worthy of your help. Rather than trying to maneuver the big, global, unwieldy version of the story, narrow it down by asking, "Are you a horrible, irresponsible person or is this a simple case of being human?"

Kid's and Teen's Emotions: Turning on a Dime

One minute, parents are scrambling to catch their child with a safety net, and the next, the child is totally fine and asking the parents to take her to the mall. Let the inconsistency be. Adults do most things more slowly than kids: We walk, eat, and think more slowly, and for the most part, we recover from our emotions more slowly, too. That kids can switch gears so swiftly and thoroughly is generally a good thing. If they need to do some cleanup with someone else—like apologizing for their behavior, or hurting your feelings—that can't slide, and you can tell them that you are happy that they are feeling better, but that you're still feeling hurt or upset by some things that were said. Other than that, if you are worried only about your own whiplash from the sudden about-face your youngster has managed to do, well, the more you expect your kids to turn on a dime, the less whiplash you will have.

Distress Is Temporary:
Uncomfortable Doesn't Mean Unbearable

Parents do their children a huge favor when they remember that their suffering won't last. Then, they won't and don't get sucked into the desperate place of trying to get rid of their kids' distress at any cost. Instead of feeling the pressure to fix it, listen and breathe. Rather than adding to the escalation of distress, you'll be showing your child by your calm behavior that this situation is manageable. Think to yourself your new mantra: "I don't need answers; questions are better."

Use Strategies as a Tool, Not a Weapon

> Bart Simpson: This is the worst day of my life.
> Homer Simpson: The worst day of your life *so far*.
> —*The Simpsons Movie*

Homer Simpson is not on any short lists for father of the year, but in his misuse of the tool of getting specific, he generously illustrates for us the point that it's to nobody's benefit to become the "cognitive error police" pointing out our children's thinking mistakes. Our goal is to free our children from negative thinking by giving them choices and alternatives from the stories in their head that are making them feel bad, wrong, or hopeless. If we approach this goal by correcting our children for going the wrong way, we aren't showing them the pathways out; we're just giving them one more reason to shut down. Instead, team up with your child and pose questions about the negativity as if it is a separate entity. Wonder aloud, "That sounds a lot like the Generalizer to me. Does it to you? Does this feel as if it's getting bigger than you want it to?" Or respond with, "I'm thinking that your brain wants you to go 'global'; can we shrink the problem down to the specific situation?"

All-Inclusive: Practice These Principles with the Whole Family

When you practice in other interactions in your family what you are preaching (or at least teaching) to your negative-minded child, he will see that things work better when we catch ourselves being globally negative, find the specific, see negative things as temporary, and attribute successes to permanent factors rather than chance. You will find that your whole family is in a better place, spending more time on positive endeavors and less time bogged down. Your child needs to see the principles in action when he's not in the hot seat; this is one case where the view is much better from a distance. If you don't want your child to globalize negatively about himself ("I am so stupid; I can't get this math"), make sure you're not generalizing about him yourself ("You are so irresponsible; you forgot to bring home your permission slip").

Catch Your Child Being Positive

If we focus only on the behavior we want our children to change, we're not practicing what we preach when we tell our children to look for the good. Parents must maintain a dual focus: one to dismantle the circuits of negative thinking and, equally important, to catch their children being "good" including when they are thinking clearly, accurately, and freely. Notice, enjoy, and luxuriate in those moments when your child is "optimizing" on her own.

When I was in graduate school, the antidote to child behavioral programs based on "punishment" was the idea of "catching the child being good." Rather than spending time and attention tracking all the problems, counting them, writing them down, something aversive to all, these programs involved noticing any prosocial behavior—"You smiled at so and so"; "You said thank you to someone"—and just as the brain does more of what it does a lot of, kids do more of what we attend to. Sometimes it takes a deep breath and creative reframing to find the good, but it is worth it, and it doesn't preclude teaching a lesson at the same time. In fact, it increases the chances your child is paying attention.

While it may be easy to spot these model child moments with younger kids, catching teens "being good" may need a little more latitude and a slightly different interpretation. Remember that teens are working on their identity, what kind of person they want to be, all the while juggling the social judgment, comparison, and pressure they feel. Not to short-change teens, they can be wonderfully enthusiastic and funny and warm, but during these challenging years, it may be the *absence* of negative behaviors that is the easily accessibly recognition-worthy act: your teen didn't grumble when you asked for his help, he didn't storm off when you talked to him about the condition of his room, he didn't get defensive and attack when you talked about curfews, and bonus: didn't eye-roll with the request for family dinner. In these instances, no need to harp on the specifics, a simple appreciation of the good, "thank you, that's really helpful," or, "thanks, that's really nice," will be a welcome surprise for all.

CONCLUSION

Our own expectations and beliefs can interfere with our helping our kids free themselves from the stronghold of negative thoughts. Most important is not to be afraid of your child's negative thinking, to expect it, to dive into it, and to learn how it works. It's a normal part of life. For some kids, it's too frequent and gets deep very quickly, and they need our help learning how to climb out, but if we think it's something we need to chase away or think it shouldn't be there, we are not teaching our children how to face it head-on and not be limited by it. Instead, we are running away from it with them.

Idea Box

For the coming week, notice your reactions to your child's distress. Are you angry, rescuing, or sending in the cheerleading squad? Instead, focus on your breathing, tell yourself this isn't urgent, and relax your face and shoulders as you exhale. While you are looking compassionately at the young person across from you, picture her competence; think of her in her strongest moment; imagine her abilities for resolving this situation. Give both of you the gift of time. Bring your compassion for the intensity of feelings that your child has, and bring your equanimity with the knowledge that this, too, shall pass. You'll notice that when you lower the urgency, the emotional temperature drops, and your child (and you) can function in an optimal zone.

PART THREE

Turning on the
Axis of Possibility

11

RESILIENCE TO GO AND
HAPPINESS TO STAY

No is always no.

—They Might Be Giants[1]

yes is a world
& in this world of
yes live
(skillfully curled)
all worlds

—e. e. cummings, "Love Is a Place"

The distance between the universes described in these two quotes can seem infinite, especially when you're single-handedly trying to heave-ho your child from one to the other and dinner is burning on the stove. I was sitting recently with Judy, the mother of ten-year-old Jesse. Judy had reached a point of true burnout as she had been trying to push Jesse up the hills of disappointment and pull him out of depths of frustration and pessimism for several years now, just to get him through school every day. Even with good things—special outings, parties, dinner at restaurants—it seemed Jesse, in his mom's words, could "suck the fun out of anything" for the whole family. I was reminded of the Greek myth of

Sisyphus, who was destined to push a boulder up a steep hill every day, only to find it back at the base again the next morning (for all eternity, no less). We all have had times when we are metaphorically dragging our kids kicking and screaming to "get to yes"; in those times, our body is saying, "Pull!," but our mind may be wondering, *Why am I the only one doing all the work here?*

The key to resilience is not pushing your child up that hill, or getting her to yes—not you all by yourself. Instead, it's teaching her a new frame, a new mind-set—to stop and think: "Is it a big hill? Maybe it is, or maybe it isn't, but if so—what do I bring to the table to climb that hill, and if it's not a big hill, what do I bring to the table to change my thinking about it?" You are teaching your child to question "Is it the situation, or how I'm thinking about it?" so she can push past her first thoughts of distortion and discouragement and focus on the parts of the situation that she can do something about. It's getting her to "go" when she is feeling stuck. When you give her the tools to create choices, she can shrink the apparent distance between the universes of negative and positive so that the "yes" may emerge—by her own discovery—even out of the world of no.

We saw in Chapter 5, about the master plan, how to bring your child from the initial stance of resistance to mobilization for action. If we think of the master plan as a full-course meal, we can consider the examples in this chapter "appetizers," or "conversation starters," to get you to the table for common trouble spots: receiving criticism, trying new things, or managing friends that trip the negative reaction in kids wired for pessimism. Rather than being rendered speechless by your child's initial resistance, discover from these brief examples of conversations how you can get her moving when she is stuck or, better yet, how to put her in the driver's seat. What stalls your child is not the problem, but her perception of the magnitude of the problem. Rather than telling her how she is wrong, ask her questions to shrink the problem down to size. Rather than seeing a roadblock, she will see a specific problem with a myriad of solutions. The second half of the chapter is about bringing the positive into our children's lives, planning and planting props for choreographing more positive experiences throughout our children's day.

RESILIENCE TO GO: QUICK STARTS
TO GETTING OUT OF THE COMMON GLITCHES OF LIFE

Recall the Master Plan Steps

- **Empathize with your child:** Meet your child where she is; accept and reflect what your child is feeling.

- **Relabel and get specific:** Figure out what really went wrong; shrink the problem back to the specific issue at hand.

- **Optimize and Rewire:** Help your child generate different perspectives on and narratives about the situation, and choose the one that is most accurate, optimistic, and opens up possibilities.

- **Mobilize:** Get your child to pick up her brain, get busy, and not dwell on the problem. Help her take action to fix it.

Getting to Go: Looking Up, Not Rounding Down: Creating Choices

In each of these vignettes, we start with a child who has shut down, deciding (not rationally, but emotionally) that the game is over (most often with the perception that the game has been ended on him). The goal is not to take the feeling away by any pleading, reassuring, shaming, promising, or other contortionist move you can think of; it is to help your child see that the ball is in his court. Rather than wearing himself out proving why he will be unsuccessful, help him identify and challenge the fear or the foregone conclusion that he is envisioning in that situation. Then, he can convince *himself* of a different choice.

Preemption: When "I Can't" Is Really "I Won't"

The Problem: Your Child Resists Trying an Activity. When your child says things like "I will hate it; it sucks; it will be stupid; it will be lame or boring," you may instantly find yourself reflexively trying to stave off the tidal wave of negativity by vigorously campaigning for "it" regardless of what "its" actual merits may be. When you are dead set on getting him to do an about-face, your child will have to dig in further because you are insisting that he do what *you* want him to do; his resistance is his way of letting you know how hard it is for him. If you approach in an overly cheerful "yes-you-can!" posture, you can expect more resistance still. The last thing we want to do is set up situations where our children feel the need to express their autonomy in opposition to us; we need them to know that we're on the same team. Remember, too, sometimes your child's resistance, while authentic, is superficial. All that protest has to be voiced to get it out of the way, but even kids themselves will admit that it's not how they feel 100 percent, it's just a feeling, and when parents get overly invested and concerned by that first response, kids may feel overwhelmed. Just as parents of infants and young children can quickly and accurately decode their children's crying for the extent of the distress, keep working on attuning yourself to the signs of whether they were only window-shopping that response, or whether they were sold on it.

The Plan. Help your child sort through his protest to identify what part is a fearful or pessimistic overlay on the situation and what part might be a legitimate preference to opt out of an activity that just isn't fun. Just presenting your child with those options may take him by surprise, but it also lets him know it is safe to investigate; you are not going to argue him into it. Once your child identifies the obstacles he is anticipating, ask him, "What part of it *can* you do?" or "What part are you willing to try?" or even "Is there a part that looks good to you?" That way he can say no to some aspects of the situation, while saying yes to others. With younger children, bring in Try-It Guy to teach Meany Brain or Mr. Perfect that nobody is an expert at first: We all need to start at the beginning, practice, and ask for help when we need it. With teenagers who have more social pressure than young kids, they also have more experience in the world and are better able to make accurate assessments for what will most likely happen in a situation. Make sure you distinguish with them what they are thinking could happen versus what they really believe will happen in a situation—how long do they think it will take to settle in? What do they think they'll be saying about the situation the next day? The gist of the plan is as follows:

- Empathize: *Tell me what's the hardest part for you. It might be really awful, and that could stink if you went and it was terrible.*

- Get specific: *What's the worst picture you are imagining? If it is bad, how will you know it? What will be happening? What are you thinking will go wrong? So, the bad thing would be having no one to talk to?*

- Optimize: *Let's figure out a couple of things you could do if that happened. What are some different ways this could go? What's the most likely picture? If things did go well, what would it look like? You would have someone to sit with and you'd have a great time. How can you make that happen?*

- Mobilize: *So, you figured out you want to ask someone to go with you, and you want to get there early? Sounds like a plan.*

Self-Criticism: Ready, Aim, Backfire

The Problem. When your child is frustrated, mad, sad, or disappointed, her default response may be to lob her reaction at the closest target: herself. Often far more damaging than the specific situation that spawned the negative reaction in the first place, a child's harsh statements of self-criticism do a lot of damage in a short period of time. Kids can wear themselves out by going on a rampage of being hard on themselves, and the original problem that set it all off gets lost in the shuffle. Bottom line: Being harsh with yourself doesn't help.

The Plan. Help your child separate the strong feelings he's having from the facts of the situation. Just feeling bad—no matter how bad—doesn't make his perception true, but it does distract him from addressing the problem at hand.

Here's a possible reaction when your child says, "I'm the dumbest person in the whole class. Everybody is smarter than me."

- Empathize: *You really felt bad when you didn't understand the math problem at school.*

- Get specific: *That situation happens a lot to people, but it really bothered you this time. What's the part that bothers you the most about that? Did everybody else understand? Do you know that for sure, or did it just seem that way because you were upset? Why do you think you didn't understand the problem? Was it something about you, or something about the situation? Oh, you were out sick the day before, so everybody else had practiced this already? Everyone else gets the problems faster anyway? Wait, does fast mean smart? Does Mrs. Smith give high marks only to kids who answer the fastest? Right, it might be nice to be fast, but it doesn't guarantee the right answers.*

- Optimize: *Okay, I suppose it's possible that this means those things you said about yourself, but you know I don't think that. Let's see what other possible interpretations are there. How would the fact-checker part of your brain tell the story of what happened? Ah, the news reporter revealed the key fact that you were absent that day. And being absent doesn't mean not being smart, does it? Even if you had been there, you might not have understood? Does that mean you aren't smart? Yikes, why were teachers invented if kids are supposed to know everything themselves? So, can your thinking brain talk to your negative brain and explain what happened?*

- Mobilize: *So, now that you know the problem—you need to catch up on what you missed—what do you want to do? Okay, talk to the teacher; that sounds good. So how about the next time you are confused? Instead of saying, "I'm not smart," what could you say? "I don't understand yet" or "I need help"—great. That sounds like a good plan.*

Frustration Situations: Persevere or Scrap It?

The Problem. While some things may be easier to learn than others, learning generally takes time. Kids don't master something right away; they have to work at it. When kids in a negative spin meet that initial frustration, which is part of the learning curve, it doesn't register with them as a passing phase; it feels as if they're never going to get it and they mistakenly attribute that anticipated failure to a permanent deficit on their part rather than a normal, expected, and temporary stop on the learning curve. Rather than calibrating their response to the manageable frustration of the temporary *now*, they bet on the frustration of the permanent *never* and quit. Kids decide that one bad lesson or even one bad note means "they stink," period. They need to accurately label that they may "stink" at being patient with themselves, but not at the activity they are pursuing.

The Plan. When your child is saying, "I stink at piano; I am terrible; I want to quit," the goal is to engage his detective work to narrow the big assessment down to the exact moment when things changed or soured. And it's important to see that an isolated event—messing up in music, or sports, or a test—doesn't change everything that came before. Identifying the facts as distinct from the feeling, distinguishing what's fleeting from what's permanent, your child will be able to make a rational decision about the best course of action for *him*, rather than feel he needs to flee the situation altogether because it feels untenable.

- Empathize: *I see that this is a really frustrating moment for you. I know it's frustrating not to be able to play as easily as you would like.*

- Get specific: *What happened to make you feel this way? Is there a straw that broke the camel's back? Your teacher didn't smile? What did that mean to you? That he thinks you stink? Can you think of any other reasons why he might not be smiling?*

- Optimize: *So, through the negative lens, you stink and your teacher thinks so, too, but last week when he was smiling, what did you think of your piano playing? Does one "off" week change your talent? Is the smiling or not smiling about you or about him? Let's take the microphone away from The Criticizer for a minute and let Specific Guy tell the story. What do you think makes a strong piano player? Talent and practice? Do you find that you haven't been practicing much at all? So maybe part of it was that your teacher wasn't feeling well, and part of it was that you haven't practiced.*

- Mobilize: *Okay. What are your choices here? You can't help that your teacher had the flu. Is this something you want to work at more, or do you want to keep it the way it is? You want to practice for fifteen minutes a day? So, does it make sense to give up on piano, now, and decide that you're a bad player, or do you need to hold off on that decision until you give yourself the chance to do what everybody else who is good does, practice?*

Compliments: Better to Repel Than to Receive?

The Problem. Kids in a negative-thinking mind-set have trouble accepting compliments. With positive experiences in short supply, we would expect them to readily welcome any positive feedback. Why is this not the case? Because since *everything* isn't perfect about them, compliments feel false. With the all-or-none rule dominating their minds, until they are all good they are bad; there's no middle ground. Rather than being a pleasant experience, compliments may be a catalyst for further self-criticism as the child is compelled to prove them wrong. Or, on the other hand, even if they are believed, compliments may be repelled because the child then feels more pressure to live up to a standard they perceive as impossible—even though they've hit it—they'd rather their work go unnoticed.

The Plan. When your child says, "I don't believe her. She's just saying that," or "That's not true; I'm not good at that," don't force her to agree with the praise. Instead, help her identify the faulty logic in why she feels she must reject the praise. You can also change the context of the conversation and rather than debating whether the accomplishment is worthy or not, teach your child that praise is simply an act of kindness, a gift from one person to the other. What do you do when someone offers you a gift? Accept it, graciously.

- Empathize: *It feels weird or uncomfortable when people say nice things. I guess you don't want to feel as if you're bragging. Or is it something else?*

- Get specific: *What's the hardest thing about it for you? Is it more of a fear that people's expectations of you are really high and that one wrong move could ruin it and they wouldn't think highly of you anymore? If you tell me that you like my dinner, I could feel pressure to always make a good dinner, but I think you just mean it to be an appreciation. Or is it that in your mind you don't deserve a compliment unless everything about you is perfect? Can you think of why that would be a problem? Would people keep trying if they deserved compliments only when everything was just right? Is that how you feel about your friends or teachers? Can compliments be about smaller things that keep growing toward bigger things instead of waiting for that one big thing?*

- Optimize: *So, one thing that happens with a compliment is "Uh-oh, better protect myself." Let's think of some different reactions. How do you think the person wanted you to take the compliment? What would your hero Eleanor Roosevelt say about it—let it in especially since you're afraid? How about your best friend—what do you think her brain tells her about compliments? What if we put the scared part aside for a minute. Is there a part of you that could feel proud and appreciated—just for a second? And what about the all-or-none rule?—What about a "some" rule—"I do some things very well, some of the time"?*

- Mobilize: *So, maybe it is about getting used to praise, letting it in just a little at a time. What's the one-liner that you want to say to yourself the next time someone gives you a compliment— "Try it on; you don't have to keep it forever, but at least see how it feels"? Maybe you can practice just saying, "thank you" and even try to compliment someone else, too—it's a gift that makes the giver feel good, too—so just take it!*

Negative Feedback: Take It in or Let It Take Over?

The Problem. Your child may see any shred of criticism as negating his accomplishments. In the flip side of the compliment issue, when a child gets a single piece of negative feedback, or a correction, it overrides not only any previous positive messages he has received, but it also recasts his identity as a complete failure. His distress is commensurate with the crushing blow—the ground he imagines he has lost—as opposed to the actual repercussions of the feedback (which will actually instruct him on how to improve rather than on how he has failed).

The Plan. Don't try to convince your child that his harsh interpretations are untrue. Instead, help him identify exactly what was actually said, and then put that one isolated piece of information in the context of other feedback that he's got. Watch how what starts as "I'm the worst soccer player; I should quit!" can be narrowed down to "The coach corrected my header today."

- Empathize: *You're feeling really upset. This is getting really big. Let's slow it down.*

- Get specific: *What did the coach say to you? What did it mean to you? Do you think the coach was trying to tell you that you're the worst player and should quit? What was the message he wanted you to get?*

- Optimize: *Let's look at different ideas: From the "I am a terrible person" or the "Mr. Perfect window," it looks as if you should quit, but let's take what happened today and channel it through the neutralizer* [see Chapter 5]. *How does that correction sound when it is said calmly to you? Your negative mind makes it seem so big and scary by yelling it at you, but your smart mind can see "That's his job, to correct me." Do you think professional athletes get feedback like that? What do they do? Was David Beckham born "bending it" like that, or do you think his coach helped him? If your coach thought you didn't have potential, would he bother correcting you?*

- Mobilize: *The coach thinks you are a very strong player, but he wants you to practice your headers, so that you will be an even stronger player—he needs you! How do you want to practice? You want to ask the coach for some pointers? Great idea.*

Hypersensitivity:
Taking Things Personally That Aren't Personal

The Problem. Your child may be convinced that people are always judging her. Kids with a negative thinking bias are excellent at noticing the nuances of others' behavior—every gesture, facial expression, the exact quality of their eye contact, but they are *not* so skilled at interpreting those observations accurately. They take in stray data that likely were not even intended for them. For example, when a teacher stares off into space because he has a headache, your child's interpretation is that the teacher is mad at her or doesn't like her, and she creates a new theory about herself by incorporating a negative connotation from a coincidental or neutral event.

The Plan. Help your child sort out what's personal and what's not, not by disagreeing with her, but by engaging her thinking skills. Take her perception that "Suzie laughed during my report, so my report sucked" as a question or hypothesis rather than as an airtight conclusion. By saying, for example, "One of the reasons Suzie may have laughed is that your report wasn't good. I'm willing to entertain that possibility even though I think it's unlikely, but is that the explanation that fits the facts the best? What are some other reasons why she may have laughed?"

- Empathize: *You're really upset about the report. Let's figure out what happened.*

- Get specific: *What's making you feel this way the most? You saw someone laughing?*

- Optimize: *Remember the minimizer/maximizer mirrors [Chapter 2]? Is the mirror playing tricks on you? What do you think is being exaggerated here? Let's think of all the different other reasons that Suzie would laugh. Oh, she always laughs at people? She doesn't usually even pay attention? Hmm, so is this personal or coincidental? It sounds as if it's coincidental, but let's just say that Suzie was laughing at you. Would that necessarily mean your report wasn't good? That's saying that Suzie's opinion rules. Is she in charge? What's being minimized? What about all the other people's reactions, including your own? Let's say that Suzie is one variable. Is she the most important one, or the most uncomfortable one? If we put Suzie aside, can you do your own assessment of what worked and what didn't? Can you think about your teacher's feedback?*

- Mobilize: *Now that you've figured out how to separate people's reactions from your own, can we think of a takeaway message for when that happens again? Maybe "I can't control everyone's reactions. I can only control mine," and "Not everything that happens is about me. Sometimes it's just a coincidence."*

Friendships: One Strike and Somebody's Out

The Problem. Your child may feel easily rejected by her friends' behavior. Friendships can be like minefields for kids with a negative bias. First, take the unpredictability and developmentally appropriate self-centeredness of young people (they're not thinking that you're waiting to sit together; they're thinking, "Ooh! Ice cream sundaes in the cafeteria! I'm there!"). Then, combine that with the tendency to personalize impersonal, insignificant social data ("She went to play on the tire swing; I hate the tire swing; she doesn't want to be my friend anymore"), and hurt feelings are a frequent result. This one-strike policy can work in the direction either of rejecting a friend or of feeling rejected by a friend, based on little to no evidence.

The Plan. The goal is to take what your angry child sees as an open-and-shut case and help her see that there are things she can do to improve the situation—or to see that once she gets specific, there wasn't really much of a situation in the first place.

Here are some possible reactions when your daughter says, "I hate her; she's awful; what a terrible friend!"

- Empathize: *You're having really strong feelings—I can imagine feeling hurt or angry or frustrated—or is it all of those? It's hard when we feel hurt by our friend. We can expect her to be the one person who wouldn't hurt us, except, I guess, everyone's human; everyone has her moments.*

- Get specific: *What happened? What was the moment that upset you the most? She didn't listen to what you were saying about the movie and blew you off? What's your thought about that? She doesn't care about you, and she's not a good friend? How is she not a good friend? Can we get more specific? Okay, she went to the movie with someone else, when you were going to go together. So, you're thinking she doesn't care. Okay.*

- Optimize: *That is definitely one way to look at it. Let's look at some different ways. Does she usually break plans, or is this more of a "sometimes" thing? Is this a trend on your friendship graph or an outlier? Was this a misunderstanding? Did she know that going to the movie together was so important to you? How do you think she would react if you told her that it did matter? What if you looked at this situation with your "we're all human" glasses? What would you see? Could you understand both your disappointment and her mistake? Let's imagine that you let this friendship go. How will you feel a week or a month from now? Does it seem worth trying to preserve it? Let's look at your facts-versus-feelings pie charts. You're 100 percent mad, but only 10 percent of you believes that she is a bad friend. That's a really important distinction to make. The anger is temporary; the friendship is here to stay. You did some really good work sorting through this.*

- Mobilize: *Are you ready to talk to her now, or do you want to wait until you're feeling better? How will you know if the conversation went well? How can you help that happen? Do you want to practice it? What if you play you first and then we switch and you play her?*

The gist of these examples is being compassionate about our children's reactions and hesitations and seeing them as legitimate, while not assuming—for their sake—that because they thought it, so it shall be. Instead, you are trying to get traction, movement, consideration of other possibilities, heading out of the "no." Because the wheels of change may turn slowly, while we're working our kids out of the negative direction, we look at how to ensure that positive experiences will be part of our children's daily routine.

BRINGING THE POSITIVE TO THEM: BRINGING THE MOUNTAIN TO MUHAMMAD

I have heard many a parent say some variation of "If I could just see him smile; if he could just get into the car and say one positive thing!" Understandably, parents get worn down by children's negative spins, but we need to remember that for some children, learning to do this "feeling-good" thing is like learning long division. It's not going to come naturally; they're going to have to work at it. In the next chapter we look at rigging the whole household for everyday optimism, but for now we focus more specifically on setting up a neural exercise routine in your child's day to build in low-effort, high-impact moments that bring, if not a smile that you can see on the outside, a release she will feel on the inside.

Choreographing the Good Every Day

Over and over, we've said that the brain gets good at whatever it does over and over. So, when your child or teen is wired for finding the bad, doing daily exercises to get the neurons moving toward noticing the good will help him change his brain programming to notice the good more and more without having to do it "on purpose." The following ideas can be introduced gradually, one every few weeks—to your whole family. It is best to practice what you preach, so plan on instituting these changes in your life, too; then you can compare notes with your child or teen and see how the plan is working. If the notion of creating more positive experiences in life will strike your child as noxious, it may be best to introduce this project as building in some brief, calming minivacations from stress. Rather than forcing him to go to "happiness school"—and doing homework for it, no less—get a conversation going about each of the topic headings below: morning routines, activity, play, and so on. Before presenting the specific suggestions here, invite your child to weigh in with his own ideas for incorporating some positive rituals into daily life. Welcome all suggestions, and be patient and encouraging. Don't feel that your child or teen needs to start this project all in one week. The goal is building good practices for life, and they may emerge slowly over time.

Wake-Up Call. What do you want to see when you first wake up—a pile of laundry or papers on your dresser, or a really cool picture of you and your cousins at the Grand Canyon? Professional organizers talk about "mission control": the place in your house that holds the keys, the phones, the shopping list for the instrumental infrastructure of your life. To choreograph a good start to the day, we can create a positive launching pad for the part of it that we can control: the first thing we see when we open our sleepy eyes. Invite your child to create a small display on a bedside table or dresser, or on the wall next to her bed. She could draw a pretty picture, write out a favorite inspiring quote or a joke that gets her laughing every time (change frequently!), a picture of a happy occasion with people they love, a vacation snapshot, an award or photo marking a proud accomplishment, or even a picture of a place she's never been that just makes her feel good when she looks at it: the majestic Mount

Everest, the deep blue ocean of the islands, whatever she chooses. Whatever may come later, by touching base with her emotional central command first thing each day, she is setting her own tone.

During the Day: Breath: The Instant Refresher. Computers don't operate well when they're on for too long. With too many windows open, searches from days before, and projects completed but not tucked back in their folders, the machine starts running slowly and it's time to shut down or restart. Our body and mind run on similar principles. Working in "offline" time—even if it is four incredible deep breaths, which take all of twenty seconds—can work wonders. The stress that children manufacture by trudging through the negative can be ameliorated with a few deep breaths, which will trigger the relaxation response in the body, create a feeling of well-being, and allow them to take in the oxygen they need and to expel the carbon dioxide they don't. No extra equipment is required. They just close their eyes and breathe deeply in and exhale out—1–2–3—from the abdomen. Young children can be encouraged to breathe like a calm cat stretching in the sun, or to relax like a seal bobbing on the water's surface. Older children can visualize a peaceful scene and use their breath to make the colors in the scene more vibrant. Smiling at the end of a deep breath sends a strong "all-clear" signal to the body's stress center and deepens the feeling of relaxation. There are many popular relaxation apps for teens; the key is finding one where the voice is calming without being, in their words, "creepy." At an opportune time, invite your teen to take five minutes to listen to some free apps and decide what voice she likes the best. Taking this first step is the hardest, once she has the app downloaded on her phone, she is more likely to try it, and if she likes it, she'll want to return to it, and the habit creates itself.

Ask your child or teen how she would like to take a five-second midday booster. Ask her to think of a cue at lunchtime to help her remember to take a deep breath and smile—while she's unzipping her lunch box, or standing in line in the cafeteria, or taking her last bite before she leaves the lunchroom. No one will notice, but just letting go of her tension for all of five seconds will help reset her stress level, and she will feel the difference when she cultivates this practice over time.

Play! Another way of going offline with some exuberance is to get in a few minutes of play. According to one definition, *play* means "to move or operate freely within a bounded space."[2] This sounds like the very prescription for our children, who rarely operate freely no matter how big or small the space. Researchers are finding that as much as play can feel like wasting time, it's *spending* time, innovating, enjoying, having fun. It may even have evolutionary benefits, according to a recent *New York Times* article: "The individual most likely to prevail is the one who believes in possibilities—an optimist, a creative thinker, a person who has a sense of power and control. Imaginative play . . . creates such a person."[3] Although our children may think that play requires a screen and a keyboard, that's not what the research suggests. There is a resurgence of interest in electricity-free play. As Bobbi Conner, author of *Unplugged Play: No Batteries, No Plugs, Pure Fun*, writes, "Electronic games are preprogrammed with finite possible responses, they limit the imagination. A child who draws, paints, builds, and invents experiences a creativity that has no boundaries. By learning that he has the ability to shape his world—either alone or in the company of others—he gains the self-confidence he needs to grow into a problem-solving, creative adult."[4] Have your child make a short list of ten quick unplugged activities, and keep it on the fridge. Think back on the most cherished activities of your childhood, or see the resource guide at the end of this book for more ideas.

Activity and Exercise. Getting your kids moving doesn't just keep them busy; it is a proven potent method of improving mood. We know that staying active helps prevent obesity and high blood pressure, reduces stress, and improves sleep, but as we saw in Chapter 6 researchers have also found that exercise on a regular basis can be as effective as antidepressant medication in treating the symptoms of depression. In one study, from Duke University, exercise for thirty minutes three times a week was as effective as sertraline (Zoloft) in reducing the symptoms of depression, and those in the exercise group had lower rates of relapse at ten months than those in the medication group.[5]

Since daily life for most of us is already filled to the brim, rather than trying to squeeze in a gym workout for your child, just think about increasing his activity quotient each week. Introducing manageable new habits will start to add up. For example, park farther from your destination and walk, take the stairs instead of the elevator, include your child in working in the garden or raking leaves, run with the dog, put on some music that your child likes and dance after dinner, play catch for fifteen minutes, or even back of the door basketball. Choose an errand to walk or bike to instead of taking the car or bus. Your child can set a goal of three such activities a week and keep track on the family calendar.

All's Well That Ends Well. On some days, it feels as if the thing we're happiest about is that the day is over! And that's okay. But on most days, we can do our own internal Google search to find something that went well, was satisfying, was interesting or surprising, something we are grateful for (more about this in Chapter 12). Rev up those search engines at dinner or bedtime. Then, compare notes: Sharing your discoveries with someone else enhances the enjoyment all over again. For young children, you may want to frame this search as a "treasure hunt" to find the good in each day: Some treasures may be more hidden than others. For older children, make this an open-ended conversation, no pressure; you might share with them a small observation of something that worked in your day, and they can choose to chime in if they wish. Even if they don't, you are reinforcing the idea that it feels good to look for the good.

In the spirit of flexibility, it is important not to feel obligated to do these exercises daily, although when you are starting a habit, it will help it "stick" if you integrate it a couple of times a week for about three weeks; it generally takes about that long to create a new habit.

Not-So-Hidden Treasure. Just as we can't always find our trusty umbrella on a rainy day, we usually can't put our finger on compliments, good memories, or banner moments when we need them most. Children with a negative bent keep a mental file of all their mistakes: They can generate at a moment's notice a list of embarrassing moments. But when it comes to the positive moments, they may scramble and still come up empty-handed—usually because when they need the positive memories most, they're in no mood to hunt. Have your child create a box or folder of golden moments: when her soccer coach said, "We really needed you today; you made this team happen," or his English teacher said, "I was so moved by your poem that I immediately read it to my family," or a friend said, "You are exactly the kind of friend I hoped to find in high school," Ask your child to "name" the collection or file. When your child is having a down moment, you might gently wonder aloud if it would be a good moment for this treasure box.

CONCLUSION

Although it feels as if you are wholly responsible for moving your child out of his unhappiness, sharing the load by asking questions rather than scrambling to convince with the right answers will help your child get in a new thinking habit: "When you have that 'things are going badly thought,' don't stop there, generate new perspectives so you can see your situation in a different light." Establishing regular routines for engineering positive experiences in kids' lives requires some initial choreography and intention, but given the benefits, this project will turn into stable practices on your child or teen's new axis of possibility.

Family Activity

Have your child ask/interview others at the dinner table, or with grandparents: "Do you ever have a day when you feel as if everything is going wrong and nothing's working out, and it feels as if it's going to be that way forever? Well, how do you handle those times?" Your child may listen for ideas, such as making it smaller; turning the feelings into a poem, a song, or a drawing; or trying to find a way to flip it over to see the other side of the coin—what went well. Talk to your child afterward about any new strategies she learned, any observations she made, such as, "Wow, I didn't know Grandma felt bad like that sometimes. She's always happy."

Next, have your child take a second poll by doing her own happiness research: "What makes you most happy in life? What do you do to make sure you have happiness in your day?" Have your child organize the results in whatever way she can: Young children may just report back what they learned; middle schoolers could organize the data in a graph and share it with the family.

12

EVERYDAY OPTIMISM

Planting Seeds for a Lifetime of Sustainable Living

And happiness . . . what is it? I say it is neither virtue nor pleasure nor this thing nor that but simply growth. We are happy when we are growing.

—John Butler Yeats[1]

Happy families are all alike; every unhappy family is unhappy in its own way.

—Leo Tolstoy, *Anna Karenina*

On many of these pages, we have focused on what might be considered effective weed control: how to identify the unwanted negative thoughts and not let them take root. This work is necessary, but not sufficient. It is only half the picture; the other half is about planting, intentionally putting in place activities that will help your child will thrive on, sowing the seeds of sustainable happiness.

Harvard psychologist Tal Ben-Shahar, a leader in the field of positive psychology and author of *Happier: Learn the Secrets to Daily Joy and Lasting Fulfillment,*[2] uses an economic model for well-being: Positive experiences are "income" because of the benefits they bring, and negative experiences are "expenses," in that they drain our resources. In that sense, kids with a negative bent are often operating at a deficit. Spending out-weighs savings, and you can see it on their face. Households can also fall into deficit spending when their attention and resources are focused on what is wrong, to the exclusion of even noticing what's right. Happier, more optimistic families use a version of the age-old investment strategy of "pennies a day," making daily automatic deposits in the emotional reserves of their children. These practices not only ease the stress of the day-to-day but will also build future emotional equity in your children, yourself, and your family.

In this chapter, we look at basic principles for setting up an optimis-tic household; think of this as a home renovation project without the dust (or the stress). Why do we want to create more optimism in our household? Research suggests that people with an optimistic thinking style enjoy better health, have stronger immunity to diseases, are less vulnerable to depression, have a higher degree of satisfaction in their lives, tend to live longer, and *are happier*. Culling results from the latest research on optimism and depression prevention, this chapter offers an array of principles for optimistic living and techniques for exercising the optimistic part of the brain. If we want our children to be pulled toward positive hubs in their lives, we need to build them. There are many, many opportunities—in the car, at the dinner table, in the evenings—however brief—that can serve as an ideal construction site for building this positivity.

It's important to intentionally clear space and time (it can be brief!) for connection. Take a look at the following drawing and brainstorm with your family what your family's "values pyramid" looks like now, and how you'd ideally like it to look. In the busyness of life, there is much that happens outside of our awareness. So, you can as parents think: What do you want the foundation of your family to be, what are small steps to making that happen? If you're not eating dinner together any night, try for one: get family interest going by having everyone brainstorm the menu and conversation topics. Then, guard that time with your life! Is it that too much of your interaction with your kids is about grades or hounding them to get to bed? Talk to them about it. Say that you'd like to have our at least one conversation of their choosing every week. Maybe they could play songs they are listening to.

What Matters Most?

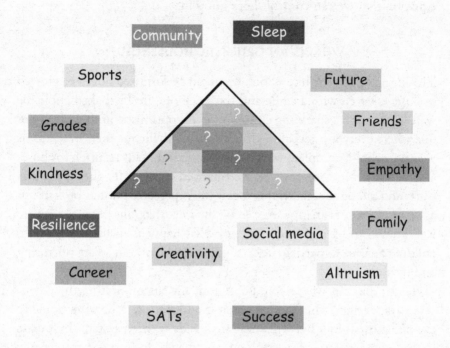

Can your family volunteer? Work together on getting more sleep. You can take back control bit by bit from the monolith that is our culture of busyness and make decisions about the shape of your life wherever possible, and in doing so, you are teaching your kids an essential lesson: we can be choosers (even if only in small ways) in what we focus on and what matters in our life. One student said that she felt she was living in the bubble of how important her grades were and her life and decided to subscribe to a newspaper feed. Another teen decided to set up art materials in his room so that when he had time, maybe instead of going on his phone, he would draw or paint. In a family of young children, parents decided that pajamas and pancakes night would be the fun solution to a busy schedule of getting home late from sports. You might decide to play a game, read a poem. Modeling this process with your kids—whether they are five or fifteen—will change the conversation in their head as they move in on in their lives to include such questions as: "Am I taking care of myself? Am I taking care of others? Am I finding meaning in what I do?" This is the part of the happiness equation that we can control. Let's jump in.

WHAT IS AN OPTIMISTIC HOUSEHOLD?

Visiting an optimistic household, we might be surprised not to be greeted by June Cleaver, with a smile and the smell of a freshly baked apple pie wafting through a sparkling clean house. An optimistic household is not one where everyone gets along in a cheerful, idyllic manner. In fact, it is *your* household, complete with dishes in the sink, kids running for buses and fighting with one another, and harried parents. It's the messy life, warts and all, but crucially, this messy life is perceived not as broken but as vibrant. Parents are not stressed by the imperfections because they are well known to be part and parcel of what happens in life. As a result, children are free to participate. Structure is evident, but so are nurturing and flexibility.

Depending on where you are in your life, incorporating these concepts may feel anywhere from welcome additions to a buzzing home to the one more thing that will crash an already frazzled system. If you are in the latter category, please read on. You may be feeling as if you have to do it all, do it all well, and do it all consistently; in other words, you must be perfect in your adaptation to optimism. None of this is the case. Read through and find the one idea that you'd like to add to your life now, and then take a minute each week—perhaps while you're doing dishes Sunday night before starting the new week—to see how you've worked the idea into that week. That's it. Maybe a few weeks later, choose one more idea. The thing about seeds is that once you plant them, they take on a life of their own, so while you'll need to give them some initial attention, you will find that these concepts and practices will start to pop up—like real seeds—in unexpected places. Your five-year-old, who wasn't even the intended audience, will remind everyone to take a moment and pause, or you'll hear your teenager use the word *grateful*, or your middle schooler will respectfully ask you to let him handle something himself because he thinks he's up to it, and it will take your breath away. Over time, you'll see your family's relationship to these ideas beginning to take root and blossom.

Agency/Action

In the classic children's movie *Babe*, the wise old cow tells the naive young pig that he needs to accept that the way things are, is the way things are. But what if the way things are strikes your child as legitimately unjust or unhelpful? We don't want to foster the cow's passivity. Dr. Martin Seligman described the state of being passive, giving up, not trying, as "learned helplessness." This mind-set is learned through a series of adverse situations in which a person perceives himself as having no influence, so he resigns himself and stops trying.

The alternative is to create and highlight experiences that allow your child to tap into her own resourcefulness and have an impact. Beyond the instant reinforcement of "I know what to do! I can do this myself," these aha! moments also reinforce an essential pathway that the child begins to anticipate and rely on: "I can get through things. I can figure them out." Knowing how to solve problems and have an impact will build your child's self-confidence more than any words of praise—however sincere.

The research on depression has borne out that learned helplessness is a key source of depression, so in our homes, we want to empower our children with a sense of agency: taking responsibility for their own experience, knowing that their actions have an impact, and knowing that when they speak up in a respectful way, they will be heard. When we solicit our children's opinions and then listen—taking seriously their suggestions for making the chore system more fair or making the bus less noisy—we are teaching our kids what I refer to as "learned agency." We are helping them know that they can advocate for themselves and do for themselves. They aren't stuck.

There are a few key corollaries: First and foremost, encouraging kids to talk and hearing them out *isn't* an instant guarantee that they will get what they want. And the child who says, "Well, then, what's the point of trying?" needs these exercises the most. He needs to see that you will take him seriously, and although you may not agree with this particular request, he will be learning to speak up for himself. The second corollary is that this "free speech" strategy doesn't mean allowing disrespect, whining, or hurtfulness. Encourage your child's expression *within* the parameters of decency, asking your whiny child to talk in a "regular voice," or your disrespectful child to "rephrase, please."

When the issue is having agency with the injustices in the world or other missions, children might wonder, "What can one person do?" Keep a running list in your household of "What One Person Can Do." You will find examples, every week, of innovative ways that individuals have taken an idea, run with it, and made a difference. Think of these long-recognized heroes: Rosa Parks catalyzed the civil rights movement when she refused to move to the back of the bus because she was African American. Alexandra Scott, though she died at age eight, raised over $16 million for cancer research when she started Alex's Lemonade Stand. Immediately on learning that he was HIV positive, basketball legend Magic Johnson founded the Magic Johnson Foundation for AIDS, which has raised millions of dollars for education and medical services. But we don't have to look back to find examples of inspiring action. We are living in a time of great courage and impact of young people taking the lead. Here are some ideas to get you started: Take the teenagers who survived the Parkland High School shooting in Florida—Emma Gonzalez, David Hogg, Alex Wind, Cameron Kasky, Jaclyn Corin—along with Matt Deitsch and Delaney Tarr, who started a movement of young people to raise awareness for gun safety, including organizing a nearly 1-million-strong March for Our Lives against gun violence in Washington, DC. Malala Yousafzai, who spoke up in her native Pakistan for the rights of girls to attend school, and was shot for her activism. She recovered and went on to win the Nobel Peace Prize in 2014, the youngest person to be a Nobel laureate. Greta Thunberg, sixteen-year-old Swedish activist, is catalyzing youth worldwide to speak out about the climate crisis.

These are famous examples of young people who went from idea to action. You don't have to be famous to make a difference. The people on this list can be local heroes who saved an injured bird, started a recycling project at your school, or collected coats or canned foods for the homeless. Encourage your family to talk about ways of having an impact that each of you admire. Write down three things each of *them* can do to make the world a better place, and check on the progress frequently. The scale of impact is not the measure of success. Helping your elderly neighbor bring groceries into her house—this is seeing an opportunity to make a difference and taking it; doing, as Buckminster Fuller said, the one thing that only you can do.

Autonomy and Responsibility: As Much as You Can Give

Helicopter parents, deplane! If we are always right there at the ready, swooping down to anticipate and fulfill our children's needs, we will truly be depriving them of the opportunity to see what they can do for themselves. Are you making decisions for your children about food, clothing, homework, or even their future? Pass the microphone back to them. Even young children can make their own choices, and with each choice, they also learn what it is like to be responsible for themselves; as children get older this is a necessary facet of their development if they are ultimately going to strike out on their own. Remember that the most effective parenting style is the authoritative approach, where the rules are clear, but children are granted as much autonomy as possible within those parameters.

So, when we find a way of making a task at home more accessible (e.g., moving the snacks down to a low cupboard, so your child can get them himself; teaching him how to make his favorite grilled cheese so he can have it on demand; or teaching him how to tie his shoelaces), we are increasing our child's autonomy.

Plants grow toward the light, and kids tend naturally toward greater independence if we let them. At the gym, you need to keep on gradually adding more weight to keep building your muscles, and children need to keep adding autonomy or responsibility, or they will atrophy. (The caveat here is to expect some moments of contradiction: Your teenager wants to assert her independence by getting her nose pierced because that's her style, she says, but she also wants you to give extra hugs when no one is looking.) Remember we don't want our children to metaphorically "leave home" abruptly; if instead they can practice steadily by doing things their way, their actual leaving will be smoother when the time comes. The other caveat is to expect a margin of error: You may grant too much autonomy. You may let your teenager go up to his room to do homework, only to find he's been talking to friends on Facebook for two hours. When these miscalculations occur—and they will—allow your child first dibs on explaining to you why *you* are upset with him (you'll be happy to know he "gets it"); let him offer some possible consequences, reparations, or revisions to the current plan. As we saw in the earlier discussion of "agency," hearing your children out doesn't guarantee that you'll adopt or endorse their plan, but they will be practicing around the hub of good judgment (better late than never), and you might even get a good idea out of it.

Nurturing autonomy and also leaving room for kids to come to you to ask for help build competence and confidence in our children by instilling the idea that asking for help when they need it isn't a sign of weakness. Ask your child whether she wants help; don't assume it. Be nearby but busy with your own activities, so that if your child is stuck and needs assistance, she can learn how to ask for what she needs. When kids do ask for help, parents should welcome their request, but return it with some compassionate but informational questions: "Where did you get stuck? What have you tried?" Your object isn't to withhold information from them; on the contrary, it is to respect that they have their own ideas about how to solve their problems.

Intrinsic Value and Satisfaction: Pride and Growth, Not Perfection

Leon is a very talented and bright teenager who wants to (and does) excel in everything he does: music, sports, acting, academics, even cooking. He told me recently that he is "never satisfied" with any project he does, any performance, any test score because he always wants to do better. On the one hand, we can applaud Leon for being driven and relentlessly pursuing perfection, but on the other hand, a quick calculation tells us that burnout is looming on the horizon. Leon has to avoid the fate of the "crispies"—so labeled by college admissions boards as the über-over-achievers who tragically crash and burn on arrival at the college they worked so hard to get into. Leon can realize his potential, paradoxically, by pacing himself. Rather than chasing that elusive carrot of perfection, children like Leon need to be taught to stop, chomp, and savor a big bite of the ones they have already earned. There are many reasons this is the right direction—for longevity, and also for confidence. Dr. Tal Ben-Shahar emphasizes that our goals can't just be about deferring of happiness to some future date, what he refers to as the "arrival fallacy": "I am miserable taking these advanced classes, but they will help me get into the right college and then I'll be happy," then "I'll be happy when I get the right job," and yet again "when I get that big promotion." The answer is redirecting your child to the intrinsic satisfaction of what he is doing in the present, in addition to planning and working toward a better future.

So, back to my friend Leon. When I asked him what would happen if he could stop and appreciate his accomplishments, he said he was afraid that if he let up, he would either fail, become complacent, or, worse, become unambitious. Like any unexplored fear, the power of this one was not in its accuracy, but in its being left unchallenged. A kid like Leon needs to take small steps to reflect on and value his achievements—what he's learned from them, how he enjoyed them—so that rather than waiting for that elusive one big day, he can appreciate all the days in between.

How can we help our children derive satisfaction from the now as well as the later? First, do no harm. Parents will benefit from listening to how we are talking to our children. Are you yourself totaling up a tally sheet of achievements, or are you taking a genuine interest in their experiences and perceptions? Don't pay attention only to the evaluation of their work. Instead, dig deeper: "What did you like about the assignment? If you were the teacher, how would you change it? What did you learn from it? What are the most interesting assignments you've had this semester? What did you like about them?" If we want our children to cultivate a lasting relationship with learning, we need to emphasize it in our interactions and help them see that every step they are taking is part of a larger path toward growth.

Destigmatize Mistakes: They Are Opportunities to Learn

I will never forget how long ago, I walked into my daughter's first grade classroom and was heartened to see a bulletin board entitled "Brave Spellers." Some examples on the board included my daughter's rendition of *psychologist* as "sykollogis"; other children had stepped out with "hotchoklit," (*hot chocolate*) "jacalatern," (*jack o'lantern*) and even "pobmiter" (*pedometer*). It reminded me of another distant memory: A professor in college encouraged us to go out on a limb and say something "outrageous" each week, rather than playing it safe and staying close to the script. Because we had the blessing of our professor, we felt safe to experiment with our comments and class was greatly enriched as a result.

What do these educators understand? That mistakes are the language of learning. I remember an old cartoon in the *New Yorker* that predated the Enron scandal by a decade or so; it depicted executives nervously sitting around a conference table, one of them saying, "I think our best strategy is to destigmatize embezzlement." While the parallel is far from perfect—embezzlement is illegal, mistakes are not—the concept of normalizing something that is endemic hits the spot. Endorsing the inevitable may be unsavory when it comes to business, but imagine if as a culture we sat around the table and came to the same conclusion about mistakes, especially for our kids. How much anguish could we avert, and how much potential could we unleash in children who dared to try?

Recall the research of psychologist Carol Dweck, who found that children with a fixed mind-set about intelligence (one that doesn't allow for mistakes) were unwilling to take risks, wouldn't work to their potential, and instead stayed in the safe zone. We can imagine a tug-of-war between children's potential and their perfectionism, and somehow their perfectionism keeps calling the shots, limiting their growth. Why are children so afraid of making mistakes or taking risks? If you think that you are risking your whole reputation, rather than just learning something new, you're going to play it safe. Children with a negative mind-set think that their intelligence is conditional, provisional, and even precarious, needing to be proven all the time and easily revoked, while their mistakes are permanent, and they can remember every single one. It is imperative that we teach children early in life that just the reverse is true. When a child makes a mistake, make your comments about that event rather than about her character: "That wasn't okay"; "I'm disappointed about that choice"; or simply, "What happened with the math test?," rather than generalizing, "You are a bad girl"; "You're always so disrespectful"; or "You're lazy with schoolwork." The model to use when processing a mistake is "Some things change, some things stay the same." Help your children see what is temporary, such as the poor judgment they exercised in that moment, and what is permanent: their positive lasting qualities as human beings.

Often parents of children who opt for the negative are surprised by how hard their children are on themselves when they make a mistake or are corrected. As twelve-year-old Mike recently told me, "When my mom corrects me, it's like I have a good trash can and a bad trash can, and the good trash can is empty, but the bad trash can just keeps getting filled up with stuff like 'I'm a brat, I'm disrespectful, I'm stupid.' It's not that my mom says those exact things—it's just how I feel." Mike's system reminds us of several points: for negative-minded kids, the "bad" trash can never gets emptied; there is no expiration date or statute of limitations on what they've done wrong, so any new mistakes just make the can overflow. At the same time, the "good" trash can seems to have holes in it; compliments slip right through. Teach your children that the mistakes should slip out because we don't keep repeating the same ones; we learn from them, whereas our positive experiences stick with us.

Make sure that your lessons about mistakes include yourself. If you, as a role model, try to pretend you didn't make a mistake or blame someone else, your kids will go underground with their own missteps. If instead you can earnestly, or even humorously, muster the courage to say, "My bad," or "Mea culpa," or simply, "I goofed," your kids will know the coast is clear. You are saying that even smart, nice, responsible people make mistakes.

Adversity Happens: Let Them Overcome

Patrick, a college student who has suffered from depression for many years, recently realized that his parents have always done *for* him—saved his neck with papers in high school, written his college applications, made his doctor's appointments, intervened with teachers in school, even filled his car with gas. And as much as Patrick was grateful for this, and his friends saw him as leading a charmed life, until Patrick's parents started to back off from their well-intentioned lifelong valet service, he was unable to really see himself as capable in the world. The trigger for this epiphany was Patrick's getting into a minor fender bender and breaking the mirror off his car. His dad said, "Son, I'm going to let you handle this." That broken mirror was one of the best things that could have happened to Patrick. In his words, he learned by fixing that mirror himself that "if parents always put a pillow under their kids so they don't fall, they'll never know that they *can* fall and still be okay. It's like changing a tire: If someone always does it for you, you could get stuck, but if someone teaches you, you will know how to do that for the rest of your life." On his own, Patrick came to this ancient wisdom: "Teach a man to fish," an aphorism that has been popularized by experts in the field of child psychology. I immediately thought of Wendy Mogul's *The Blessing of a Skinned Knee*,[3] which encourages parents to give up the superparenting job of taking every pebble out of our children's path, as—in addition to being impossible—it raises a generation of fragile children who don't know how to fall, fail, struggle, persevere, and ultimately overcome. Instead of creating a template where adversity means defeat, we can look at these "skinned knees," broken toys, broken hearts, forgotten homework, and rejections as building a template in the mind where adversity is equated with strength and growth.

Few of us set our GPS system with the destination "overprotected, dependent child," but we find ourselves led there by our own compassion for our children and the cultural squeeze not to let them fall behind (read "making sure they stay ahead"), especially when everyone else's parents are *overdoing* for their kids. We have to be brave enough to stretch our belief to ride out our children's discomfort (just as we want them to learn that they can), *even though* we know we could short-circuit this process by giving in or taking over.

We can look to the last line of the Serenity Prayer as a guide. Parents need to have the "wisdom to know the difference" between letting their children struggle with disappointment or adversity out of a lack of compassion and giving their children room to struggle and overcome out of a true compassion and knowledge that without these experiences, they won't be prepared for life. You will be helping them see they don't have to crumble every time they fall; instead, they can regroup, perhaps even better than before, and move on.

A caveat: Although *you* know you are not hanging them out to dry, sometimes that's the message kids get. If you're really conflicted about setting limits, you may get *angry* at your children for putting you in this difficult position of having to say no to them. It's not rational, but that's par for the course. Statements like "You're just going to have to deal with this yourself" and "It's your choice; I'm not solving this; this is your problem" can slip off the tongue of the most compassionate parents when they're in the squeeze of *feeling* like bad parents, while doing the good (brave) parent thing of setting a limit. Use your empathy to instead draw a line compassionately: "I know this is not easy for you, but I am here to listen"; "If you think this through, I'd be happy to hear your thought process." The late child psychiatrist Donald Winnicott referred to the "good enough [parent]"—the one who is in tune with her child's needs but not perfectly—as the optimal relationship in that it leaves room for children to develop the resilience to tolerate the discomfort in the space between need and relief.

Working smarter not harder, if you take your imaginary remote and silence all the emotion around a disappointment or struggle, it comes down to problem solving—defining the problem, brainstorming possible solutions, choosing one, and going for it. So when your child is struggling—whether it's the wrong peanut butter for your toddler, or the math book left in the locker for your teenager—rather than trying to solve the problem at warp speed, *pause and ask*. Pose the question "What do you want to do?" or "What do you think we can do about this?" Enlist your child as a collaborator, and he will learn to problem-solve. If you want your child to be able to tolerate frustration, allow him to practice on the smaller stuff. Sometimes putting a name on an experience can contain it and remind you that even if you feel a situation *is* impossible, it is in the category of solvable chaos. Invite your family to invent a name for this category of experience, how many of us raising kids in the 1990s got a little comic relief during our toddler's meltdown, when we labeled it "The End of the World as We Know It" from the REM song, or "Here Comes My Nineteenth Nervous Breakdown" from the Rolling Stones. Children (outside the heat of the moment) may come up with their own labels. One child called this category of experience the "highly uncomfortable, totally temporary thing," or HUTTT for short. Being able to refer to it as HUTTT allowed him to anticipate that it would be over soon and helped make the experience itself more tolerable. Labels like this also counter the feeling that these experiences *shouldn't be happening* and instead make it clear that they happen to all of us.

Chores: Contributing to the Common Good

Could it be that the universal trigger for grumbling and eye rolling among children has actually been identified as one important factor associated with success in later life? You don't need to wave the data in their face, but you should know that in the right measure of time and difficulty, household chores offer your child an opportunity to build up his work ethic and get a sense of accomplishment from a job well done. Start small. If your kids are currently doing no chores, brainstorm what they might *like* to do (for younger kids who like to participate) or might *be able* to do (for teenagers who'd rather, politely or not so politely, decline). Toddlers can play games with you to clean up their toys: "Which blocks do you want to put away, the red or the blue?" Preschoolers can put their clothes in the hamper and help set (or decorate) the table. School-aged children can empty trash cans, organize mail, clear dishes, and more. You may be pleasantly surprised that once your child feels ownership over a domain, he will guard it fiercely (especially if it provides a built-in opportunity to tell people what to do). For example, if your child is on counter duty, he's going to keep after all who leave their stuff on his territory, or if she's in charge of unplugging unneeded charger cords, she will likely be all over you when you forget. If she's in charge of watering plants, she will be really concerned when they look limp.

Remember to help your child choose a chore that capitalizes on his strengths. As we saw in Chapter 4, if your child is an excellent organizer, "hire" his services to clean up your books, or magazine collection. Ask your child who is a techy to type up instructions on how to set up a shared electronic family calendar on everyone's phones, or set up a password for your Wi-Fi. If your child is not good with his hands, folding laundry is going to be a recipe for disaster, so don't go there. Not every chore can be tailor-made to your child's liking, so you should expect complaints, but don't get pulled in; try to have some humor: "I guess whistling while you work is not going to cut it, but what about playing some music on your phone?"

Spending Time Together:
A Couple of Meals a Week Goes a Long Way

Norman Rockwell painted warm family dinners apparently to express a wish for what he longed to have in his own chaotic home—a nice meal around a shared table. These days between sports schedules, homework, late shifts on jobs, or jobs that never end, we are eating more fast food than ever, in cars on the go, and the idea of a family meal may feel relegated to the realm of just that: an idea. Research supports the fact that we all benefit from eating together—with phones and TVs off. Kids do better in school and have a better vocabulary, and teens are less likely to engage in drug use and in general have better mental health and less depression or suicidal thoughts. Even if it's once or twice a week, make it a family affair, take suggestions for the menu, switch off who is in charge of "entertainment," feel the connection—your kids will, too!

Discipline Is About Learning

As much as kids like to get away with things now and then, most parents know that children thrive on structure. Just look what happens when dinner is not on the table at the usual time; they are up in arms: "Hey, what's going on here? Where's dinner?" Knowing where the line is helps children predict how things work on the *outside*, which translates to regulating their actions on the *inside*. When there is no limit setting, they may feel that they are uncared for, that what they do isn't important enough (and this might invite more negative behavior until they finally get your attention), or they may just feel disorganized and be unproductive or even decompensate. Discipline is the checks-and-balances system that maintains a healthy structure in the household. Rather than being about shame, punishment, or embarrassment, it is a way of bringing children back into the order of the household.

When a child or teen makes a bad choice, breaks a rule, or hurts someone in the family, if the goal is truly to make sure he learns a better way, you don't need to be the one lecturing him about it. The working-smarter-rather-than-harder strategy is instead to "check his work"; likely he already knows the lesson and will be able to respond to your prompts: "What do you think I'm going to say here?" or "What do you think we should do about it?" Then, this lesson becomes a win-win: You know that your child does understand the rules, and he gets credit from you for knowing them. Especially with kids prone to go into a negative-spiral, when they mess up, it may be so intolerable to them that they blurt out all sorts of things—"I hate myself, I'm so stupid!, I want to die!, I hate you!" While alarming, they don't necessarily mean these things, but the feeling behind this is "I'm overwhelmed." Giving them the opportunity to "self-correct" by telling you what they did wrong will help them not feel worse than they already do (and they really don't need to feel any worse, you've got their attention!). Whenever possible, use reparations (e.g., having your teenager do a positive thing to reestablish his good citizenship by washing the family car he trashed up with fast-food containers), rather than punishments. At certain times removal of privileges makes sense, but rather than the purpose being punishment, the rationale is that your child is not ready to handle those privileges on his own.

At its best, discipline turns a bad situation into something better and incorporates many of the concepts we've discussed: accepting mistakes, encouraging resilience for dealing with an adverse situation, agency. Your children have a chance to participate in the outcome. If you are disappointed in your child's behavior because she *should* have known better, let her know, but keep in perspective (so that she can, too) that this is one false move, and even though she needs to re-earn your respect for that particular behavior, she isn't back to square one in her status as a person in your home and in your heart. State the obvious: "I still love you even though I'm mad right now. I know that you need to learn by making mistakes, and I know you probably won't make *that* mistake again. You'll make a different one."

Savoring: Multiplying Positive Experiences

We all understand what it means to dread a future event with all the negative, catastrophic trimmings. If we think of this type of anticipation as *borrowing ahead* on trouble, then the opposite—anticipatory savor-ing—can be thought of as *borrowing ahead* on enjoyment, pleasure, or satisfaction. This term, coined by Loyola University psychologist Fred Bryant, suggests that we can look ahead in a positive way, relishing the future rather than fearing it. He and his colleague Joseph Veroff describe three temporal forms of savoring: anticipatory, in the moment, and rem-iniscent.[4] Children know well how to savor the big things—Christmas, summer vacation, their birthday—and by imagining in advance how sweet it will be, they are multiplying the impact of that positive event. Savoring and focusing on the positive can be a practice cultivated in daily life, even on days that aren't circled in red on our calendars. The challenge is to set up your coordinates to look for the good, even on an ordinary day, to discover, as poet William Blake said, the "moment in every day that the devil can not find." While this practice can enhance anyone's life, it is vital to put the positive on the mental map of children headed for the negative. The best way to teach this practice is to engage in it yourself and share your findings with your family. You can define savoring as "catching a moment" and stretching ahead to enjoy it before you get there ("I am thinking about seeing you on that stage for graduation next spring, and it makes me smile"), stretching back to remember something really nice that happened ("I'm remembering when you made those pancakes for me for Mother's Day"), or catching the moment as it is happening and enjoying it ("I love watching you play baseball—you are so at ease and at one with the game"). These descriptions are fitting for young children as well as adults: Select a picture and then dive into it. Pretend it is happening now. What feels good about it? What makes you smile?

You can start the savoring practices by focusing on big things—a playdate, a special day with grandparents, or the prom—but smaller-scale occasions can yield profound savorings if you're looking for them. I asked twelve-year-old Benjamin, who seems to find darkness more easily than light in his life, if there was a part of today that he'd like to savor. His answer: "What's to like about one day—isn't it like any other day?" I asked Benjamin, "Why do people like sunrises and sunsets?" "They're beautiful," he said without missing a beat. "Exactly," I said. "They *are* beautiful, and yet they happen every day, kind of in the same way. It's not as if suddenly the sun is going to rise in the west. But we can find extraordinary experiences even in things that are ordinary. So, think back on your day, your classes, lunch, recess, any moment that felt like something you might want to focus on for a little longer." "Well, I guess there was a really cool moment at lunch when my friends were joking about this book we needed to read for school, but we were all just saying these funny things, and I was thinking it was like we were all passing the ball to each other, playing this great game of catch, being superclever, but there was no ball—but we were passing to each other—sort of with words—anyway, it just worked out perfectly." "That's neat. So, it sounds as if you were savoring your connections with these kids," I said. "And our wit!" Benjamin added.

Savoring something from the past stretches its presence in our lives, like getting two for the price of one. Savoring the future can do the same.

Roy was having trouble going to school in the morning. He thought ahead about the whole day and felt overwhelmed, as if he couldn't do it. In addition to slowing him down and just thinking of one class at a time, we also had him focus each morning on one moment he was looking forward to—not just the final bell at the end of the day. Then at night, he would check in with his dad to see if that was actually the good point of the day, or if something else had happened that made him happy. Although this activity may seem small, over time, putting our attention and focus on these circuits of positive feeling—enjoyment, friendship, love, humor—makes these hubs more accessible to us. Rather than your child having to do an intentional exercise to find the positive to savor, these experiences will start to take the neural expressway that he has built and will find their way to him effortlessly.

Gratitude and Compassion

What's so funny about peace, love, and understanding? Nick Lowe posed this question through the voice of Elvis Costello a couple of decades ago. The serious answer is that scientists have found that people who bring compassion and gratitude into their daily awareness are healthier and happier, experience more positive moods, and are more contented—not to mention the benefit they provide for others around them. Some children who are pulled to the negative are also wired for these qualities, but for other children, spending time in unhappy places in their mind has put up a wall around them, and their empathy count may be very low. By a process called *reciprocal inhibition*, the positive emotion that results from engaging in moments of connection *competes* with negative emotion, and the feeling that feels better wins. The following exercises will help you to slowly introduce these concepts into your family life. Be patient: Just as a sincere apology is worth more than a forced one, it is better to wait for the spontaneous words of true appreciation and concern than to have your child pull a muscle trying to manufacture them on the spot.

Gratitude. We have all heard the caricatured "You should be grateful!" statement on television if not from our own mind or lips. Typically it is uttered with a putdown comparison along the lines of "I never got a new toy when I was a kid, and I was grateful!" Or even the hyperbolic "We lived in a cardboard box, and we were grateful." Wrestling gratitude from our children rarely brings the desired effect, unless making them feel guilty and berating ourselves for sounding like our own parents is what we were going for. Feeling gratitude is something entirely different. It's not wrestled into existence; it is born. It is something that makes your heart expand rather than contract in shame, guilt, or anger. And perhaps this is why researchers are finding that these off-grid moments of pure being, when our body is in a state of letting go, rather than clutching, are actually remarkably good for our mood and our health. Expressing gratitude does much more than just put a smile on someone's face. It can increase good mood and well-being in those who practice it, and it can even increase healing in those who have experienced trauma. In his book *Thanks! How the New Science of Gratitude Can Make You Happier*, Robert Emmons of the University of California at Davis wrote, "Our ground-breaking research has shown that grateful people experience higher levels of positive emotions such as joy, enthusiasm, love, happiness, and optimism, and that the practice of gratitude as a discipline protects a person from the destructive impulses of envy, resentment, greed, and bitterness."[5]

In one study, psychologist Emmons, along with his colleague Michael McCullough, looked at what happens when ordinary people (of no particular religious background) begin a habit of gratitude. In one study, several hundred people were divided into three groups. One group was asked to record the events of the day; the second group recorded unpleasant experiences; and the third group made a list each day of the things for which its members were grateful. The gratitude group participants reported higher levels of alertness, enthusiasm, determination, optimism, and energy; they were less depressed and stressed; and as if that were not enough, they were more likely to help others.[6] Another thing about gratitude is how incredibly good it feels when you really dive into it, and that is likely why the "attitude of gratitude" has caught on so quickly.

While we may have our sights set on saintly expressions of gratitude, encourage even the smallest gestures. If we were to discourage our children's gestures that don't quite fit the mold, the journey will likely end right there. For instance, Benjamin, whom we met earlier, was hard-pressed to find anything to be grateful for in his day. Today was just like any other day, and on and on. "Dig deep," I suggested. "Was there an unexpected gift—someone's doing something nice for you like lending you a pencil when, if they hadn't, it would have been a drag?" "Okay, well, I guess it was good that I didn't have to go to gym class today because the teacher was sick. I don't like gym." "You know what, Benjamin?" I said. "That is a good start."

Researchers have found, perhaps not surprisingly, that forcing gratitude does not yield positive results. Dr. Sonja Lyubomirsky of the University of California found that people who wrote in a gratitude journal once a week were happier than those who wrote three times a week; making it a regular practice but not a chore made the difference.

Individually, you can express your gratitude to your family members, and as a family you may express your gratitude to important people in your life, such as teachers and neighbors, and share something that you are truly grateful for informally at dinner. Encourage and model writing thank-you notes or appreciation or gratitude notes to someone you don't know well; help your child imagine and *savor* how the recipient will feel when this generous gesture is received. Although some research has suggested that it isn't necessary to send gratitude letters, that writing them gives the author the boost; of course sharing that joy multiplies the benefit.

Compassion: What You Give, You Receive

> The actual beneficiary of the practice of compassion and caring for others is oneself. We may have the impression that the main beneficiaries of the practice of compassion are those on the receiving end; that the practice of compassion is relevant only for those concerned about others and irrelevant for those who are not, because its main benefit goes to others. This is a mistake. The immediate benefit of practicing compassion is actually experienced by the practitioner.
>
> —the Dalai Lama, *Illuminating the Path to Enlightenment*

Some children feel a great depth and breadth of compassion—are always the first ones to offer to help, even seeing the need before it arises—but there is a break in the circuit when it comes to showing compassion for themselves, and instead they switch over to self-criticism and accusation. For other children, negative spins and dissatisfactions are such a distraction and preoccupation that they act seemingly obliviously to others' needs, to the point where an initial scanning of your parental database for the keywords "your child" and "compassion" yields no results. It is only when you persist with an *advanced* search that you are able to unearth times when your children have stepped out of their bubble and cared. Interestingly, however, it appears that the instinct to care is just that: a built-in, irrevocable, and inalienable instinct, although more or less developed in different individuals. Researchers at the National Institutes of Health have used brain scan technology to find that subjects thinking altruistic thoughts (donating money to charity rather than keeping it for themselves) activated a primitive part of the brain that usually lights up in response to basic needs, such as food and sex. What this landmark study suggests is that compassion is a basic, hardwired need, and that satisfying it makes us feel good.[7]

But how do we convince kids who are often miserable themselves to have compassion for others? You can certainly explain to children of any age that apologizing, doing something nice for someone, or just thinking good thoughts about someone else actually makes us feel good. After all, who gets first dibs on holding the "good thought"—even before your friend or family member knows about it? You! Your middle schooler or teenager may be interested to know about the research just described and the lessons of the Dalai Lama. Some examples of beginning to practice compassion include giving compliments, exercising good sportsmanship during a game, or holding a door for someone. Ask your child at dinner for examples of "random acts of kindness" that they have witnessed in their own milieu.

One of the things that can interfere with compassion is our judgment about one another. It's virtually impossible to be both critical and understanding—like trying to take a picture and be in it at the same time. Another way of looking at this dilemma, however, is that being judgmental can create a vicious circle, and compassion can interrupt it. So, while our *first reaction* may be to judge—your child may complain that someone was very mean at school—we can also help our children cultivate a *second reaction* to stretch themselves to imagine a reason why the person might have acted that way (and there are always reasons for everything).

If we approach this problem with a judgment of our own—"That's mean of you; the boy's parents just got divorced!"—we shoot ourselves in the foot as role models. We are also going to turn off the thinking part of our kids' brain, shutting them down with feeling guilty or angry or likely both in quick succession. Instead, ask your child without judgment, but with curiosity (so you can try to cultivate her own), "I understand that really hurt your feelings. I might feel that way, too. Hmm, why do you think somebody might do that?" If your child answers, "Because he's mean," remember to use the magic word *different*, and reply, "Yes, that could be, but can you think of a *different* reason why he might do that?" As with any of these skills, doing as you are saying is a powerful model, and sincerity is required. So, deliver your reply with no strings attached. Let go of where you want your child to go and start where she is.

Kindness Leads to Happiness and Right Back Atcha

We want our kids to be kind, and the more opportunities we give them to act kind, the more the habit will stick. Kindness is compassion put into action. Holding the door for your teacher or classmate, giving a compliment to a friend in gym class, participating in a fund-raising walkathon, including your child in the choosing for donating food and clothing for those in need. Give your kids early and often opportunities to witness the positive feedback loop: What we give, we receive. If you are donating to a charity, find a way that your child can choose which charity, do chores to contribute, or be the one to hand in the donation even if you are the behind the scenes funder. Share the job; share the happiness. Research supports the finding that we get a greater happiness "boost" when we think away moments of kindness to each other (buying a gift) than when we think about a gift we gave to ourselves.[8] So, giving makes us feel better and it makes others feel better; when we feel better we are more likely to be kind. Round and round it goes. In the words of Lady Gaga: "Just be kind. The act itself is free and it's priceless."

Decisions Without Tears: Making "Good Enough" Choices

In our culture, we are flummoxed by making decisions. As adults, we may put off buying a new cell phone, or appliance, or just about anything these days because the numbers of features and combinations of features leave us stunned and overwhelmed. Children with a negative bias may have an especially difficult time with decision making because it is easier for them to stew in disappointment—anticipating that they will regret the decision, and lamenting after the fact that they made the wrong choice, as that possibility is always dangerously nearby. Children may spend hours wondering whether they've invited the right friends to the movies, chosen the right sport to try out for, picked the right electives in school, and then there is the question of material choices. I have spent many sessions with children who are tortured with doubt about whether they bought the right game systems. These stakes are much higher than whether you're choosing Crest or Colgate. When we recognize that children are marketed to more than any other age bracket, it is no wonder that our kids are overwhelmed. As fourteen-year-old Mike explained to me recently, "We're the bratty generation. We can't help it. We don't want to act ungrateful or selfish, but we buy something and then two months later somebody buys something that's better—so the thing that was so great before isn't the greatest anymore, and then you're really mad and you want that new thing." Apt social commentary from Mike aside, the fact is that children are burdened with more choices than ever before but have no apparatus with which to make them.

Researchers have found that actually less (choices) is more when it comes to making decisions. Barry Schwartz, author of *The Paradox of Choice: Why More Is Less*,[9] sheds light on why decision making gets hard and what we can do about it. He uses the term "maximizer" to describe someone who compares absolutely everything in detail with the intention of making the "perfect" choice. In contrast, a "satisficer" is someone who makes a fairly quick choice, considers the choice "good enough," and anticipates feeling content with having made a decision and finishing something.

Parents can help kids learn to make choices early and often with little things, but don't give them too many options. In the much cited Jam Study, researchers found that when consumers were faced with choosing a jam, they were ten times more likely to make a purchase if they chose among *six* varieties than if they had to choose among *twenty-four* flavors of jam.[10] So, step one for your kids is to "limit the jam," or reduce the number of options. Step two is to ask your children whether the "jam" is a forever decision or a short-lived one. What it comes down to is not thinking that there is one perfect or right choice, which will make us happy forever (realistically, the shelf life for happiness from any one decision is very short), and that there are devastatingly wrong choices that will make us miserable for which there is no recourse.

In business, Parkinson's law states that a task will expand to fill the time available. So, too, with decision making: The longer a child has to make a decision, the longer she will anguish over it. Set a time limit, or better yet, ask your child how much time she wants to give to weighing the options, and how soon she wants to move on and start enjoying the outcome of that decision.

Help your child reset the mind-set and lower the stakes. First ask, "Is this the most important decision of your life, or just a little one? If it doesn't work out great, how long do you really think it will impact you?" When your child right-sizes the likely repercussions, the decision suddenly feels less daunting. When she thinks there is one right answer and the rest are *wrong* answers (instead of thinking there is a good enough answer), she gets into depressive thinking. There is a cost deducted from our happiness when we maximize. Those painstaking decisions usually don't feel that great anyway because of the ordeal we underwent to reach them. Not surprisingly, Schwartz has found higher rates of depression and perfectionism in people with a maximizing style; they are also more likely to experience deep regret and compare themselves negatively to others. The second step is to brainstorm the options but limit the "jams"; third, consult an "expert" on the topic (for example, when trying to decide which camera to buy, ask your buddy who is a photographer) or make a pros and cons list; fourth, when you've narrowed the choices to the last few, make a "good enough choice." I've found that when kids get stuck at this last stage, you can put the choices in a hat and pick one out. Interestingly, taking the control away from them and leaving the matter to chance seems to help some kids tap into their true preference, and they'll comment, "Oh good, I got the one I wanted." For others, the anger over someone else's choosing for them cancels out the fear of making the *wrong* choice. So, if the option pulled out of the hat is not the one they want, they can override it and say, "Nope. I really want the other one." Either way, the problem is solved: A decision has been made!

Everyone Counts

At one time, children were to be seen and not heard; then the pendulum swung back to create child-centric households where parents were at the mercy of their children's picky appetites and singular interest in screen-related activities. Now we may find ourselves singing along to KIDZ BOP in the car when there is ne'er a child in sight because we don't even know where (or what) *our* music is. As well-intentioned parents, we want the middle ground. Soliciting your children's opinions about things is a way of honoring their presence and input (and getting them used to articulating their opinions and needs), but it does *not* give them free rein to run your household. Get your child's vote on projects: the route to take on a family walk, possible destinations for family vacations, new additions to the weekly dinner menu, or the color of the flowers or the kind of vegetables to be planted in the garden. So, part of "everyone counts" is including children in the family agenda, and the other is to include everyone in your child's agenda from time to time. For instance, step into your teenager's world and ask him to share with you the music he likes these days (he may be shocked that you're not asking him to turn it down); sit down and play a round of those video games that you are constantly trying to extricate your middle schooler from; if for your school-aged child it's drawing and making collages, grab the scissors and glue and make one, too. You will enjoy these rare windows into your child's world, and in return, your child will relish the opportunity to be the tour guide rather than having to travel on someone else's itinerary.

Reasonable Risks

As part of the renovation of our first house, we planned to replace an exterior door with a window to make our front room cozier. Marveling at the construction that my husband had undertaken on his own, I asked him, "Where did you learn how to do all this?" "I didn't," he replied. "I'm figuring it out." Although it was not the answer I expected, all's well that ends well. There is a term in business that comes from an old Irish saying, "Throw your hat over the wall; you'll be committed to go get it."

Trying something, even when you can't see exactly what's on the other side of the wall, is exactly the formula that came out of Carol Dweck's research about children with a growth mind-set. Often children with a negative mind-set don't want to try something unless they are absolutely sure they can do it. With all-or-none thinking at full throttle, they perceive the difficulty as a sign that they aren't smart, so the last thing they would want to do is engage further in that doomed activity. They never want to appear not to know, and rather than take a chance, they may melt down or refuse to try.

You can model taking reasonable risks by showing your child the seams of how things work in your house—with a recipe, a building project—and then he can do the same when asking a girl out on a date, performing at the school talent show, or trying something new. Cultivating this idea in your home could prevent a tremendous amount of frustration by paving the way for your child to try either things he wants to do but is afraid, or things he really needs to do but doesn't know exactly how. While you can't see exactly how things will turn out, your children will get more comfortable with making a commitment to trying things with the conviction that they will get to the other side and retrieve their hat!

Getting Enough Sleep

If we are honest with ourselves, we likely don't get enough sleep and neither do our kids. Did you know that the American Academy of Pediatrics (AAP) recommends kids aged six to twelve should get nine to twelve hours of sleep a night? And that teens should get eight to ten? We may tell ourselves that we and our kids can "afford" a small sleep debt—after all, what's being a little tired; aren't we all?—but the costs are far greater. We can all point our fingers to technology as the problem, but until the day that smartphones walk themselves into our hands and insist that we scroll (and that day may come!), we do have some choice in the matter. Study after study has concluded that teens with a sleep deficit translates to difficulties with academic performance: memory, focus, attention, and importantly, psychological risks—and most studies and surveys conclude that all teens are sleep-deprived to varying degrees. Teens who have less sleep are less resilient in the face of stress-ors, have greater difficulty keeping adverse events in perspective, and may act more impulsively. They also have greater difficulty modulating their reactions to events and are more likely to have suicidal thoughts. A recent study found that teenagers who go to bed at midnight or after were 24 percent more likely to suffer from depression, and more than that, were 20 percent more likely to have suicidal thoughts than teens with parent-set bedtimes of ten p.m. or earlier.[11] The issue is complex. Early school start times clash with teenagers' circadian rhythms. One recent study found that starting school an hour later gave high school students an increase in daily median sleep of thirty-four minutes of sleep per night and 4.5 percent increase in median grades, and atten-dance also improved.[12]

We can't abdicate our role—as with any other staple or decision, kids need our help in seeing the big picture, translating that into little picture details like when to start that bedtime routine. Taking the au-thoritative parent approach, it's best to not just tell your kids what to do about sleep, but to talk to them about why this matters and enlist their help to make each member of your household part of the sleep-well team. Remember the table for two: If you're asking your kids to sleep, you need to, too!

Here are some ideas:

Set a Target Bedtime. Kids need to have a set bedtime; otherwise, they figure out tons of way to bargain for more time: "I'm hungry; I want to cuddle; I need a glass of water." Also, your child's body clock will set with a routine and will anticipate sleep on cue. Teens need to have a target, too; even if they go to bed later, the target will be an anchor from which they won't stray as far.

Make Sleep Inviting. For kids, this means snuggling and being read to, or reading themselves. Some teens enjoy meditations apps, such as Headspace and Calm and OMG I Can't Meditate. Yes, it does mean that they have their phone, and that is tricky, but if they download the app, they can put their "do not disturb message" in a creative way, not see their notifications, and get into their Zen place.

Institute a Last Call. For kids, make a half-hour bedtime announcement. After that, the kitchen closes.

Do Your Turn-Down Early. Kids who do homework up to the last minute or are on their screen are asking their body to suddenly do an about-face and relax on demand. Instead, do what fancy hotels do. An hour or so before bed, dim the lights in the house, turn down the volume on devices (or, just turn off the devices; the AAP consensus is no screens thirty minutes before bed). Have your kids and suggest that your teen wash up and change into their pajamas so that their body gets the message that it's off duty. Then, as they naturally get more tired as the evening goes on, they'll be ready to pop in bed and won't have to interrupt the flow by having to stop and get ready for bed (which—with its transition-heavy activities—often wakes kids up!)

Establish a Routine. Decide on your wind-down activities and repeat nightly—a warm bath, a cup of tea, a book.

Keep Out Blue Rays. If you or your kids have to be on their computer or phone in the evening, consider downloading a free app that filters out the blue light on screens that is known to interfere with sleep.

If these suggestions sound too wholesome or just impossible, especially for your teenager, please know I've suggested to many teens that they monitor their tech time and see how it correlates with stress. It's all about reframing. When kids decide to take the bold move and rather than feeling the FOMO, actually decide on purpose to unplug, over and over, these brave teens, pioneering in the land of healthy choices, end up setting off a domino wave of others deciding that they'll be signing off early, too. . . . Seeing how much better it feels to be rested and not heading into your day already stressed out is worth passing on a late-night conversation. Kids need to see it to believe it, so talk about a trial period of a few weeks (it takes three weeks to establish a habit) and see how it goes. Getting more sleep strengthens our cognitive, emotional, and physical foundation and increases our capacity for making accurate interpretations and sound decisions in our life; the inside job of happiness rests, we could say, in large part on our getting enough sleep.

Orienting Your Life Toward Joy and Happiness

Last but not least, make room in your life for the things you enjoy, but don't leave that up to chance. Set up your life so that you trip over those things regularly. Especially since one consequence for children with a pull to the negative is that they may lead very serious lives, experiences that make them smile, laugh, and feel satisfied need to be within arm's reach, as they may not seek them out. Remember that it's not that children with a negative bias don't *want* to have fun; it's that the gravity of their thinking is bringing them down. If they are around humor and levity, typically they will get pulled up into the positive spiral. The situation is sort of like the one with kids and vegetables: Although kids will never ask for vegetables, they will start to munch on the ones put out in front of them, without even realizing it. Start by asking your children what they most enjoy doing as a family—playing games, listening to music, rocking out dancing, cooking, watching movies, telling jokes, reading poetry, making music, doing yoga; then, together, figure out how to make those things a part of daily life. Some ideas are scheduling a family game night; leaving the box of Boggle or cards on the dining room table; keeping a joke or riddle book in the kitchen and, yes, even in the bathroom; keeping CDs of family-friendly comedians in the car for a good chuckle during even those brief commutes. Designate a basket (or place on your fridge), and have each member of the family put an item in it, switching every couple of weeks. Items can include jokes, thoughts, silly pictures, novelty toys, and cartoons. Put the basket out in the family room, and watch what happens when your children (or spouse) pick something up and—without effort, pressure, or expectation from anyone—find themselves transported to a better mood.

CONCLUSION

As you incorporate these small gestures into your everyday routine, your child will be unaware that she's learning something new, but everyone will find that there is more give in the family system. Implicit in all of these strategies is the idea of undertaking them together—with family, with friends, with your community—because our ability to connect and find meaning in what we do is the greatest predictor and sustainer of our happiness.

Idea Box

Have your child (or you) write down the buzz word from each strategy on a separate piece of paper (e.g., *autonomy, gratitude, decision making*). Put the pieces of paper in a basket. Have your family choose one or two from the basket and discuss their recent experiences with the idea, and ask them to set a goal for one way they would like to bring that idea more actively into their life. This is a one-size-fits-all activity. Kids of all ages and their parents can participate in their own way. Repeat frequently.

Have a family reading of one of the greatest resiliency books of all time, Dr. Seuss's *Oh the Places You'll Go!* filled with wisdom and encouragement for success while navigating the bumps in the road. This classic is a fun read for kids, and is often given as a graduation gift for high school and college students. Read it with your family—everyone can participate!—and you'll likely pick out pearls of wisdom that will become family mantras.

13

LIGHTING UP THE FUTURE

Keeping Your Child on Track for the Long Run

Ellie is starting to catch herself from "falling down all the stairs," when she's upset. She slips down a couple, but she pulls herself back up. Before, when something got her down, there was no talking to her. Now it feels as if she's keeping a foot in the door of what's real and what's hopeful. She is staying more balanced, and as she is feeling better, she is more open to my help; we're getting to be a good team.

—mother of a twelve-year-old

The other day I was trying to balance my checkbook, and I said under my breath, "Why does this always happen? I'll never fix this." My six-year-old son turned to me and said, "Mom, I think the meanies are attacking *you* now!" I had to laugh but I felt this deep sense of relief. If he can catch my negative-thinking slips, I feel so hopeful for the future that he'll be able to catch his own, and he won't always need me there trying to convince him to let it go.

—mother of a six-year-old

If you do not change direction, you may end up where you are heading.

—Lao-tzu

SEEK AND YOU SHALL FIND

Parents of children wired for negativity want to know, "How do I get him to *stop* being so negative?" As we've seen throughout these pages, the answer is not about stopping the negative, but stopping the tyranny of the negative by changing the *attention* you give to it. By stepping back and recognizing that familiar, unreliable voice whispering in your ear, kids can create the opening to start a new feed that leads in a more promising direction. Rather than being trapped in the world where problems loom large and solutions are elusive, our children learn with our coaching to reverse the ratios; get specific (shrink the problems to their true size); and optimize (open up to the myriad of nearby possibilities far beyond the constraints of negative thinking). Kids tune up their brain by choosing what to tune in to and what to tune out. Change for these children comes from even the smallest shifts in thinking, which register dramatically. They can change how they are feeling just by changing how they are thinking and talking to themselves. Suddenly, they've found how to climb out of the hole rather than dig into it deeper. Repeat that pattern many times, and the brain learns an essential new trick: don't stop at the first pessimistic thought—pivot, and look at the myriad possibilities that are more accurate and more encouraging, too!

FLEXIBILITY: THE SOUNDS OF CHANGE:
A NEW THEORY OF RELATIVITY: OUT WITH THE ABSOLUTES

We are reassured that our kids are well on the way to a life of sustainable happiness when we hear them *catch themselves*—sometimes even in midsentence—thinking negatively. More reassuring still is seeing them "right-size" their problems to make them manageable. An exasperated "This term paper will never be done!" transforms into a centered, "Well, it *seems* impossible, but *something* must be happening. I'm not going to be writing this when I'm a hundred!" There is even humor in the mix from time to time, as when one child explained dramatically that she "would *never* trust her friends *ever* again because they *always* let her down." Her mother responded with "Wow! That's quite a construction!" to which the daughter replied with a smile, "Thanks! I made it myself!" When kids can identify the entry points into the negative spiral, they can also navigate—sometimes even with a touch of flintiness and moxie—their way around them. Let's listen.

In the middle of what had become a very typical story for nineteen-year-old Lei, explaining how she couldn't sign up for a certain college course because she might not get an A, and then she'd know she wasn't smart, something quite unusual happened. She stopped herself in mid-sentence and said, "Wow! That is really 'fixed mind-set' of me! First of all thinking that I'm going to fail, and then thinking that not getting an A means I'm not smart. Does that sound absurd?" She went on, "Shouldn't I take the class that really interests me—instead of one that is going to be easy but boring?" Suddenly, Lei was hearing her own familiar patterns in the story and how they were limiting her. No amount of convincing from throngs of adoring fans could have approached the impact of her own realization in that aha! moment when she was able to pick up her thinking and head it down another path.

One mother described how after just a few weeks of working on these issues, her fifteen-year-old daughter, Emma, had been swept up in a nightly rant about how much homework she had, and how impossible this night and her life in general were; Emma caught herself mid-tirade, stopped, steadied herself, and said, "No, I'm not going to do that. Let me try to put this in a more positive way," and went on to reframe the work she had to do in much more manageable terms. Tired of the rant and how it made her feel, even though it had become second nature to her, she realized that all the work it would take to dig herself out of that hole of gloom was not worth the temporary release of diving into it.

Sitting on the edge of my seat with Jackie, a very articulate and sincere nine-year-old girl, I had her read to me from her journal of highlights and lowlights of that week. She was recounting all the mistakes she had made, the grades that weren't up to par in her mind, and selectively comparing herself to classmates who, for the purpose of that particular moment, were in better shape. I asked Jackie whether she noticed any patterns in what she was observing, and she replied, "I always focus on what other people did right and what I did wrong. I think I need to focus on . . . " I held my breath to see if she was going to simply flip it—"good me, bad them"—or realize that her mind needed to focus on the good all around. She finished her sentence: "Yeah, I'm going to focus on what we both did right." Not only had she seen the changes she needed to make for herself, but she had also realized that shining a negative light—whether on herself or on others—didn't help anyone. Seeing the good, surrounding herself in the good, was going to result in a much more satisfying week, and beyond.

For other children, the sounds of change are more the sounds of quiet, an absence of fighting, anger, and despair when they do get into a tough corner. Parents are hearing their children, now familiar with their own process, not fight it but manage it.

One mother said, "I realize that I don't have to solve Anna's discomfort. I can let her be with it. It is a big relief and very freeing for me. I don't feel unkind anymore; I see how it's helping her grow. She is doing more for herself, and we're both a lot happier."

This change, detected practically in the very molecules floating in the air, is described by the mother of fourteen-year-old Joe about his reaction to an oral presentation he had done at school—one on global warming that he had thrown himself into heart and soul.

He walked through the door and I could tell immediately that it didn't go well. He had a pained look on his face, his shoulders were shrugged, and he definitely was not making eye contact. I started to feel anxious inside. I was bracing myself for the meltdown, or explosion, or some of each, at the same time I was frantically scrambling to figure out how I was going to avert the disaster, make it all better, save him from crashing, and me from being pulled down, too.

But then a strange thing happened. It was milliseconds, but it was almost as if we were moving in slow motion. I don't know who sent the signal first—if it was him or me—but somehow it was as if we both decided to soften to this experience. Something shifted and I just stopped panicking for him. Instead, I found myself starting to breathe in slowly and deeply, and I felt this wave of calmness come over me. I closed my eyes, nodded my head, and thought to myself, "He's going to be okay." At the same moment, instead of the barrage of complaints that I was expecting, Joe looked at me and said, "I just need some time. I'll be all right." He sequestered himself in his room, put on his music, and hid in his shell for a while, and by dinnertime he was back with the family, laughing at the antics of his little brothers. He came over to me for a hug after dinner and said,

"Thanks." I didn't ask him for what. I realized that he was thanking me for letting him go, for believing in him, and for not chasing after him to fix it. The relief that I felt at that moment went much deeper than that afternoon. That's when I realized how far he had come in his life. He didn't need to beat up on himself with me, have me reassure him, or argue with him about how terrible things went and always do. Instead, he just needed to let it wash over him and come out the other side.

I could see his life open up for him that day, and even though I knew there would be challenges, I could see him going out in the world and not needing to take me in his suitcase. I felt the deep sense of contentment that he was being launched and that he could manage.

INTERACTIONAL OPTIMISM FOR LIFE: FREEING YOUR CHILD FROM NEGATIVE THINKING—AND YOURSELF

What we see in this last interaction is that Joe's mother needed to keep a level head and not spiral with her own pessimism ("This always happens to him. He's so vulnerable. He'll never figure this out"), or her own anxiety ("What's going to happen in college if he can't take criticism or rejection? How will he ever manage?"). Her ability to keep these impulses in check—while not easy!—helped leave room for Joe to step in, and rather than having to defend himself from his mother's worries and foregone conclusions, getting tangled in her wires, he could just straighten out his own. There's always going to be that next time when something goes wrong for our kids and we want to (and do) react by rescuing, worrying, being impatient, or some combination thereof, and while we can forgive *ourselves* for that first reaction, just as we are asking our kids to do, we need to cultivate our second reaction: to step back and support lovingly, more and more letting our children find their own way.

With the pressures on kids and parents to succeed today, it may be difficult at times to take the courageous step of letting our children pull into themselves as Joe needed to do that day. There could be a million and one good reasons for the swoop-and-rescue maneuver, yet there is another response that virtually cancels all of those reasons out: If we never let our kids flounder, they won't learn to swim, and they won't learn to shine. When we let our kids hold their own—in the right amounts—they learn to trust themselves, and we can behold that miracle in motion, that most sublime happiness, of watching our children growing.

If you need any more convincing that optimism is at least a two-person job, look at what happens when a family—inadvertently—opts for interactional pessimism. Twelve-year-old Benjamin, whom we have met before, came to me beleaguered by anxiety and negativity. He is a very bright, young, and articulate boy whose wit is, by his own admission, more appreciated by adults than by his bathroom-humor-loving peers. Life hit Benjamin hard. Whenever he made any misstep in sports, in school, with other children, his worst moment was spotlighted and replayed over and over like the news feed at the bottom of a TV screen: "Benjamin is a loser. He missed the ball at soccer. He didn't know the answer to the geography question. No one ever laughs at his jokes at lunch." Despite all the odds against him, Benjamin really wanted to feel better and caught on quickly to how these broadcasts and pronouncements of things "never" changing, things "always" going wrong, only served to make him feel much worse. He understood that they were like news "hype," playing up the drama of events in his life that were unpleasant but manageable.

After we had been meeting for a couple of months, Benjamin and his mother were talking in session about preparing for the upcoming exams at school. His mother, a very bright woman who can pull toward the negative herself, was feeling nervous about Benjamin's studying enough and said, "This isn't elementary school, you know. These exams count. You need to take them seriously. How are you going to get to college—and stay there—if you can't organize your time!?" Benjamin's mother was watching a scary movie in her mind. Wanting to support her concerns, but also recognize that this movie was *not* what was happening now and was *not* going to help Benjamin in any way right now, I paused for a moment to choose my words carefully. But before I could say anything, Benjamin himself jumped in and said it as clearly as could be: "Mom, you're putting pressure on me to work harder by looking at things too much from the future. Scaring me doesn't do it. Don't you get it? Part of me is convinced that if I don't do well in school, I'm going to be a homeless person, but that's the part I'm trying to change." There it was. Benjamin did not need to hear fear and pessimism in stereo; he was trying to turn down the speaker in his own mind. In the best spirit of co-operative learning, Benjamin's mother looked at him, smiled, and said, "You're absolutely right." Benjamin—who loves to be right—nodded his head and smiled, too, a big, wide smile of pride. Not only was he finding his own way out, but sometimes, his mother was following his lead.

In moments like these, parents can feel confident that from interacting with the ideas in this book, their kids have in their pockets a great many strategies to get them moving in a new direction. They have been hearing new words around the house—*sometimes, not yet, temporary, occasionally, partially*—and when they hear the old ones—*always, never, impossible, disaster*—they are most likely to call their parents on it. Is there anything more reassuring than being corrected by our children? Not only do we have the profound reassurance of knowing that *they* know what's right, but we can be equally relieved knowing that they have the gumption to say it.

In other moments, parents may witness their children spontaneously and genuinely sharing—in random acts of compassion—the knowledge that has become second nature to them. This was the case for ten-year-old Bobby, who upon overhearing his mother second-guessing a decision she had made years ago, said, "Mom, I think you're walking in through the wrong door. That's the negative one. I think you should try another one." Visualizing many different doors through which to approach a situation was a strategy that had given Bobby his freedom—taking the daunting and making it doable—with just a pause and a rethink; he could see that array of possibilities standing before his mother—and he was going to hold a new door open for her.

When children are solidly rooted in their own understanding of and compassion for themselves, there is a contagion of health: They are free to grow and have compassion for others. Not only are they free to have compassion, but as they wrestle themselves from their oppressive self-loathing and critical thoughts, they are free to be encouraging, supportive, and excited about other people's growth, too. Once the early work of rewiring in new directions has been done, these gestures become automatic, nearly effortless. Not only are we preventing our children from sliding down the slippery slope from negative thinking to depression, but we are also providing them with the opportunity to live in their optimal range, a place where the beneficiaries are unlimited. No longer depressives-in-training, these children have become ambassadors—not every moment of the day, but in their spirit—ushering themselves, their friends, and their family toward a new pole of possibilities.

TAKING THE LONG VIEW

Every journey begins with the first step. As hard as it can be to witness your child's struggles—each time—this also ensures that you get a front-row seat to see the fruits of all those labors when she is able to ride out the wave of negativity and emerge triumphant. All parents wish that the bumps in the road that they face with their children were just that—minor detours that lead to smooth sailing again. When kids' own thinking style is the obstacle, rather than our running ahead to take it out of the way, our children learn to be agile and climb over themselves. Parenting a child with a negative thinking style means understanding that while challenges will emerge and are the givens in the equation of life, our commentary about why those problems happen to us, how solvable or unsolvable they are—those quantities are the variables. It is entirely up to us how we define those terms. Our children bring other givens to the equation of life: their strengths, their knowledge, and their desire to connect and be happy. With all this in hand, we can be confident that they are prepared to come up with the answers they truly need, and build not only resilience and happiness for themselves, but in so doing, create a better world for all.

Resource Guide

*Denotes an organization that provides names of qualified treatment providers.

ORGANIZATIONS AND WEBSITES

Mental Health Resources

*Academy of Cognitive Therapy**
(610) 664-1273
www.academyofct.org

*American Academy of Child and Adolescent Psychiatry**
(800) 333-7636
www.aacap.org

*American Association of Suicidology**
(800) 784-2433
www.suicidology.org

American Psychiatric Association
(703) 907-7300
www.psych.org

*American Psychological Association (APA)**
(800) 964-2000
www.apa.org

Anxiety and Depression Association of America*
Main phone number:
(240) 485-1001
www.adaa.org

Association for Behavioral and Cognitive Therapies (ABCT)*
Central Office phone:
(212) 647-1890
www.abct.org

Children and Adults with Attention Deficit/Hyperactivity Disorder*
(301) 306-7070
www.chadd.org

Child and Adolescent Bipolar Foundation*
(847) 256-8525
www.bpkids.org
www.depressedteens.org

Depression and Bipolar Support Alliance (DBSA)*
(800) 826-3632
www.dbsalliance.org

Federation of Families for Children's Mental Health
(703) 684-7710
www.ffcmh.org

National Alliance on Mental Illness (NAMI)
(800) 950-6264
www.nami.org

National Center for Learning Disabilities*
(888) 575-7373
www.ncld.org

National Suicide Prevention Lifeline
(800) 273-TALK (8255)

International OCD Foundation*
(617) 973-5801
https://iocdf.org/

Worry Wise Kids
www.worrywisekids.org

Bullying and Peer Issues

National Association of School Psychologists
(301) 657-0270

Fact sheets on bullying prevention for parents and administrators: https://www
.nasponline.org/resources-and-publications/resources/school-safety-and-crisis
/bullying-prevention

National Youth Violence Prevention Resource Center
www.safyouth.org/scripts/topics/bullying.asp

Prevent Cyberbullying
https://www.stopbullying.gov/cyberbullying/prevention/index.html

Cyberbullying Research Center
https://cyberbullying.org/

University of Nebraska: Bullying Prevention and Intervention Initiative
https://cehs.unl.edu/empowerment/

US Department of Health and Human Resources
www.stopbullyingnow.hrsa.gov/index.asp?area=main

Integrative Health

National Center for Integrative and Complementary Health
https://nccih.nih.gov/

*Townsend Letter for Doctors and Patients. Townsend Letter,
the Examiner of Alternative Medicine*
(360) 385-6021
www.thetownsendletter.com

Mindfulness

Association for Mindfulness in Education
www.mindfuleducation.org
(650) 575-5780

Suicide Prevention

National Suicide Prevention Lifeline
(800) 273-TALK (8255)
Crisis Text Line: by texting TALK to 741741

The Trevor Project
Hotline for 0, transgender, and questioning youth, (866) 488-7386

BOOKS

About Depression

Barnard, M. U. *Helping Your Depressed Child: A Step-by-Step Guide for Parents.* Oakland, CA: New Harbinger, 2003.

Fassler, D., and L. Dumas. *Help Me, I'm Sad: Recognizing, Treating, and Preventing Childhood and Adolescent Depression.* New York: Penguin Books.

Miller, Jeffrey. *The Childhood Depression Sourcebook.* New York: McGraw-Hill, 1999.

About Distress Tolerance/Dialectical Behavior Therapy (DBT)

Van Dijk, S. *Don't Let Your Emotions Run Your Life for Teens: Dialectical Behavior Therapy Skills for Helping You Manage Mood Swings, Control Angry Outbursts.* Oakland, CA: Instant Help Book, 2011.

About Cultivating Empathy and Improving Mental Health

Borba, M. *Unselfie: Why Empathic Kids Succeed in Our All-About-Me World.* New York: Touchstone, 2017.

About Problem Solving

Shure, M., and T. F. DiGeronimo. *Raising a Thinking Child: Help Your Young Child to Resolve Everyday Conflicts and Get Along with Others.* New York: Pocket Books, 1996.

About Temperament

Bernstein, J. *10 Days to a Less Defiant Child: The Breakthrough Program for Overcoming Your Child's Difficult Behavior,* 2nd ed. Boston: Da Capo, 2015.

Cary, W. B., and M. Jablow. *Understanding Your Child's Temperament.* New York: Macmillan, 1997.

Kurcinka, M. S. *Raising Your Spirited Child,* 3rd ed. New York: Morrow/Avon, 2015.

About Mindfulness

Snel, E. *Sitting Still Like a Frog: Mindfulness Exercises for Kids (and Their Parents).* Colorado: Shambhala 2013. www.stillquietplace.com.

Brach, T. *Radical Acceptance: Embracing Your Life with the Heart of a Buddha.* New York: Bantam, 2004.

Willams, M. G., J. D. Teasdale, Z. V. Segal, and J. Kabat-Zinn. *The Mindful Way Through Depression: Freeing Yourself from Chronic Unhappiness.* New York: Guilford Press, 2007.

About Celebrity and Historic Failures

Boyer, C. *Famous Fails!: Mighty Mistakes, Mega Mishaps, & How a Mess Can Lead to Success!* Washington, DC: National Geographic Children's Books, 2016.

Green, J. *Famous Failures: Hundreds of Hot Shots Who Got Rejected, Flunked Out, Worked Lousy Jobs, Goofed Up, or Did Time in Jail Before Achieving Phenomenal Success.* Los Angeles: Lunatic Press, 2007.

Green, J. *The Road to Success Is Paved with Failure: How Hundreds of Famous People Triumphed over Inauspicious Beginnings, Crushing Rejection, Humiliating Defeats and Other Speed Bumps Along Life's Highway.* New York: Little, Brown, 2001.

Young, S. *Great Failures of the Extremely Successful.* Los Angeles: Tallfellow Press, 2002.

About Psychopharmacology

Wilens, T. E., and P. G. Hammerness. *Straight Talk About Psychiatric Drugs for Kids, Fourth Edition.* New York: Guilford Press, 2016.

Acknowledgments

About fifteen years ago, I scribbled an idea on a piece of paper, "freeing your child's negative mind," after weeks of seeing children struggling with classic pessimistic thinking and had the privilege of turning that slip of paper into the first edition of *Freeing Your Child from Negative Thinking*. The dramatic changes that have occurred in kid's and teen's lives in the ensuing ten years have made the need for depression-prevention that much more urgent, and I am so grateful for the opportunity to return to these ideas for the second edition. For recognizing the need for this revision to further bolster the resiliency skills of our young people setting out into this complex world and bolstering the skills set of parents, who want their kids to do this sure-footedly, much gratitude to Miriam Riad and Renée Sedliar at Da Capo. For picking right up on that need and supporting my work, deep gratitude, to Gareth Esersky and Carol Mann. Thank you to Cisca Schreefel and Dan Ambrosio for bringing the book to the finish line.

There have been many changes in my own life in ten years! Our kids are grown up and launched into lives of their own, but as book writing becomes one's world for a time, thank you to my daughters, Mer and Raia, for your flexibility and support in birthing this, another book sibling. Taking a big look back, I never would have been able to do this project, or any of my other books, for that matter, without Phillip Stern, my husband, first line editor, manager of all things when a book is cooking, and really, there's always a book cooking, and translator of my often vague and inscrutable wishes (even to me!) into illustrations that are exactly what I want. Your devotion to my strivings and to the greater cause of better health and well-being for all is something for which I am eternally grateful.

As much as happiness comes from the inside work we all must do, it is absolutely multiplied by the company we keep, and finding community to support you doing that work is one of the best antidotes to negative thinking one can have. I feel so lucky and grateful for the communities that keep me going: Our dear friends, my amazing Wordspace writing group, my Facebook family, my indispensable assistant, Abby Buffington York, my colleagues and mentors "in real life" and those whom I've met on social media, and all the wise people—from strangers in supermarket lines to the healers in my life—who keep me on my rails. A big, big thank-you to you all.

While it's true that a therapist spends much time in the darkest corners of people's lives every day, it is also such an honor and privilege to surround yourself by the light, the living proof of the potential of the human spirit for growth and resilience. I want to thank all of my patients for believing in their own happiness and taking the opportunity to take on the work for that hard-earned growth. Special appreciation goes to the families who agreed to share their experiences here so that others may learn from them, too.

We know that the brain, for the sake of survival, scans for negativity and threat. We are living in times where there is sadly no shortage of negative events to locate. It is understandable that we could quickly connect the dots of adversity, to the exclusion of everything else, and land in a despondent place. But sitting right next to those dots are the bigger dots, the bright lights of humanity: Our limitless capacity for caring, for compassion, innovation, creativity, excellence, and even for fun that our children and our world possess. It is these bigger dots that, especially in the difficult times, we must visualize, support, and develop with daily intention. I am confident that as we work together in supporting especially the bravery and resilience of the younger generations given the challenges they face, that our vision for a better world will be realized. Thank you, reader, for being part of that unstoppable upward spiral.

Notes

INTRODUCTION: THE WORK OF HAPPINESS
IS ALWAYS ON THE INSIDE

1. A. T. Beck, A. J. Rush, B. F. Shaw, and G. Emery, *Cognitive Therapy of Depression* (New York: Guilford Press, 1979).

2. E. Gillham, K. J. Reivich, L. J. Jaycox, and M. E. P. Seligman, "Prevention of Depressive Symptoms in Schoolchildren: Two-Year Follow-Up," *Psychological Science* 6 (1995): 343–351.

3. J. Schwartz and S. Begley, *The Mind and the Brain: Neuroplasticity and the Power of Mental Force* (New York: Regan Books, 2002).

4. J. M. Twenge, T. E. Joiner, M. L. Rogers, and G. N. Martin, "Increases in Depressive Symptoms, Suicide-Related Outcomes, and Suicide Rates Among U.S. Adolescents After 2010 and Links to Increased New Media Screen Time," *Clinical Psychological Science* 6, no. 1 (2018): 3–17.

1. UNDERSTANDING NEGATIVE THINKING

1. Sharon Begley, *Train Your Brain, Change Your Mind: How a New Science Reveals Our Extraordinary Potential to Transform Ourselves* (New York: Ballantine Books, 2007), 8.

2. M. E. P. Seligman, *Authentic Happiness* (New York: Free Press, 2002), 45.

3. S. Lyubomirsky, K. M. Sheldon, and D. Schkade, "Pursuing Happiness: The Architecture of Sustainable Change," *Review of General Psychology* 9, no. 2 (2003): 111–131.

4. E. Hagen, "The Bargaining Model of Depression," in *Genetic and Cultural Evolution of Cooperation*, ed. P. Hammerstein (Cambridge, MA: MIT Press, 2003), 95–124.

5. M. Levine, *Teach Your Children Well: Why Values and Coping Skills Matter More Than Grades, Trophies, and "Fat Envelopes"* (New York: Harper Perennial, 2016).

6. M. Levine, *The Price of Privilege: How Parental Pressure and Material Advantage Are Creating a Generation of Disconnected and Unhappy Kids* (New York: HarperCollins, 2006).

7. L. Pappano, "The Incredibles," *New York Times*, Education Life, January 7, 2007.

8. K. A. Mclaughlin, K. C. Koenen, E. D. Hill, et al., "Trauma Exposure and Posttraumatic Stress Disorder in a National Sample of Adolescents," *Journal of American Academy of Child and Adolescent Psychiatry* 52 (2013): 815–830.

9. Ibid.

10. A. H. Mezulis, J. S. Hyde, and L. Y. Abramson, "The Developmental Origins of Cognitive Vulnerability to Depression: Temperament, Parenting and Negative Life Events in Childhood as Contributors to Negative Cognitive Style," *Developmental Psychology* 42, no. 6 (2006): 1012–1025.

11. J. M. Twenge, "The Age of Anxiety? Birth Cohort Change in Anxiety and Neuroticism, 1952–1993," *Journal of Personality and Social Psychology* 79 (2000): 1007–1021.

12. J. M. Twenge, T. E. Joiner, M. L. Rogers, and G. N. Martin, "Increases in Depressive Symptoms, Suicide-Related Outcomes, and Suicide Rates Among U.S. Adolescents After 2010 and Links to Increased New Media Screen Time," *Clinical Psychological Science* 6, no. 1 (2018): 3–17.

13. W. R. Beardslee, E. M. Versage, and T. R. G. Gladstone, "Children of Affectively Ill Parents: A Review of the Past Ten Years," *Journal of the American Academy of Child and Adolescent Psychiatry* 11, no. 37 (1998): 1134–1141.

14. S. B. Campbell and J. F. Cohn, "The Timing and Chronicity of Postpartum Depression: Implications for Infant Development," in *Postpartum Depression and Child Development*, ed. L. Murray and P. Cooper (New York: Guilford Press, 1977), 165–197.

15. W. Beardslee, T. R. G. Gladstone, and E. E. O'Connor, "Transmission and Prevention of Mood Disorders Among Children of Affectively Ill Parents; A Review," *Journal of American Academy of Child and Adolescent Psychiatry* 50 (2011): 1098–1109.

16. Michael Yapko, *Hand-Me-Down Blues: How to Stop Depression from Spreading in Families* (New York: St. Martin's Griffin, 1999).

17. C. E. Durbin, D. N. Klein, E. P. Hayden, M. E. Buckley, and K. C. Moerk, "Temperamental Emotionality in Preschoolers and Parental Mood Disorders," *Journal of Abnormal Psychology* 114, no. 1 (2005): 28–37.

18. E. M. Cummings and D. Cicchetti, "Toward a Transactional Model of Relations Between Attachment and Depression," in *Attachment in the Preschool Years:*

Theory, Research, and Intervention, ed. M. T. Greenberg and D. Cicchetti (Chicago: University of Chicago Press, 1990), 339–372; K. D. Rudolph, H. Constance, D. Burge, N. Lindbert, D. Herzbert, and S. E. Dalie, "Toward an Interpersonal Life-Stress Model of Depression: The Developmental Context of Stress Generation," *Developmental Psychopathology*, 12, no. 2 (2000): 215–234.

19. G. S. Diamond, B. F. Reis, G. M. Diamond, L. Siqueland, and L. Isaacs, "Attachment Based Family Therapy for Depressive Adolescents: A Treatment Development Study," *Journal of the Academy of Child and Adolescent Psychiatry* 41, no. 10 (2002): 1190–1196.

20. D. Baumrind, "The Influence of Parenting Style on Adolescent Competence and Substance Use," *Journal of Early Adolescence* 11, no. 1 (1991): 56–95.

21. S. Suomi, cited in Yapko, *Hand-Me Down Blues*, 41.

22. M. Kovacs et al., "A Controlled Family History Study of Childhood Onset Depressive Disorder," *Archives of General Psychiatry* 54, no. 7 (1997): 613–623.

23. M. E. P. Seligman, *What You Can Change and What You Can't* (New York: Vintage Books, 2007).

24. Jeffrey Schwartz and Sharon Begley, *The Mind and the Brain: Neuroplasticity and the Power of Mental Force* (New York: Regan Books, 2002).

2. CHANGING YOUR CHILD'S MIND

1. W. Knaus and E. Ellis, *The Cognitive Behavioral Workbook for Depression: A Step-by-Step Program* (Oakland, CA: New Harbinger, 2012), 82.

2. S. Klein, *The Science of Happiness: How Our Brains Make Us Happy and What We Can Do to Get Happier* (New York: Marlowe, 2006), 35.

3. G. Vallortigara et al., "Asymmetric Tail-Wagging Responses by Dogs to Different Emotive Stimuli," *Current Biology* 17, no. 6 (March 2007): R199–R201.

4. Judith Viorst, *Alexander and the Terrible, Horrible, No Good, Very Bad Day* (New York: Aladdin Paperbacks, 1987).

5. Tara Brach, *Radical Acceptance: Embracing Your Life with the Heart of a Buddha* (New York: Bantam Books, 2003).

6. M. White and D. Epston, *Narrative Means to Therapeutic Ends* (New York: W. W. Norton, 1990).

3. WEATHERING THE STORM OF BIG, NEGATIVE FEELINGS

1. John Gottman, *Raising an Emotionally Intelligent Child: The Heart of Parenting* (New York: Simon & Schuster, 1997).

2. Joseph LeDoux, *The Emotional Brain: The Mysterious Underpinnings of Emotional Life* (New York: Simon & Schuster, 1996).

3. Myrna Shure, *Raising a Thinking Child: Help Your Young Child to Resolve Every-day Conflicts and Get Along with Others* (New York: Pocket Books, 1994).

4. R. J. Semple, E. F. G. Reid, and L. Miller, "Treating Anxiety with Mindfulness: An Open Trial of Mindfulness Training for Anxious Children," *Journal of Cognitive Psychotherapy* 19, no. 4 (2005): 379–392.

5. M. A. Fristad and Jill S. G. Arnold, *Raising a Moody Child* (New York: Guilford Press, 2004).

4. SHINING THE LIGHT ON YOUR CHILD'S UNIQUE ABILITIES

1. Carol Dweck, *Mindset: The New Psychology of Success* (New York: Random House, 2006).

2. Robert Brooks and Sam Goldstein, *Nurturing Resilience in Our Children: An-swers to the Most Important Parenting Questions* (Chicago: Contemporary Books, 2003), 258.

3. C. Peterson and M. E. P. Seligman, *Character Strengths and Virtues: A Hand-book and Classification* (New York: Oxford University Press, 2004; Washington, DC: American Psychological Association, 2004).

4. Dweck, *Mindset*, 6–7.

5. Ibid., 6.

6. "But They Would Not Give Up," accessed February 20, 2008, from Emory University Division of Educational Studies, www.des.emory.edu/mfp/efficacynot giveup.html.

7. Robert Sternberg, *Wisdom, Intelligence and Creativity, Synthesized* (New York: Cambridge University Press, 2007), 71.

8. Brooks and Goldstein, *Nurturing Resilience*, 3.

5. GOING FROM THE "NO" TO THE "KNOW"

1. K. Reivich and A. Shatté, *The Resilience Factor: 7 Keys to Finding Your Inner Strength and Overcoming Life's Hurdles* (New York: Broadway Books, 2002).

6. WHEN NEGATIVITY TAKES HOLD

1. D. J. Whalen, M. Chad, M. Sylvester, and J. L. Luby, "Depression and Anxiety in Preschoolers: A Review of the Past 7 Years," *Child and Adolescent Psychiatric Clinics of North America* 26, no. 3 (2017): 503–522.

2. R. M. Ghandour, L. J. Sherman, C. J. Vladutiu, M. M. Ali, S. E. Lynch, R. H. Bitsko, and S. J. Blumberg, "Prevalence and Treatment of Depression, Anxiety, and Conduct Problems in U.S. Children," *Journal of Pediatrics* 206 (2019): 256–267.

3. Ibid.

4. American Psychiatric Association, *Diagnostic and Statistical Manual of Mental Disorders*, 5th ed. (Arlington, VA: American Psychiatric Association, 2013), 327.

5. Ibid., 349.

6. M. A. Reinecke, N. E. Ryan, and D. L. DuBois, "Cognitive-Behavioral Therapy of Depression and Depressive Symptoms During Adolescence: A Review and Meta-analysis," *Journal of the American Academy of Child and Adolescent Psychiatry* 37 (1998): 26–34.

7. A. Cipriani et al., "Comparative Efficacy and Tolerability of Antidepressants for Major Depressive Disorder in Children and Adolescents: A Network Meta-analysis," *Lancet* 388 (2016): 881–890.

8. Ibid.

9. TADS Team, "The Treatment for Adolescents with Depression Study (TADS): Long-Term Effectiveness and Safety Outcomes," *Archives of General Psychiatry* 64, no. 10 (2007): 1132–1143.

10. A.T. Peters, R. H. Jacobs, C. Feldhaus, D. B. Henry, A. M. Albano, S. A. Langenecker, . . . J. F. Curry, "Trajectories of Functioning into Emerging Adulthood Following Treatment for Adolescent Depression," *Journal of Adolescent Health: Official Publication of the Society for Adolescent Medicine* 58 (2016): 253–259.

11. A. Spirito, C. Esposito-Smythers, J. Wolff, and K. Uhl, "Cognitive-Behavioral Therapy for Adolescent Depression and Suicidality," *Child and Adolescent Psychiatry Clinics of North America* 20 (2012): 191–204.

12. K. Goldapple, Z. Segal, C. Garson, M. Lau, P. Bieling, S. Kennedy, and H. Mayberg, "Modulation of Cortical-Limbic Pathways in Major Depression: Treatment-Specific Effects of Cognitive Behavior Therapy," *Archives of General Psychiatry* 61 (2004): 34–41.

13. National Institutes of Health Office of Dietary Supplements, "Omega-3 Fatty Acids and Health: Fact Sheet for Health Professionals," accessed June 16, 2019, https://ods.od.nih.gov/factsheets/Omega3FattyAcidsandHealth-HealthProfessional/.

14. American Society for Biochemistry and Molecular Biology, "Study Links Brain Fatty Acid Levels to Depression," May 25, 2005, accessed May 2, 2008, www.sciencedaily.com/releases/2005/05/050525161319.htm.

15. H. Nemets, B. Nemets, A. Apter, Z. Bracha, and R. H. Belmaker, "Omega-3 Treatment of Childhood Depression: A Controlled, Double-Blind Pilot Study," *American Journal of Psychiatry* 163 (2006), 1098–1100.

16. G. Grosso et al., "Omega-3 Fatty Acids and Depression: Scientific Evidence and Biological Mechanisms," *Oxidative Medicine and Cellular Longevity* (2014).

17. Office of Dietary Supplements, National Institute of Health, "Dietary Supplement Fact Sheet, B–12," accessed February 20, 2008, http://ods.od.nih.gov/factsheets/VitaminB12_pf.asp.

18. J. Hintikka, T. Tolmunen, A. Tanskanen, and H. Viinamäki, "High Vitamin B12 level and Good Treatment Outcome May Be Associated in Major Depressive Disorder," *BioMed Central Psychiatry* 3 (2003): 17.

19. E. U. Syed, M. Wasay, and S. Awan, "Vitamin B12 Supplementation in Treating Major Depressive Disorder: A Randomized Controlled Trial," *Open Neurology Journal* 7 (2013): 44–48.

20. M. A. Oldham and D. A. Ciraulo, "Bright Light Therapy for Depression: A Review of Its Effects on Chronobiology and the Autonomic Nervous System," *Chronobiology International* 31 (2014): 305–319.

21. J. E. Gangwisch, L. A. Babiss, D. Malaspina, J. B. Turner, G. K. Zammit, and K. Posner, "Earlier Parental Set Bedtimes as a Protective Factor Against Depression and Suicidal Ideation," *Sleep* 33, no. 1 (January 2010): 97–106.

22. J.A. Blumenthal, P. J. Smith, and B. M. Hoffman, "Is Exercise a Viable Treatment for Depression?," *ACSMs Health Fitness Journal* 16, no. 4 (2012): 14–21.

7. PREVENTING THE WORST

1. CDC, "10 Leading Causes of Death by Age Group, United States–2017," National Vital Statistics System, Nation Center for Health Statistics, accessed June 16, 2019, https://www.cdc.gov/injury/images/lc-charts/leading_causes_of_death _by_age_group_2017_1100w850h.jpg; Centers for Disease Control and Prevention, "QuickStats: Suicide Rates for Teens Aged 15-19 Years, by Sex—United States, 1975–2015," August, 2017, p. .816, accessed June 16, 2019, https://www.cdc.gov /mmwr/volumes/66/wr/mm6630a6.htm.

2. https://www.cdc.gov/mmwr/volumes/66/wr/mm6630a6.htm; J. A. Bridge, L. M. Horowitz, C. A. Fontella, A. H. Sheftall, J. Greenhouse, K. J. Kelleher, . . . J. V. Campo, "Age-Related Racial Disparity in Suicide Rates Among US Youths from 2001 Through 2017," *JAMA Pediatrics* (May 21, 2018); *CDC, NCIPC, "Web-Based Injury Statistics Query and Reporting System (WISQARS)" (2010, August 1, 2013), available from www.cdc.gov/ncipc/wisqars;* CDC, "Sexual Identity, Sex of Sexual Contacts, and Health-Risk Behaviors Among Students in Grades 9-12: Youth Risk Behavior Surveillance," Atlanta, GA: US Department of Health and Human Services (2016); R. A. Leavitt, A. Ertl, K. Sheats, E. Petrosky, A. Ivey-Stephenson, and K. A. Fowler, "Suicides Among American Indian/Alaska Natives—National Violent Death Reporting System, 18 States, 2003–2014," *MMWR Morbidity and Mortality Weekly Report* 67 (2018): 237–242, doi: http://dx.doi.org/10.15585/ mmwr.mm6708a1.

8. LOSING, FAILURE, PERFECTIONISM, AND JEALOUSY (OH MY!)

1. T. Curran and A. P. Hill, "Perfectionism Is Increasing Over Time: A Meta-analysis of Birth Cohort Differences from 1989 to 2016," *Psychological Bulletin* (December 28, 2017, advance online publication), http://dx.doi.org/10.1037/bul0000138.

2. J. Campos, K. C. Barrett, M. E. Lamb, H. H. Goldsmith, and C. Stenberg, "Socioemotional Development," in *Handbook of Developmental Psychology*, vol. 2, ed. P. H. Mussen (New York: Wiley, 1983).

9. NAVIGATING SOCIAL MEDIA

1. J. M. Twenge, T. E. Joiner, M. L. Rogers, and G. N. Martin, "Increases in Depressive Symptoms, Suicide-Related Outcomes, and Suicide Rates Among U.S. Adolescents After 2010 and Links to Increased New Media Screen Time," *Clinical Psychological Science* 6, no. 1 (2018): 3–17.

2. R. Mojtabai, M. Olfson, and B. Han, "National Trends in the Prevalence and Treatment of Depression in Adolescents and Young Adults," *Pediatrics* 138, no. 6 (2016): 1–10.

3. M. Borba, *Unselfie: Why Empathic Kids Succeed in Our All-About-Me World* (New York: Touchstone, 2017).

4. J. Pujol, R. Fenoll, J. Forns, B. J. Harrison, G. Martínez-Vilavella, D. Macià, . . . J. Sunyer, "Video Gaming in School Children: How Much Is Enough?," *Annals of Neurology* 80, no. 3 (2016): 424.

5. Twenge, Joiner, Rogers, and Martin, "Increases in Depressive Symptoms."

6. K. Eagan, K. E. B. Stolzenberg, J. J. Ramirez, M. C. Aragon, M. R. Suchard, and S. Hurtado, "The American Freshman: National Norms Fall 2014," Los Angeles: Higher Education Research Institute, UCLA, 2014.

7. Twenge, Joiner, Rogers, and Martin, "Increases in Depressive Symptoms."

10. THE PARENT'S ROLE

1. E. J. Gibson and R. D. Walk, "The 'Visual Cliff,'" *Scientific American* 202 (1960): 67–71.

2. Sara Lawrence-Lightfoot, lecture, University of Pennsylvania, Graduate School of Pennsylvania, March 1989.

11. RESILIENCE TO GO AND HAPPINESS TO STAY

1. They Might Be Giants, "No!" Rounder Records, 2002.

2. Free Dictionary Online, accessed February 24, 2008, www.thefree dictionary. com/play.

3. R. M. Henig, "Why Do We Play?" *New York Times Magazine*, February 17, 2008, 75.

4. Bobbi Connor, *Unplugged Play: No Batteries, No Plugs, Pure Fun* (New York: Workman, 2007), x.

5. M. Babyak et al., "Exercise Treatment for Major Depression: Maintenance of Therapeutic Benefit at 10 Months," *Psychosomatic Medicine* 62 (2000): 633–638.

12. EVERYDAY OPTIMISM

1. J. B. Yeats, *Letters to His Son W. B. Yeats and Others 1869–1922* (New York: Dutton, 1946), 121.

2. Tal Ben-Shahar, *Happier: Learn the Secrets to Daily Joy and Lasting Fulfillment* (New York: McGraw-Hill, 2007).

3. Wendy Mogul, *The Blessing of a Skinned Knee: Using Jewish Teachings to Raise Self-Reliant Children* (New York: Penguin Group, 2001).

4. F. Bryant and J. Veroff, *Savoring: A New Model of Positive Experience* (Mahwah, NJ: Erlbaum, 2007).

5. R. A. Emmons, *Thanks! How the New Science of Gratitude Can Make You Happier* (New York: Houghton Mifflin, 2007), 11.

6. R. A. Emmons and M. E. McCullough, "Counting Blessings Versus Burdens: Experimental Studies of Gratitude and Subjective Well-Being in Daily Life," *Journal of Personality and Social Psychology* 84 (2003): 377–389.

7. V. Shankar, "It Feels Good to Be Good, It Might Be Only Natural," *Washington Post*, May 28, 2007, A1.

8. E. O'Brien and S. Kassirer, "People Are Slow to Adapt to the Warm Glow of Giving," *Psychological Science* 30, no. 2, (2019): 193–204.

9. Barry Schwartz, *The Paradox of Choice: Why More Is Less* (New York: Ecco Harper Perennial, 2004).

10. S. Iyengar and Mark Lepper, "When Choice Is Demotivating: Can One De-sire Too Much of a Good Thing?," *Journal of Personality and Social Psychology* 79, no. 6 (2000): 995–1006.

11. J. E. Gangwisch, L. A. Babiss, D. Malaspina, J. B. Turner, G. K. Zammit, and K. Posner, "Earlier Parental Set Bedtimes as a Protective Factor Against Depression and Suicidal Ideation," *Sleep* 33, no. 1 (January 2010): 97–106.

12. G. P. Dunster, L. de la Iglesia, M. Ben-Hamo, C. Nave, J. G. Fleischer, S. Panda, . . . H. O. de la Iglesia, "Sleep More in Seattle: Later School Start Times Are Associated with More Sleep and Better Performance in High School Students," *Science Advances* (2018): 4.

Index

AAP. *See* American Academy of
Pediatrics
abnormal feeling, social media and,
234–235
abnormal thyroid functioning, 163
absolutes, in negative thoughts, 13,
18
acceptance
empathy and, for failure, 199
sadness in, of worst, 2
accuracy, of positive events, 64
accurate explanations, for happiness, 3
accurate thinking, 122
action plan and, 123
formula for, 70
problem solving and, 246
action plan, for negative thinking
accurate thinking and, 123
empathy and, 121
levity and, 124–125
long-distance learning approach,
123–124
reminders to shrink view of problem,
121–122
See also master plan, on negative
thinking
active
activities, for mindfulness, 88–89
treatment, of CBT, 165

addictive behavior, social media and,
234
ADHD. *See* attention-deficit
hyperactivity disorder
adolescents
CBT for, 166
CDC on suicide rates of, 175, 184
depression rates for, 9
developmental stages of, 157–159
heightened suicide risk of, 186
identity and, 157–158
medication for depression in, 170
normal negativity in, 158
red flags for depression of, 159
relabeling with, 134–135
script explanation, for negative
thinking, 128–129, 129 (fig.), 130
(fig.)
sleep and depression of, 174, 310–311
social media experiences of, 233–234
suicide open-ended discussion with,
178
thought gathering of, 40–41
adversity, 192
lowering expectations and, 193–195
moving through feelings, 196
optimism overcoming, 295–297
parent role in handling, 195–196
strengths in, 108–109